THIS

—

Joanna
Eleftheriou

—

WAY

BACK

WEST VIRGINIA
UNIVERSITY PRESS
MORGANTOWN

Copyright © 2020 by West Virginia University Press
All rights reserved
First edition published 2020 by West Virginia University Press
Printed in the United States of America

ISBN
Paper 978-1-949199-66-6
Ebook 978-1-949199-67-3

Library of Congress Cataloging-in-Publication Data
Names: Eleftheriou, Joanna, author.
Title: This way back / Joanna Eleftheriou.
Description: First edition. | Morgantown : West Virginia University Press,
2020. | Series: In place
Identifiers: LCCN 2020011864 | ISBN 9781949199666 (paperback) |
ISBN 9781949199673 (ebook)
Subjects: LCSH: Eleftheriou, Joanna.
Classification: LCC PS3605.L378 B A6 2020 | DDC 818/.603—dc23
LC record available at https://lccn.loc.gov/2020011864

Book and cover design by Than Saffel / WVU Press

THIS WAY BACK

IN PLACE

Jeremy Jones, Series Editor
Elena Passarello, Series Editor

The Painted Forest
Krista Eastman

Far Flung: Improvisations on National Parks, Driving to Russia, Not Marrying a Ranger, the Language of Heartbreak, and Other Natural Disasters
Cassandra Kircher

Lowest White Boy
Greg Bottoms

On Homesickness: A Plea
Jesse Donaldson

For my teachers

Contents

The Rope
of Desires

The easternmost village in the Cypriot Republic's southern state, Asgáta rests five miles from the island's coast and 140 miles from Beirut, which lies southeast across the sea. Mud brick houses sink into a valley, the stone Church of the Twelve Apostles hovers over a creek bed, and hills rise up all around. From their peaks, the waters of the Mediterranean, or the haze above it, are visible. Gullied roads cut through the underbrush of terebinth, sage, and thyme and into a sparse forest of juniper, wild carob, olive, and pine. When the rains come, brown hillsides turn green. Poppies bloom red against this green, then almond trees blossom, also yellow daffodils, rock rose, and spiny broom. When my father died, this green that he loved had not yet dried in the summer sun—it was April, the hills still bright, for the winter that had preceded his burial was a good one. Rains filled the dams so that after many dry years, they spilled over, and long-empty riverbeds bore water.

After a lifetime of moving back and forth between his birthplace and America, Andréas Eleftheríou made his way back, and with eleven months to live, arranged a garden, planted gardenias and roses round a new home, and set near the front door a trellis for the jasmine that would welcome summer visitors with its sweetness, and at night, bid them goodbye.

It is uncommon to praise a burial, its just-rightness. But I cannot ignore the comfort of my father's place in Asgáta's graveyard. He loved people, but not all of them—he was particular in his choice of company, and took measures to secure substantial space between himself and his neighbors. He chose houses precisely for the empty space—the nothing—at the borders of the property: Queens, 1974, an enormous backyard; the Troodos mountains, 1989, a ring of pine forest; Asgáta, 1993, a carob-strewn tract belonging to the squabbling children of his aunt Melaní; Parekklishá, 2011, a dirt road, an enormous hedge, and a thicket of weeds too narrow to build on (ever). Before he left Parekklishá for the last time, my father spent eleven months looking over his thicket at the city and the sea.

Burial plots are given without charge to people from Asgáta, no matter how long ago they left the village, and the next grave is dug as it is needed, so the snaking rows tell a chronology of loss. My father's place in this chronology gave him neighbors he'd liked when they were alive, so I imagine him comfortable spending an afterlife in proximity to them. He also has a view of the one-room schoolhouse that had left him memories so fond, he'd had an architect design our Asgáta house so that the living room's bay window framed the school's pale blue shutters and roof of red clay. And so, when I saw him lowered into a corner plot with a tall cypress on the right, a quiet kinswoman on the left, my grief softened with a sense that he might be glad his years of illness had now ended.

My father's death summoned me to Cyprus in the last

week of April, too late for me to return to school in Missouri, but early enough to cut my semester short—adding an extra week to my time on the island where he had wanted me to stay.

As the funeral bells tolled and the priest said, "Give rest to the soul of your servant Andréas in a place of light, a place of green grass, a place of rest, where there is no sorrow," the sun flooded the cemetery with light. The men were comfortable in their suits, not sweat-drenched like they would be in Cyprus's late May, yet I was warm enough in a short-sleeved dress. It was the balm of warm sunshine and cool wind that my father had once assured us Cypriots enjoyed every day. The perfect temperature for a funeral. My brother and his oldest friends bore the coffin. I walked behind them with my mother and sister to my right. A few yards to my left walked my own old friends who had visited me there, in that very place, when I lived with my parents in the village.

As we stood in the same church my mother, brother, and I had attended week in and week out for a decade, listening to the same chanters and the same priest, surrounded by neighbors wearing the same clothes they always wore, by people who belonged in Asgáta where Andréas was born at home, death folded itself into life. The ground he entered was the ground from which he pulled root vegetables, into which he dug irrigation ditches, and on which he played soccer every Christmas with the bladder of a slaughtered pig.

And when the priest scattered onto that body wheat, the wheat too had risen out of that ground. The oil poured onto my father had been pressed from olives grown in that place. The plate thrown into the grave to shatter in the coffin below, like the wheat scattered into the wind, would become part of that earth again. Into the ground of our everyday lives my father's friends and son and students dug their shovels, and out of it they heaved the dirt of the place onto the box that bore his body.

After that, Dino and Cathy returned to their American lives, but I stayed behind on our father's island because mine could wait until the fall semester. My fellow English instructors in the States asked for my Cypriot address and sent sympathy cards to my parents' house. I spent the summer there, in their house, alone with my mother, reading. My mother read theological books in English and reread the gospel in the original Greek. I read theoretical books on mourning—Harrison, Butler, Derrida—and I pulled my father's journals from a drawer and typed their contents up, driven, I guess, by a need for work. Sometimes, I translated what I'd typed into English. I typed in Greek, and I typed again in English. This typing, and this retyping, too, was the work of mourning. I did the typing when my mother was out, not because I thought she would forbid it, but because I could not speak about my desire. For every act of grief that wasn't part of a ritual, I had only silence. There was language for what were the customary duties of the bereaved. For my desire to read and type up my father's language, I had none.

First among the nameable labors of mourning was the making of *kólyva*, a wheat-based food offered on the ninth day after the death during a memorial at church. On the eighth day, my mother and I invited friends up to the house, littered though it was with piles of my father's clothes, washed and folded for donation. I'd gone to high school with Erika, and we had spent a lot of time in each other's houses— mostly hers, since she lived in the city close to school. When we had activities in the afternoon on a school day, I would stay at her house instead of taking the village road all the way back home to Asgáta. Erika and her mother Ivi showed us how to prepare the boiled wheat and decorate it with pomegranate, aniseed, raisins, sesame seeds, and blanched almonds. They directed us to place the almonds in the shape of a cross over the wheat.

After the ninth-day memorial, my mother and I stood behind tables set up for this custom outside the church, and as villagers left the churchyard, they took a handful of boiled wheat and said, "Memory eternal." Once, as a picky teenager, I refused to take this handful of kólyva and the widow took hold of my arm and pulled me back. "Eat. For his soul." I took in my cupped palms the wheat of the dead, and I placed the undesired food inside my mouth and chewed. Under the grieving woman's gaze, I let pomegranate seeds break sweetness onto the earthy flavor of smooth wheat, and never refused kólyva again.

Next, we had to pay visits to the cemetery. There wasn't much to do while visiting, although according to our mayor, who'd dug the grave, there was water to spill. Buckets of it. The mayor explained that before a stone memorial could be built on top of my father's grave, the heap of raised earth needed to settle, and we could speed this settling process up by carrying buckets of water and sloshing them onto the earth. Because the task gave my hands something to do, I ignored my suspicions about the logic (how much earth could a few buckets of water move, especially since we had a whole winter ahead before we could build the memorial?). I continued to fill that red paint bucket with water and haul it, sloshing, to spill onto the pink-brown rocky mound. I got my clothes a little wet but didn't mind, since it was now late May, and hot. My mother and I spilled buckets and buckets onto the earth while his photo, on the temporary wooden cross, looked on. Andréas had thick, long sideburns because in the photo he was young.

After the day's water spilling was done, and weeds were pulled from the grave, I passed the rest of the visiting time by walking around the graveyard. I looked at fading pictures and the flowers, some new and some plastic, some recently alive. Nearby were the large family tombs of neighbors I'd known during the years when we lived together here, in the village. Asgáta's four-hundred-odd residents were easy to remember. I didn't know everyone's name, but I knew all of their faces. Mothers and sons, uncles and nephews, grandparents and grandchildren, and husbands and wives now shared tombs here, the way they had once shared a single village house in life. A stone's throw from my father's grave, in the direction of the old Twelve Apostles Church, lay my father's maternal grandparents, in a shared grave marked with a gray stone crucifix. It bore the dates of their deaths, and I learned that my great-grandfather had died before my father's birth. I saw on it also the printed evidence of what I had known—that my great-grandmother had died while my father was away at boarding school, so that he learned of the loss long after it had occurred, when he stepped off the bus after school had let out for Christmas break. All this memory-laden stone, all these memorialized generations, provided comfort to me as the tangible markers of lives I'd heard of only in stories.

I spent my high school years in that village and four more after college. I ran past the cemetery often while exploring the hills. I had entered it only during funerals. I don't know why I had never before walked around inside. What I do know is that the comfort of a visible lineage for myself there, in a particular place, set distance between Thoreau and me, who was in his thirties when he wrote in *Walden*, "Deliver me from a city built on the site of a more ancient city, whose materials are ruins, whose gardens, cemeteries." I have come to love living among cemeteries and ruins. As I've travelled around the Mediterranean Basin, I've often come across piles of unmarked antiquities—in Lésbos a fallen column and in Thássos a cracked sarcophagus; in Athens a metro full of ancient art and in Thessaloníki the Vía Egnatía's pavestones—all half-heartedly fenced off or grown over with weeds. In Asgáta, a Roman skeleton turned up during my visit in 2019, and when I left, the grave was still covered up with boards from old crates, cordoned off with yellow police tape, and protected by a night guard until its significance could be assessed. This ancient cemetery, or the ruins that suggest one's existence under the ground, lies less than a mile from the Church of the Twelve Apostles where less ancient relics lie. Chances are, the archaeologists won't excavate. So very many generations have left records of themselves in stone that there is no space left in the museums, or in the museums' crowded storerooms, and the cities remain strewn with ruined memorials. Sometimes, archaeological finds are reburied after excavation because the best preservation material is the earth.

I wonder if Thoreau ever changed his mind and acquired a taste for ruins in the way my father, still happily in America in his twenties, later yearned toward ancestral gardens.

A few weeks after the funeral, my mother and I were once again tending to these little graveyard duties when a neighbor entered and told us not to worry about a third mourning custom we'd been neglecting. The living are supposed to keep alight an oil lamp, which is housed in a miniature cupboard fixed to the back of the wooden cross. The lamp is really just a glass of oil with a floating wick in it.

Only pretending to veil her reproach, the neighbor said, "Don't worry! I have been lighting Andréas's lamp when I come to tend my mother-in-law's grave."

When we thanked her but showed no remorse for our neglect, she said, "You do know it has to be kept lit for the soul to go up!"

We assented, and may even have lit the oil lamp. But my mother is very religious and also very American, and so quite unworried about practices that, like the lamp-lighting, were not based in official Orthodox church canons. She lit it a few times during our visits after that, but always agreed when I suggested we snuff the flame before leaving. Every summer, wildfires decimate large parts of Cyprus' forest, and the trees killed take many human lifetimes to grow back.

Some days later, late at night outside my parents' house, I reported to Erika the way the neighbor had chastised us for our neglect of my father's needs as he progressed in the afterlife. She imitated the exasperated voice my dad would use if he were to become stuck in the grave, unable to go up, because of my mother's strict no-folklore, dogma-only religious allegiance. This allegiance had frustrated him when he was alive. Growing up in Cyprus, my father was used to bending the rules of Orthodox Christian dogma and prioritizing cultural practices that sometimes reach back as far as pagan times.

Erika and I were laughing when a bird whooshed down from the sky flapping large wings, waited a moment, and then disappeared.

"What was that?" Erika asked.

"An owl!" I explained that I'd been finding them perched

on telephone wires above me while I ran, flapping before me on my long walks in the hills—more in the first weeks after his death than in the sum of all my previous several years of running in the Cypriot hills.

"It's my dad," I said, and she accepted the answer.

>>·<<

Two years later, I was considering all this—the lingering of souls, the appearance of owls, and the importance of flames—when my cousin Dina and her husband (also called Andréas) drove me to Asgáta. They are the only family my parents were close to in Cyprus, the others having fallen out of touch due to illness, age, or misunderstandings. Dina and Andréas had visited my father in the hospital during the weeks when I thought he would live—long enough to leave the hospital, or at least until April 26, 2012, when I would duck out of my spring semester in Missouri a week early to visit him. They said that in the last weeks, my father spoke ever more urgently about something I had heard him lament from time to time— that his own parents, Agáthi and Constantínos, were buried in New York. I remember him speaking of his parents as if they had not been buried at all, but left, like Polyneices, for the vultures to eat. He spoke of them as though they were hostages, held in a foreign land against their will. Later, we would know he was talking about himself.

"Do you think he felt guilty his parents didn't get what *they* wanted, or was it because it was his desire they be buried in Cyprus?" I asked as we pulled up to the cemetery gate.

"Oh, *he* wanted them here in Cyprus, definitely. It was your father's wish," Andréas answered. When he died at seventy-two, my father had just returned with my mother to Cyprus yet again, even though all three children had settled in America. All their living parents and siblings, too, were in New York. But my father insisted on moving to Cyprus for a fourth time, "for good." I wondered if, most of all, he wanted to spare his children the guilt of abandoning a parent in a foreign land.

>≫·≪

During our last conversation, my father said, "I would like to live another ten years." He said it in an offhanded way, the way we might say we'd like to get another graduate degree, while very much resigned to the impossibility of fulfilling that wish. What I heard him saying was, "I'm glad I made it back before it was too late." Eighteen years had already passed since that first diagnosis of heart disease. I remember learning as a teenager that an undetected heart attack had caused irreparable damage. For eighteen years, he took many different medicines and stayed alive, growing weaker and, in the end, more eager for the village where his life had begun.

My New York-born mother, for her part, returned to her own New York birthplace six months after her husband was laid to rest. Then she drove up to Mount Olivet Cemetery in Maspeth, just north of Brooklyn, and bought grave plots for her mother, her brother, and herself. That meant the just-opened family tomb in Asgáta would house my father's bones alone. I am the only thirty-three-year-old I know who wonders on which of two continents she should be buried, I thought when my mother told me about her purchase.

I would read, much later, in *The Dominion of the Dead*, "each of us must choose an allegiance—either to the posthuman, the virtual and the synthetic, or to the earth, the real and the dead in their humic densities." And I would wonder if my mother's choice of a burial in a place without ancestors meant she had chosen what Robert Pogue Harrison terms "the posthuman, the virtual." I would wonder if she had invested in religion's soul in a way diametrically opposed to my father, who after a lifetime of vacillation decided his allegiance was to the very ancestors he'd tried to escape when he emigrated, so that he made a hurried final effort to secure a place within the land that housed his forebears.

When my parents were planning that final move together, from New York back to Cyprus, I suggested they rent rather than buy yet another house. Having recently turned thirty, I had found a career path at last, and it appeared incompatible with a return to Cyprus. Cathy had married before we ever moved, so had never lived in Cyprus. Dino had also begun a career in America and had no plans to live in Cyprus again. We all sensed our parents would have difficulty staying in Cyprus without any of their children.

After we had toured, the summer before the eventual purchase, the house he would eventually end up buying, my father asked my opinion. "I disagree," I said to him, for the first time in my life.

"But you are *a hundred percent Greek*," he argued, insisting this identity should cause me to support a purchase that no one considered wise. My love of Greek music and literature, along with the Greek landscape's hold over my imagination, should have made me sympathetic.

I countered, "Isn't Dino Greek too?" My brother and I have the same parents.

"No," he said, dismissing my appeal to fact, perhaps annoyed that I was ignoring other facts—that my brother took an interest in business, listened to American music and watched television, and didn't return to the island after college, or share with my father and me a certain way of being in the world that is ruminative and nostalgic.

"Dino is an American," my father said, ending the argument. He looked at me like I had betrayed something—not *him* so much as something he knew was in me, something he had given me and only me. That look of betrayal recalled a time three years before, when he had sold off all his property in Cyprus, having accepted bad offers because he wanted so badly to leave.

"*Me píkrane aftós o tópos,*" he had said many times. ("This place has embittered me." "Με πίκρανε αυτός ο τόπος.") He'd been betrayed by the happiness of his youthful memories, and by the promises of the large swaths of land he had inherited from his parents. Those memories promised him a happiness he never found when he returned.

I never understood what it was my father wanted. He wanted so much at once: for all his children to live in Cyprus, and for us all to be in New York with the extended family, where his parents were buried. To teach history, and to grow on his own land enough food for a family. To be surrounded by us, and to be alone. He asked his three children to visit him in the hospital, as though he wanted to have us around when he passed, but when we arranged flights to Cyprus, he eluded us and died alone. He eluded even my mother, slipping away in the wee hours of the night on a rare occasion when she'd left the hospital to get a little sleep at home.

I learned nothing, in the end, but this: that human desire is a rope, one braided with thickly conflicting wants—and so, my father kept on shepherding his wife and children to Cyprus, and then out of it. He longed for a life on a mountaintop, and when he got it, he left for proximity to schools. He longed for the spoils of modernity: the city, sweatless intellectual work, emancipation from the backbreaking demands of livestock and crops. And when he got that, becoming a teacher in a New York City school, he longed for gardens, grew vegetables in Flushing, Queens, and still that wasn't enough so he went home, where he planted whole fields of potatoes, and without machines, harvested them over long days. He wanted his children to be independent, joyful adults, but he begged me, too, to pick up where he left off, embody his own desires, and make my life a realization of his abandoned dreams.

Young Andréas's journals document a resistance to the village, but the stones of the memorial I would eventually have built for him document his desire to return. When I read about my father's teenage eagerness for the city, with its electric lights and hot water, its theaters and cinemas, its promenades and dancing, and when I read his eager documentation of the process of acquiring emigration papers, I think of *The Dominion of the Dead*: "We have worked the earth to death and borne the curse of our earthbound race in every way imaginable. We have suffered endless hardships and indignities in the name of our obligations to the dead and the land. Haven't we paid our dues several times over? Don't we have the right to settle, once and for all, our debts with the dead, with the earth, even with God, if it comes to that?"

My father paid his dues as a child, shoveling out irrigation ditches in the heat and guiding toward village warehouses uncooperative donkeys laden with the harvest. His sisters, once they'd settled in America, described the long, grueling

hours of 1960s factory work as light compared to their relentless regimen, back in Cyprus, of agricultural chores.
Their father's neck hurt from straining up to the sky, seeking
a rain cloud, because without rain, the enormous amount of
land the family owned would still leave them hungry.

My paternal grandfather, Cóstas Eleftheríou, "The
American," got his name in 1936 when he returned from
a stint in Pittsburgh with enough American money to bring
Asgáta its first car. Cóstas drove a twelve-passenger Ford
from the capital of Cyprus back to Asgáta, and the village
priest, flanked by banner-bearing altar boys, greeted him at
the village entrance for a blessing. Cóstas opened a grocery
store, too, which supplemented his income from the land, but
in 1947 Cyprus's nationwide co-op grocery opened a store
in Asgáta, and my grandfather couldn't compete. In 1955, a
copper and iron mine a mile outside the village closed down,
leaving laborers without work. Jobless, they begged The
American to give them groceries on credit and he did. In
the meantime, drought parched his fields. The once lucrative carob and olive harvests shrank, while the potato and
wheat crops failed. Back in Pittsburgh, my grandfather had
dreamed of Asgáta the way prisoners dream of sky. But in
Cypriot skies, the sun can keep on shining for months. And
the sunshine drove him out.

I heard, many times, this dramatic story of their depar-
ture. Before they left, my grandfather Cóstas asked my
grandmother Agáthi to call him over when she next lit the
wood oven in their yard. When she did, Cóstas put inside
it their general store's ledger full of names and purchases
made on credit. The first of the family to leave, my grandfather Cóstas ate his last Cypriot meal with bread baked upon
the ashes of forgiven debt. Agáthi and the children followed
Cóstas after my father Andréas finished high school a few

months later. The Ford had stopped running long ago and, with no mechanics around, had been pushed off a cliff where it rusted among the reeds.

My father's teenage voice laments, in the journals he left behind, the long summer days when he was stuck in the village, when he could not do the teenage things he enjoyed when he was in the city for school: rehearsals with his drama club, volleyball matches, walks on the seafront. The two volumes he left for us to find document his last years of high school, 1957 until 1959. On the first pages, he is seventeen and sick of being stuck in the village—because for a year, the British colonial government has closed Lanítion Secondary School in retribution for the students' sit-ins. The students have demanded decolonization. My father writes of being miserable without class and without his friends, just as I would be, in those same hills, forty years on, when my own school was out. A few pages in, Lanítion has been permitted to reopen. Though the boarding schools remained closed for good, my father had an aunt who lives near Lanítion, and was able to continue his education by moving in with her family. Once he was back in the city, my father recorded kebabs and ice cream on the boardwalk, volleyball games, movies, dancing, and girls. He noted in his journal the nights on which he went to the cinema, often earning his ticket by serving as an usher. He saw Greek films and American ones, *The King and I* and *The Opposite Sex*. One of the theaters, the Rialto, was closed for decades when the area around it (called the Plaza of Heroes) became a red-light district. But now a university has opened nearby, and dorms and cafés have reverted the area to the way it was in my father's youth.

With my own friends I have sat in the renovated Rialto for films, concerts, and plays. In the summers, we've sat on the steps of the Plaza of Heroes just outside the Rialto for an international music festival. Andréas recorded excursions to the Troodos mountains and the birth of his aunt's first grandchild. He helped out with the newborn and took the baby for a walk in the *amaxoútha*, or pram.

I'm the only one of his children who can read his teenage scrawl.

And I'm the daughter whose academic job affords her time to go back to take care of our parents' unfinished business: renting out the house they bought in spite of us all, tracking down out-of-the-way plots of land that still belong to great-grandparents, and building a memorial on the space that received my father's body.

After three years, even though no amount of water-spilling had flattened the rocky heap of rust-colored earth above the grave, I decided to order the *mnemío*. *Monument*, I guess, best approximates the word *mnemío*, though monument sounds so public, as if strangers would be flocking to it. Maybe *tomb*. Some dictionaries suggest *sepulcher*, a word that recalls, for me, Jesus and Jerusalem. It would be a cement structure covered with either marble or stone.

I went to Asgáta and in the cemetery met with Asgáta's mayor and the builder whom he had recommended to do the job. My parents taught the mayor's children English, and my father grew up with his father in Asgáta, and out of love, I guess, or respect, he had used his own excavator to dig the grave for free. The mayor's father's mnemío was one of the few that matched what we all knew my father would have wanted. Unlike the majority of people, who lie beneath stately marble tombs, the butcher and the church chanter both rest under tombs made of marl, chalk, and sandstone from Asgáta's hills. The mayor helped me negotiate a price and schedule with the builder, and ensured that he understood my simple request—no need for an oil lamp cupboard, and a mnemío built of local stones.

They are the stones my father chose to pave the patios of the house in Asgáta, the one whose window framed his schoolhouse. They are stones hewn from the hills around this village, this village which, as a teenager my father tried so desperately to escape, and which—all through his thirty American years—kept calling him back. Not once, but again, and again.

The stones called him back with promises of everything he remembered. Before independence from colonial rule and the shift from an agricultural to a tourist economy, owning farmland gave a man status in Cyprus. My father's large inheritance augured respect. Leaving the village was exciting, necessary for a boy with intellectual needs. Those were well met in American universities, but none of his learning prepared him for how different life in his village would be after the decades he had spent in America. They were the decades during which the destitute, heavily taxed crown colony became a self-determined island nation, sent electricity to its villages, and turned olive presses into tourist attractions. Donkeys no longer bore the harvest, but rested in a vast donkey sanctuary run by British pensioners, who now paid taxes to the Republic of Cyprus. Even the grammar had modernized, so that whenever I typed up notes for my father, I had to update his verbs. Cyprus had entered modernity in a way it hadn't before he left it, and while he was getting his American education, alternative ways of acquiring capital and status had emerged in Cyprus. In the years after my family moved away, the tenant farmers and the hired hands went to work at the electrical plant nearby, or at a gravel quarry, or on construction sites for hotels. They earned more money than my teacher parents and built houses larger than ours with their own hands.

In the time my father spent away, being the son of a rural landowner had changed its meaning. When my father inherited his parents' tracts of earth, he received with them none of the old, ceremonial respect that they'd enjoyed. He paid taxes and hired tractors to plough to prevent wildfires, but I don't know whether my father ever reckoned with the way land ownership had once afforded a privilege he could not appreciate until it was gone.

Yet even after the disillusionment about what a plot of stony earth could yield, even after my father took his whole family back to America because he had been, by the earth's promises, disappointed, the earth on which he was born kept on calling. And I feel it too—desire for that earth. I long for my village even though what I most desire is the academic job I've got. Because although the earth has stopped being able to promise that it will feed us, although land ownership no longer gives us power over our neighbors, the earth still pulls us with its promise that it can lend to us a permanent home. People buy houses even when they can't afford them because the houses make them feel secure against the future.

We build little houses for the dead above the ground and we call them mnemía, memorials, as though their work is to preserve our memories of the dead. Really, what we're remembering is that they aren't here anymore, that they have a new home now, inside this particular bit of earth where they must stay forever. And that the future is the responsibility of the living.

We build those homes for our dead on a particular piece of land—or we scatter ashes on a well-chosen, discrete, and significant place—so that we can resist the illusion that they are everywhere, that their death never happened and that they are watching to ensure we live our lives according to what they may have wanted. *The Dominion of the Dead* teaches me that "the sanity of the community depends on the willingness of the dead to take their leave." Our rituals are designed to "appease the dead, to secure their goodwill, as it were, so that they might go gently," Harrison writes, "without rage or reluctance, into that good night." On the fortieth day, I danced, ending a period of public mourning. The owls stopped appearing, and for the rest of the summer I ran in the company of only swallows and bats. After four months, I went back to my job in America.

And just like that, I was done with traditions that render it permissible to take steps beyond the first, raw shock and the liminal space between speaking to a man and speaking for him. I stepped into the necessary separation between those upon the earth and those inside it. One day this separation will stop feeling like a betrayal. To make peace with the earth and with my own life—with a life lived according to my desires rather than his—I keep on performing one part of the work of mourning. I study his paragraphs.

My father's last years of high school coincided with the end of Cyprus's guerrilla war against British control. The Greek Cypriot freedom fighters' appeal for union with Greece was met with a compromise of independent statehood. On the last day of February 1959, Andréas wrote of bringing a little earth to his aunt's house to plant some jasmine, and then playing cards in the evening. The next day, he rose at five in the morning to travel by bus to the capital, where he joined the crowds receiving the Archbishop, exiled to the Seychelles by the British colonial regime. "Nicosia was full of people," my father recorded. Decades on, in an encyclopedia, I would read of an "unprecedented reception in Nicosia, where almost two-thirds of the adult Greek Cypriot population turned out to welcome him." The Archbishop would negotiate the colony's independence. All these events, which have now become the backbone of Cypriot history, punctuate the daily tally of girls sighted, ice creams eaten, movies seen, and baskets scored.

Men who fought for independence were released from British captivity on the day my father did poorly on a physics test, but well in Latin. News of passports and developments first with getting to Australia, then to America, also entered his pages, with only enough comment to suggest the same ambivalence I have felt when nearing any graduation—the eager anticipation of freedom mixed with regret, a premature nostalgia for the soon-to-be-lost sweetness of being a senior who has at last mastered high school, or college, or graduate school. Once warm weather came, my father studied for exams between eating kebabs and watching films in the open air.

On the day of his last final exam, he wrote, "*Tis mathitikís mou zoís.*" ("Today is the last day of my school life." "*της μαθητικής μου ζωής.*") With that ending came also the end of bicycle-riding, of promenading and movie-going, of serenading girls from under their windows. Young Andréas would be sent back to Asgáta to help with the carob harvest, plant lentils and pick oranges, restock the family grocery store with sugar and beer, and oversee the tilling of the fields. By the time Andréas graduated high school, his father had already left for America again, and was working in New York as a sous chef. His father wrote him letters with directions he recorded but did not obey. The journal concludes with this line:

Μου έστειλε 10 δολάρια ο πατέρας. Με προτρέπει να πάω στο χωριό.

Mou ésteile 10 tholária o patéras. Me protrépei na páo sto horió.

Father sent me ten dollars. He urges me to go back to the village.

—

Of Acacia
and Maple

—

I don't garden. A planted cactus placed in my care quickly perished. I don't talk about saving trees, and when I once hugged one, it was because I felt anxious and had read an article on the calming power of such an embrace. What I love about plants is their names, and the way that naming a plant brings people into a life I once lived. To lure other humans into my world, to be less alone with my memories, I say, "aleppo pine," "sugar maple," "blue spruce," "spiny broom," "oleander," "Turkish filbert," "hoary rock rose," "hackberry," or "littleleaf linden." After my father died, I wrote a poem about the *Jasminum officinale*, poet's jasmine, that had overgrown his house entrance but which, without his directions, I could not prune.

By the time I was born, my parents had gained enough American capital not only to feed me but also to buy a house more capacious than all their own previous houses combined. Half our backyard was devoted to tomato, cucumber, and lettuce plants, while the other half was all grass. Ivy climbed up all the fences and the visible backs of each neighbor's garage. My brother and I played endless soccer matches on that grass, and when we tired of running, we'd build forts out of sticks. A stately sugar maple, *Acer saccharum*, commanded the corner of our yard. I seek, still, for it a fitting metaphor that is not a king or a prince, for it didn't rule at all, but stood quietly and *gave*. It gave the grownups their shade. It gave to us a wall for our forts. With the brown picket fence opposite and the neighbor's adjacent garage forming the second and third wall, we only needed to build the fourth by filling in the empty space with sticks or, in winter, with snow.

Down the street in Bowne Park, I played among the branches of a weeping willow and hid within a stand of firs. More maples and oaks filled the grassy park, too. There were dandelions in spring, and I assumed everyone lived like this, among so much green. I read about treehouses in books, and I prayed weekly, in church, for such a structure to come to our trees. I didn't think about how hard it would be to make a treehouse in the maple or the oak whose branches didn't begin to separate from the trunk for many, many feet above our heads. It wasn't yet clear to me that I had a father who could grow almost anything, but was not inclined to build. Yet I thought of a treehouse as the solution to one of my childhood's fundamental problems: the maple and the oak next to it were unclimbable, and I couldn't scramble up trees like Jo's boys or the Ingalls children. My memory of that large, beautiful maple remains that of a great, breathing organism whose branches remained forever just out of reach.

My prayers for a treehouse weren't answered. Or perhaps, in that mystical way the world has of granting our wishes, I was taken to a new continent at the age of ten, and gained in that unexpected way the access I'd desired to the upper story of the world. For when my parents decided to move us to the island of my father's birth, I found in Cyprus trees with low branches, olives tended for centuries in a way that kept their precious oil-bearing fruit accessible to generations of farmers. I found squat carob trees and the sleek almond trees whose sloping branches I could hang from, monkey style, as I climbed.

Before their wedding, my father told my mother, Georgia, that he intended, one day, to return to Cyprus. My mother agreed, even though her only acquaintance with the island was a comment her father had made once when she was a teenager, as they passed the island on an ocean liner that was taking them to Egypt for a tour. Her father Spyros had said the people of Cyprus spoke Greek, but in an unintelligible dialect. Her fiancé painted a more enticing portrait, describing with gusto the cool, mountain towns where his Boy Scout troop had pitched their tents and lit campfires in the quiet, pine-covered Troodos forests. After the wedding, they went back to being the English teacher and the Social Studies teacher at St. Demetrios High School in Jamaica, Queens. I was born, then Dino was born, then Cathy moved out, married, and had a baby. My parents' New York lives proceeded as if the promise would remain an abstraction forever.

One day, though, there arrived a big envelope from an architect whom my father called his best friend. I sat on my father's lap in our kitchen, soft New York sunlight brightening the blue pages of the building plans he had spread before us. Reaching over his coffee mug and plate of toast and bitter orange marmalade, he showed me where my bedroom would be.

"See here? This is your room. This is your veranda." I learned a few years later what a veranda was, and because I had encountered mountains only in books and on television, I employed descriptions from the novel *Heidi* to help me picture my balcony on the second floor of a cottage perched atop a peak of our very own. There was probably grass on the vision's hill, since I pictured myself rolling down a hill to school. My dad promised me a goat of my own (I would even get to milk it), and we'd have chickens for fresh eggs.

On another day, I was bent over my mud pies in our grassy backyard, my brother was playing with an inflatable toddler-ball, and my dad was pulling weeds from around his prize tomato plant. He told me to look at the sky.

"You see what kind of a day it is today, Joanna? No clouds. In Cyprus it's like this every day of the year." He described the house his best friend was building for us, with verandas where we'd sit each morning to enjoy the always-mild breeze. There would be a stone patio and a magnificent view. "In Cyprus it never gets too cold to sit outside," he said. My father used to say that he remembered such a promise, but argued that he didn't say what I remember him saying next: "or too hot."

Cyprus most certainly was too hot, but the freedom of our outdoor lives made up for that, and once we had finally made the move in the summer of 1988, my brother and I made the best of it as children do. We especially loved the freedom we gained when we left New York City. My parents relaxed in a place where abductions were unheard of and assaults on children rare, so they let us learn for ourselves the hazards of the new Cypriot landscape. In the Cypriot places where we would live—first "the mountains" of my father's dreams and eventually the village of his birth—there were no fences, and as long as we avoided trampling our neighbors' crops and watched out for snakes, my brother and I were free to roam the hills. Happily, aside from the usual childhood scrapes, the worst event was getting stuck with the many thread-like spines of a cactus while reaching for its prickly pear (Cypriot: *papoutsósiko*, Greek: *arapósiko*). We built houses and forts in any tree that lent itself to modification. The ubiquitous *Acacia saligna*, or golden wreath wattle (an

Australian species that Cypriot environmentalists consider invasive and threatening to endemic flora), was like a willow in miniature. We would claim a tree for a while, pull out the weeds around it, bring some toys, and spend time there. We'd say, "This is my house." There was hoary rock rose, *Cistus criticus*, for an ephemeral decoration.

New York City had raised me. When I left, I missed my friends, but when I fell for rural Cyprus, I fell hard, and before long, my city memories had grown faint. On the day we visited Asgáta for the first time, my parents parked on a dirt road just above a large plot of land belonging to my grandfather. I took off on my own and walked up and down the hills for more than an hour alone. I'd never seen so much raw earth before; my suburban birthplace was buried under asphalt and grass. I returned to my parents holding strange leaves, and my father named them: the roundish carob, slim almond, and little gray-green olive. I begged for a few more minutes and scrambled back up the hillside, where the pinkish earth slid beneath my feet. Veins ran through the rocks, white glistening quartz and dark red, like clay. My fingers grew sticky from the twigs I broke to watch them ooze their viscous milk. Dry stalks of asphodel broke in my hands with satisfying cracks as I collected the pieces to make a raft. The underbrush ran downhill as far as I could see. Even the smell—of oregano, sage, and dust—hinted of a wildness that was new and yet familiar, as if all my life I had been searching for this place.

More than thirty years after that first day in Asgáta, I look back now and consider the way that, at ten, I felt I was arriving home to a place I had never seen—as if my father's home had lurked in some inherited recess of my imagination. This place was in my dreams and in my blood; it held my father's story and the story of his father before him.

Your Schedule
Depends on the Sky

My mother's evergreen wool skirt reaches my knees, and like the navy sweater I am wearing, it is both itchy and warm. A long, puffy coat further shields me from the cold. Until today, we hadn't had snow in our yard in Cyprus. Snow in the yard would bring us back four whole years, to when my brother was four and I was nine and our yard in Flushing was covered in white. It feels as if we are in New York again, where we belong.

My father sits in the kitchen sipping coffee. He is smiling at my mother's decision to drag her children to church in the snow. As a native of Cyprus, he knows it isn't wise to do battle with the weather. In Cyprus, you let weather win. You do not go out walking in the scorching midday sun; you wait until evening when the light smiles orange, gentle, sweet. Your schedule depends on the sky. No hat, no visor, and no sunscreen protects enough for a walk at midday in the sun. Streets turn to rivers when it rains and nothing can be done. When snow falls, you stay home. Cypriots wait the weather out, sleep through the heat and shiver through the cold. They watch flooded streets from their balconies, see snow flurries from their firesides, and hope for the best. But my mother is a New York, and when it snows, she puts on boots and she walks.

We have brought from New York a plastic sled, a long black one with a seat back and brakes, though one brake is broken so the sled can turn but can't stop. It's not really very good for sledding down snowy hillsides. It is perfect, though, for towing a seven-year-old who whines when you ask him to walk. I will walk in my snow boots, bought large last year to fit thick woolen socks. We put on scarves, and Dino a hat. I refuse to wear a hat because I never wear hats, and we set off down the road.

Soon, the snow has stopped but for a few flurries. The main road will be cleared eventually, but not until much later in the day. For now, the ground is buried under two or three inches of fluffy snow, the kind that reflects even gray light as beautiful. Asphalt scrapes against the sled when we reach a place canopied by trees. I cannot remember any of the things we say except that we complain a lot, and our mother talks of the hot chocolate we'll get when we return.

I have been feeling pine needles or something poking into me for the fifteen minutes we've been on the road. When the scraping gets to be too much, I bend down to upturn the hem of my mother's skirt. I find not needles but pins. My mother has been meaning to shorten her skirt to fit me better because it is made of wool and wool is the warmest thing there is. I show her the pins to emphasize how much I have suffered already in this strange religious rush. My mother has been towing Dino faster than perhaps she should, if you consider she's had back pain this year. Short of breath, she apologizes to me, throws the pins into the snow, and keeps on moving because church is starting any minute; it is already eight.

"Your father will have a fire waiting," she coaxes us on, promising cinnamon-sugar toast or the packaged croissants we love.

Even back in New York, our mother let us eat our favorite things only after church. There, we got two Dunkin Donuts each, and here in Cyprus my brother and I buy Today chocolate bars or 7 Days Croissants with chocolate-hazelnut filling from the village store. My mother doesn't think anything available in Cyprus can compare to Dunkin Donuts, and says Cypriot commercial sweet things are a waste of money, so she fries pancakes for herself at home.

We reach the main road, which is empty. My mother looks at her watch and urges me to walk faster. Dino says he is cold and my mother tells him he'll feel warm when we get to church. But the church is old, and one little round gas heater doesn't do much to warm a tall building made of stone. Women with just-baptized infants crowd around that heater and so older kids like Dino and me never get a chance to stand close.

In this parish of Moniátis, no one uses new candles. I wonder where the loads of used candles come from as I drop coins into the box and lift my stump of wax with its blackened wick from the tray. In New York, we always lit new candles, which tapered into soft white threads. When I lit my first used candle before the icon of the Virgin Mary, I felt a little strange, like I'd worn a torn sweater to church or made a gift of a book I'd already read. But at some point during the gospel reading each Sunday, watching an old candle grow even smaller, I forget about the thrift of this particular devotion, and consider only the molten wax cooling and hardening around my fingers.

In this parish, rasping, tone-deaf men chant the service quickly, and make the normally two-hour service last only forty-five minutes, so my brother and I prefer this off-key church to any other. We speak some Greek, but can't understand the dialect here in Cyprus. We have never spoken to any parishioner, and we are the only children ever in church. Often, we are also the only people receiving communion.

As we trudge on through the snow, I try to estimate how much liturgy will be left when we arrive. Twenty minutes, I guess, and am pleased. This walk has taken a while. The snow has stopped falling, and when I look up at the sky I see a patch of cloud that looks thinner, where the sun might just poke through. I shiver. Dino yells about the cold.

And then the first vehicle of the morning rounds a bend ahead of us and seems to be inching forward in our direction. The pickup truck uses four-wheel drive, and I wonder if my mother will come to her senses and ask the driver to please just take us back home. When the window rolls down, I see the figure is wearing black and his eyes shine with the brightness of prayer because it is the Moniátis village priest. He asks us where we are going; when my mother replies, he tells us to get in because there is no church on a day covered in snow.

At home, my father laughs at my mother, and after our promised hot chocolate, my brother and mother settle down to a game of checkers while I run up to change out of church clothes into my sweatshirt and jeans.

The too-long woolen skirt (which my mother will never end up hemming) lies on the floor where I have tossed it. I put my thick tights in the hamper and put on fuzzy socks, which ease the dull ache of frosty toes. I think about the black-wicked candles by the icon of the Virgin Mary, who is alone this Sunday. All that walking for nothing, I think. The black-wicked candles by the icon of the Virgin Mary are without flame, and our Lady will be gazing out at no one. And I think: This is my first Sunday without church.

—

The Actress
Who Isn't Acting

—

Melina Mercouri entered my life just as she was leaving her own behind. I was fifteen going on sixteen, and I had just started watching the news. Melina was seventy and a terminal cancer patient, but her professionally dyed and blown-out hair, along with her meticulous makeup, made her look younger than my mother, who was forty-nine. My mother had herself recently survived the disease and had, after a mastectomy, been pronounced cancer-free. Melina's own prognosis, on the other hand, grew ever bleaker, and as it did, our Greek Cypriot television stations spent more and more airtime on her. Melina mattered to audiences not so much because of her current post as Greece's Minister of Culture, but because of her activism to restore democracy to Greece twenty years earlier, and because of her iconic roles as a movie star.

I watched Melina speak into microphones in her silk dressing gown. She held press conferences in New York, not far from the apartment where I used to visit my grandmother Joanna on Sundays, before we moved away. When journalists asked Melina about her health, she refused to talk about

her personal pain. Instead, she praised the people who had
stood by her and given her a reason to stay alive, both at
Sloane-Kettering and back home in Greece. "If you should
hear that I have died," she told one reporter, "cross-check the
information again and again. Chances are, I will not actually
be dead." The ferocity of the Greek people's love, she said,
had the power to restore her health.

Melina laughed at death the way she had laughed at
the colonels who, on April 21, 1967, staged a coup d'état
that usurped the democratically elected Greek government. Melina was in New York when the tanks rolled down
her city's streets. The junta took control of all media and
censored every song, newspaper, radio show, and book.
When the junta took power, Melina was on Broadway
starring in *Ilya Darling*, an adaptation of her hit film *Never
on Sunday*. She wanted at once to use her platform in New
York to move American political opinion. Melina's husband
urged her to remain silent. An American filmmaker who
had been blacklisted, under McCarthyism, by the Special
Committee on Un-American Activities, Jules Dassin had
in fact met Melina because he had been living in self-
imposed exile in France. Once he had expressed sympathy for
the Left, he could no longer find work in the US. Knowing
first-hand the consequences of dissent, Dassin argued that
speaking out against the junta might have equally brutal consequences for Greece's biggest star. Already, in the first few
days of the dictatorship, many poets had been thrown in jail.

Melina kept silent for weeks, but once the press began to
ask her questions she could not bear to be, by her silence,
complicit with tyranny. She called the colonels clowns. She
called them gangsters. She asked American tourists to stay
away from her country so as to starve the regime of funds.
The retaliation that her husband had predicted came swiftly.

The dictators named her an "enemy of Greek tourism," confiscated her property, and revoked her Greek citizenship. At five in the morning, New York time, on July 12, 1967, the *Daily Mirror* called Melina to get the star's response.

"I was born Greek, and I will die Greek," Melina Mercouri said into the phone. She rose from bed then, at that ungodly hour, called a press conference, and told the whole world what she'd said to the *Mirror*. Made up like the 1960s movie star she was, she wore bold eyeliner and mascara around the enormous eyes that no one can forget, and spoke with the defiance of her greatest roles: Medea, Lysistrata, Blanche DuBois.

Melina said to the cameras, "Mr. Pattakos and the four Colonels were born fascists, and they will die fascists. If they want to make of me a Joan of Arc, let them try."

When reporters asked her where she based her claim that they were fascists, she pointed out what they'd done to her: "I exercised my freedom of speech, they didn't like what I said, and so they took away my citizenship. This is the very definition of fascism."

Each night thereafter, once the curtains fell on her Broadway show, Melina would tell her audience that the carefree and joyful Greece they'd just seen portrayed on stage no longer existed. Pro-junta forces hated her for this and made death threats, so that during every show, three FBI agents sat in the audience while two stood in the wings, pistols cocked.

Over the course of the seven-year-long dictatorship, Greece's Joan of Arc produced some of the greatest obstacles to the colonels' rule. Her experience as a movie star made her especially effective as a political activist. Leveraging her international celebrity, Melina helped keep global public opinion opposed to the junta. Thus, foreign governments felt domestic pressure to help restore democracy to Greece. Addressing the politicians who had been democratically elected but usurped by the coup, and were now in exile, she called to the resistance, referring to her role as Ilya: "I am a whore of international radiance; put me to use."

In 1968, one year into the junta's grip on Greece, Melina filled Trafalgar Square with British and Greek-British supporters and proclaimed into the microphone: "Today is Easter. Greek Orthodox Easter. But alas, it is also the anniversary of shame, the shame of the colonels, who buried democracy in Greece. Boycott the junta! Isolate the junta! *Give them hell.*"

At least once, during an inspection of the premises where she would be speaking, security forces found, tucked under the podium, a bomb. Melina defied this intimidation. She'd insisted that pleasure was her life's guiding principle, yet here she was, risking her life and thus all possibility of pleasure.

After seven years of protests, after the murders and brutal torture of thousands of artists and political dissidents, the colonels took a fatal misstep. They pushed their luck. They tried to overthrow the elected government in Cyprus, too, so that they could install a Greek nationalist regime and make Cyprus a pawn or a part of the Greek military state. When this risky move prompted the Turkish invasion of Cyprus, the junta lost so much political capital and credibility, their regime finally toppled.

Exiled politicians flew back home to form a democratic government. The perpetrators of the coup would be put on trial and jailed for life. Melina boarded a flight full of political exiles returning to Greece. Having had her passport canceled by the dictators, Melina traveled on documents that declared her an international refugee. Upon her arrival, she was embraced so vigorously by euphoric fans that she left the tarmac with bruises. All of this I learned in my parents' living room in the village of Asgáta in Cyprus, while she was dying and I was watching television, in March 1994.

At fifteen, watching Melina prepare herself to die, I was thinking hard about what it means to live. I hungered for meaning, and felt desperate to make sense of a certain kind of beauty that I had just begun to see. I was reading Eastern Orthodox theology books that a priest had lent me during confession, and in them I learned that in the sixth century, Saint Maximus the Confessor wrote that we must recognize "the equal value of all" in God's sight. I liked how this tied Christianity to social justice, which was starting to become an obsession for me. It is typical for a teenager to feel that the world isn't fair, and I expanded my personal grievances to connect with injustice and marginalization on a grand scale. There was no internet back then, or (in my region) even a library. My window to the outer world was the radio, a handful of television channels, and books. And it was in theology books that I first located a promise of what I sought, which was justice, beauty, and the truth.

And it was books, too, that promised to explain what I felt, which was mostly longing. We must "engrave His beauty on our memory," and when we do, Maximus went on, we'll be overcome with an "ineradicable longing for divine love." Such love, the ascetic wrote, "is always imprinting this beauty on their intellect." I set out to discover what all this bright, blessed beauty meant. On top of religious books, I was reading the Victorians and Modernists for school (Austen, the Brontës, Henry James, D. H. Lawrence) and pulling Plato and Plotinus from my parents' shelves. I was trying to understand love through Heathcliff, Catherine, Rochester, Bertha, Jane, the Brangwens, and the Symposium's tipsy philosophers, who each argued that *he* was the most earnest and ethical among all of those lusty lovers of boys.

I plastered my bedroom with song lyrics that held meaning for me, such as "anything that matters hurts and takes work," and indictments of anything fake, like "when I see friends, I hope that they don't recognize me because I don't want to hear more dead *good evenings*." The beauty I had begun to see in the world was attached to being *real* and unafraid. Like most teenagers, I raged at the hypocrisy that I saw all around me, especially in politics, and Melina Mercouri struck me as the one politician who had lived and served without hypocrisy. Her words didn't sound hollow. Hers would not be dead "good evenings." Melina's gravelly, smoke-husky voice, in love with vowels and consonants and clear in its enunciation, filled the radio waves as well as the television screens. I took to listening nonstop: light-hearted songs from her popular films, jaunty political songs in French, and the militant, serious songs from her underground work against the fascists. And, though I didn't have the word for it then, I thought Melina was hot.

For the first few days after Melina started appearing regularly on the news, I wondered, simply, "Why is this tall, sexy Athenian giving interviews from New York? Why is she assuring Greece that she will stay alive?" I didn't try hard to find answers. I just kept on looking at the woman as she spoke fiercely, as though death were an aggressor to be defeated like the junta, or like the British Museum which refused to return the Parthenon Marbles. And just as Melina marched in Washington and Boston and London and Paris in her finest movie-star clothes, so she maintained a diva's confident charm as her health continued to decline.

As I sought to figure out what gave a life meaning, Melina's story seemed to be a score for politics. I wanted what Melina had, I believed, though in hindsight I think I was a little hazy on whether I wanted to be *like* Melina or if I just plain *wanted* Melina. The fuzziness of childhood perception was giving way to adult consciousness in that maddening, non-linear manner that turns adolescents into difficult kids-but-not-kids. In fact, looking back, I might have even begun to suspect that there was another layer of complexity to my world that would remain for years out of my reach. Melina lent to politics an erotic charge. Seeing this sexy politician speak with the air of a movie star suggested that instead of figuring out whether meaning hid in religion, science, literature, or love, there might be a special sweetness to mixing it all up: theater with politics, intellectualism with art, discipline with fun, and everything, everything with desire. God himself, wrote Maximus the Confessor after all, is someone who "thirsts to be thirsted for, longs to be longed for, and loves to be loved."

I watched Melina's funeral on television. Greece's first woman cabinet member, Melina was the first Greek woman to be buried with the honors of a head of state. Her body traveled back over the ocean from Sloane-Kettering in the Boeing 747 *Olympic Eagle*, and the plane bearing her body slid between a formation of Phantom jets for its final arc toward the ground. Young women brought cigarettes to her coffin and called out "Melina is alive and needs a light!" Now, in death, Melina could indulge in a pleasure that her cancer had forbidden. All of Athens poured into the streets to receive her, and a sea of black-clad bodies surrounded her flower-covered hearse. "This is not a funeral," someone said. "This is an apotheosis."

>>·<<

Twenty winters after Melina's death, on March 6, 2014, I would be visiting my sister in New York, not far from Sloan-Kettering. Greek stations came to her television via satellite. I would watch a tribute that commemorated the day Melina died. I would watch Melina dancing in her glorious pantsuits, large sunglasses over her head, tapping the time, directing a protest film. The 2014 tribute was called *Twenty Twenty-Year-Olds Twenty Years Later*, and the twenty-year-old artists would describe what they knew of the great woman whose life had ended when theirs began.

All the young artists knew a little bit about Melina. They described her as a beautiful woman (ωραία γυναίκα), seductive and feminine, but also tough as nails, ballsy, dauntless, valiant, bold. She is both a *kokkéta*—a coquettish, feminine woman—and *andráki*, a little man, a mensch. Although on the internet one can still find misogynists who decry outspoken women by using "mannish and Mercouri-like" as a slur, for most, Melina's androgyny is part of her allure. As a tenth-grader I didn't know of any such manly women. In twelfth-grade Greek class, I would read about Hathoúla, the grandmother who despairs about the plight of women on Skiathos island. In our edition, the novelist described her as an *androgynéka* (αντρογυναίκα). I remember trying to imagine such a woman, an *androgynéka*, a *man-woman*. She would be tall, broad-shouldered, and muscular, I figured, dressed in stern, ruffle-free clothing, and accustomed to heavy outdoor work.

Twenty Twenty-Year-Olds Twenty Years Later glosses over

Melina's early years, when she wasn't so comfortable with risk. Melina's first husband stayed rich during the Nazi occupation of Athens. The only way to do that was to trade on the black market, extorting fellow Greeks who were being starved by the Nazis' policy of requisitioning food and burning fields, livestock, and fishing boats. Melina ended up married at seventeen years old because her respectable family refused to let her study theater, so she eloped with this rich, much older man who promised to help her go to drama school. Melina was nineteen when World War II broke out, twenty-one and a recent theater graduate when the Nazi troops invaded Greece. Melina's only regret in life, she once said, was her decision, back then, to stay on the sidelines in the shelter of her husband's house while most Greek youth joined the Resistance. During the bitter Greek Civil War that followed, Melina remained politically inactive. Her family had been right-wing royalists, but as an actress she would have moved in left-wing circles. She probably became conflicted as her life diverged from her family's. When tyranny returned to Greece, she was forty-seven, and determined not to repeat the mistake.

Melina wrote one book, *I Was Born Greek*, which reads like a typical celebrity autobiography in the beginning. She writes of her girlhood in Athens and her rise to success in the theater. The cover of my edition features a barefoot Melina sitting on a rock on the sunny Acropolis, and suggests the typical celebrity "how I got here" narrative. Halfway through, the book's real purpose becomes clear. *I Was Born Greek* was published in 1971, the dead center of the dictatorship, and in it Melina told the world that Greece was not free.

Like those of many authoritarian regimes, both in Latin America and Europe, the colonels continued to throw artists in jail. Not only the poets but also the composers, directors, actors, musicians, even comedians. They threw the journalists in jail, too, assassinated those they feared most, and exiled those too internationally famous to assassinate or imprison. The best music and the best plays—even *Antigone*—were banned. Later, in my twenties, I would learn how widespread these practices were among authoritarian regimes all over the world, but as a teenager, I thought the brutality of the Greek junta was unique. I had grown up a child of the Cold War and yet long remained ignorant of how many American artists were silenced in its name. I didn't know about the Red Scare in America or the blacklisting of Hollywood artists like Melina's American second husband, let alone all the other countries that had had basic freedoms taken away in the name of "containment." As pieces of the puzzle came together gradually, over decades, I would begin to see that desiring freedom—*elefthería*—is common to all people, but fighting for it is a decision far more fraught than my elementary school plays suggested. Those school plays had presented an obvious tyrant—the Ottoman rulers of Greece—and made out the decision to fight the Ottoman government as obvious. They suggested that anti-government martyrdom was a no-brainer. As I learned about activists like Melina, I began first of all to see that good and bad might be hard to distinguish. The law-abiding could be barbaric while the law-breakers could later become the pillars of the nation-state. I saw how very much a resistance fighter stands to lose. Not every hero lives.

Melina spoke at every university, every parliament, every microphone that would have her. She traveled all over the world, still dressed as a movie star but talking about politics, history, and human rights. In *I Was Born Greek*, she says:

So-called friends came to warn me that "an artist who meddled in politics would finish by destroying his career." I took recourse to the first dirty word I learned in English. "Bullshit." The narrowness and inhumanity of the notion that fighting for your freedom is "meddling in politics" makes me furious. I suggested that they brush up their history and etymology. History would tell them what role the artist has always played in the fight for justice and freedom, and the *demos* in *democracy* means *people*. Artists are people too. Thank God, many artists refuse to accept the role of court jester, or sequestration in ivory towers.

Around the same time that I became enchanted by the silk-draped shoulders of Mercouri, long, troubled passages in my teenage journals began to fret over my identity. I filled pages of my journal asking myself whether I was Greek, American, or Cypriot. I settled upon the word *Greek*. It held weight. I had never lived in Greece, and I remained restless, itching to resolve the contradiction. I'd read books about American kids, and about Greek kids, and I'd lived among Greek American kids until I was ten, but I'd never seen a representation of a kid shaped by both American and Greek Cypriot culture. Melina's love songs to Greece came closer than anything to giving me that feeling of recognition that I sought. I listened to Greek radio all the time. I learned as much as I could about recent Greek history and politics. I wrote a long, nationalistic, and embarrassingly erotic poem to a female personification of Greece (Lady Hellas). I wanted to forge for myself an emblem.

All that listening to the radio provided a piecemeal education about American imperialism. I pieced together bits of information the radio announcers gave as context before and after playing Greek songs. I listened to Greek rock music, which advocated workers' rights, rights for the poor, and recognition and commemoration of the Armenian Genocide. All this made me eager to renounce my American identity and to identify with these Greek leftists. I identified with Greek workers in songs like "I Fábrica" ("The Factory," "Η Φάμπρικα"), even though I'd never been inside a factory, and my hours of voluntary, agricultural labor always ended as soon as I felt tired.

You might say that Melina became political with her first film, *Stella*. In *Stella*, a man who cannot persuade his girlfriend to marry him tries coercion instead. One of the film's final lines is now a Greek touchstone: "Stella, I'm holding a knife."

Stella premiered in 1955, five years after the Greek Civil War ended and old gender roles were just beginning to be questioned. The title character's refusal to accept her boyfriend's proposal expresses the nation's anxiety about women's liberation. Stella kisses her lover with relish on screen, and it is suggested plainly that she also gladly agrees to have sex; she just will not marry. She leaves her soccer-star fiancé at the altar, and for refusing to need a man, Stella receives her lover's knife. To an American reviewer, the film was a "grimly lugubrious drama." He decries as old-fashioned the trope in which the "inevitable climax was the violent murder of the femme fatale," but misses how rare and radical it was to find an attractive, confident female protagonist uninterested in marriage. It continues to be rare well into the twenty-first century. Instead, the reviewer responds to Stella's indifference to marriage with this somewhat cryptic remark: "The situation is slightly Sapphic, and Miss Mercouri takes it in a stride that marks her a likely descendant of the sires of the Olympic games." The reviewer goes on, with a gusto of his own, to point out that Melina, thirty, is "not a noticeably youthful girl," but nevertheless "leaps into singing and dancing as though she was off for a 440-yard dash; at a football game, cheering her hero, she almost cripples herself jumping up and down." He concludes that "when she kisses a fellow, it resembles a Greek wrestling match. Miss Mercouri is hot-cha all over, even when gurgling her last with a knife in her back."

Looking back, Melina recalled how difficult it was to land that first film role. Casting directors, she said, favored actresses who had tiny mouths. They thought that, with her large mouth, Melina "would not be photogenic." Even the author of the screenplay, the prominent Greek playwright Iakovos Kampanéllis, who was eager to have her play his leading role, nevertheless used to call her *agoráki*, little boy. Over and over there seems to be an insistence on Melina's boyishness, both from Greeks at home and from reviewers abroad. Only Cacoyiánnis, *Stella*'s Greek Cypriot director, who would go on to write and direct *Zorba the Greek*, seemed to appreciate Melina for who she was and for what her particular physicality could do. Melina claimed that Cacoyiánnis single-handedly changed Greek cinema forever just by shooting a closeup of her not-tiny mouth.

"The camera got right up in my larynx," she said, and explained that those closeups made *Stella* the film that made Greeks capable of actually seeing a woman with a large mouth.

Melina was nominated for Best Actress at Cannes for *Stella*, and though she didn't win an award, she met the

American Jules Dassin, who had. He told her she should have won, not Spencer Tracy (they didn't give separate awards to men and women Best Actors until 1957). Dassin soon became the man Melina would call the "love of her life," a partner in both love and art. He wrote the lead role of the film *Never on Sunday* for her in the late 1950s. To economize, Dassin played the protagonist's dorky American suitor himself.

Never on Sunday became the greatest commercial success Greek cinema had ever known, and most Americans my parents' age recognize the film, or at least its Oscar-winning score. Some Greeks were scandalized because Melina's character, the prostitute Ilya, enjoys her life, refuses to be subservient to anyone, and is unapologetic about her line of work. She won't take a client just because he can pay; she takes the clients who give her pleasure. Melina said that her character Ilya *is* Greece, an unruly lover that the West kept trying to rein in, make chaste, and tame. Melina's arguments were remarkably prescient, given that postcolonial theory hadn't been born yet, and that she did not even live to see northwestern Europe, fifty years after *Never on Sunday*, castigate Greece for being indulgent, and profligate, and poor, and entirely too awash in pleasure.

Back in the 1970s, it was predictable that the international press would express disdain for Mercouri's work toward democracy's return to Greece. Interviewers ostensibly interested in her activism asked why she didn't stick to acting. Elizabeth Taylor urged Melina to stop. A *New York Magazine* article called "The Actress Who Isn't Acting" complained that she was not doing her job.

"Do you feel that this is a good and proper role for entertainers?" one journalist (along with many others) asked Melina.

And one more time, she answered: "I am an actress by profession and vocation. I am a citizen by obligation and responsibility. And I salute every actor that feels like me." She was asked this so often that sound clips exist of her giving the same answer in Greek and also in French: *je suis par profession une actrice, mais je suis par volonté et par devoir une citoyenne.* She cited the company of Vaclav Havel, actor-activists Jane Fonda and Vanessa Redgrave, and folk singer Victor Jara, who had not yet been assassinated. She said that the very question—whether it is appropriate for an artist to do political work—is a fascist question.

Melina distinguished between her *obligation* as a citizen and her *vocation* as a professional actor in a way that has continued to intrigue me even long after I first heard it as a vocation-seeking, obligation-exploring teenager. The unspoken link between citizenship and art for Melina is desire—desire for what is beautiful, for what is good. The Greeks used the word *calós* for both beautiful (think calligraphy, calisthenics, kaleidoscope) and good (think *Philokalía*, love of goodness). Sometimes I worry that to equate beauty and goodness might imply that people who aren't as physically attractive as others are also less good. So, after all, the cartoonists who portray evil stepmothers as big-nosed, pointy-chinned, and pock-skinned would have it. And we know about the insidious stereotype of the tawny, ugly villain. Nevertheless, it bears consideration, this link between beauty and goodness via desire. That the word *fair*, Elaine Scarry explains in *On Beauty and Being Just*, can denote both a just verdict and a fair or attractive woman has its roots in the complexities of human perception.

Virtue and pleasure aren't binary opposites, as the Puritans would have it, but profoundly interconnected aspects of the one desirable *good*. And so it is that, as Minister of Culture, Melina tried to put into school curricula information that was good to know and also aesthetically pleasing. She wanted to make the educational parts of Greek tourist attractions satisfying for the senses. Learning needn't be a chore simply because it is virtuous. Learning can be beautiful and fun and desirable at the same time that it remains our duty as Greeks, and an activity that is good. Melina believed that travel, art, and education should all be suffused with joy.

Here is Maximus the Confessor again, with his own thousand-year-old ascetic Christian take on the link between beauty and the good: "The Cause of all things, through His beauty and goodness and His intense love for everything, goes out of Himself in His providential care for the whole of creation." God, here, is named the "Cause of all things." God is beautiful. God is the ardent lover of creation. The cause of beauty's existence, my religion was telling me, was a nameable person, a nameable God, who loved ardently like I did and whom I could come to know. A person who prays, Maximus wrote, earns a special, transcendent knowledge— a knowledge of God. She becomes herself "a faithful copy of archetypal beauty." A copy of God. As I grew more alive to beauty like Melina's, and to the injustices that beset great swaths of God's creation, my need to know God grew ever deeper. I began to want to be a person who prays.

In Melina's life, the problem of aesthetic justice is manifest in all its thorny complexity. Melina made money from pandering to America's fantasies about an exoticized Greece, and also made Greece famous that way; she brought in tourist money to offset the destitution caused by the Nazi occupation and ensuing civil war. *Never on Sunday* single-handedly increased tourist revenue many times over. It was the most well-received Greek film ever, yet I think it was exploitative, too, or problematic at the very least. One scholar articulates the problematic nature of the film thus: "Mercouri, as a Greek woman and as a personality, is thus made to testify to the truth of the blatantly phallocentric assumptions about female 'nature' on which the representation of Greekness in *Never on Sunday* (via the American film musical) depends." By the same token, the very film that opened the gateway for women with not-so-small mouths, *Stella*, brutally reinstates the patriarchal status quo. The film ends when Stella's sexual partner drives a knife into her back, never suggesting any retribution for the murderer, as if the act of suggesting that a woman might live for herself and stare her jilted lover-murderer in the eye as he kills her was all the film could dare.

The endings of both *Stella* and *Never on Sunday* ultimately undermine the films' claims to a progressive agenda. Yet participating in such films didn't stop Melina from dedicating the rest of her life to fighting the West's imperialist, exploitative stance toward Greece. Nor did it compromise her resistance struggles. Melina owned all her choices, even ones that compromised aesthetic accomplishment and political integrity in the name of commercial success. I'm not interested in moralizing about those choices. I'm interested in learning from Melina's ability to make concessions in order to reach an enormous global audience. Melina knew that every artistic choice produces a political effect. On a visit to the Reagan administration as Greek Minister of Culture, a reporter challenged her intervention into foreign relations—he suggested that as Minister of Culture she should stick to apolitical art—and her response turned into a *New York Times* headline: "Every act is political, even to eat."

Knowing the political force of all art, Melina chose to be flexible and fearless, and to make movies that served the greater good. There's something healthy about resisting aesthetic extremes. In the name of high standards, artists can become rigid, unadventurous, puritanical, rigid. I don't have to be an ascetic leftist to be a good leftist, Melina teaches me, nor do I have to die on the cross of anti-imperialism. The "happy whore" named Ilya *does* represent modern Greece, just as Melina claimed in an interview. The whore of *Never on Sunday* knows how to live, whereas the scholar she seduces does not. He's stuck in the past and refuses the joyous disorder of the present. Homer's character (or caricature) matches the white marble statues whose wild original colors are omitted in Western Europe's reproductions of classical art. This, Melina saw clearly.

When asked whether she considered herself "an optimistic," instead of *yes* or *no* Melina replied simply, "I'm Greek." She employed not the word *ellinída* but the old word *romiá*, conjuring a Greekness that's post-Hellenistic, from the time when the Roman Empire became Byzantine, then Ottoman. Romiá evokes the bloodred, gold-leaf hues of Byzantine icons, the minor key of Orthodox chanting that sounds the same as the mu'addin's call to prayer; romiá conjures a Greekness not nameable in English. Melina explained, "I'm a romiá, which means I'm freakishly pessimistic about little things and then, when tragedy strikes, I'm an optimist." When asked what was most important to her, Melina responded with one word, *elefthería*, or freedom.

During a visit to London to give a lecture titled "Democracy and the Arts," Melina encountered the director of the British Museum, and challenged him to return the Parthenon Marbles to the monument off which they had been broken. Rather than stand-alone statues, these sculptures were part of the Parthenon when, with what variant of a hacksaw we'll never know, a bankrupt Briton had them sawn off. The bankrupt Briton, Thomas Bruce (or Lord Elgin), was a military man serving as ambassador to the Ottoman Empire. The museum director moaned that Mercouri's activism would "ruin the British museum," and she replied, fiery yet calm: "They are part of the monument." Melina died with that battle begun but not won. The Marbles are still in London. Inspired by her, activists continue to fight in the courts for the Marbles' return. They claim that unlike other looted, moveable artifacts, this particular set of statues is a component of an immovable monument which can become whole again only when it is refitted with the broken-off pieces that Britain retains.

For Melina herself, though, and for her memory, there isn't a monument in the world that seems fit. To memorialize Melina, I think the only suitable act is to embody her principles of dedication to justice and to art, to pleasure and virtue, and to pleasure *as* virtue. A proper memorial is the making of new art—art enjoyable *and* moral—in Melina's name. The Melina Mercouri Foundation makes possible artistic ventures that unite beauty, politics, justice, truth, and desire in an experience that is intellectual, spiritual, and transcendent.

A stationary stone Melina makes no sense. Yet a statue of her exists, as I discovered many years after her death. I came face to face with a white marble bust of Melina while on a run through the center of Athens. The bust stands a few blocks from the foot of the Acropolis, across the street from the National Garden and the Temple of Zeus. I recognized

Melina's face, but barely, and her big hair. For the marble betrayed her. This Melina wasn't moving, and the eyes were blank. Colorless marble is appropriate for the sedate faces of unartistic men. White stone is well suited to western colonizers and their acolytes, who whitewash history, and who insist on forgetting that in the days of Euripides and Sappho, every marble statue was painted in indulgent reds, purples, greens, and bright, bright blues.

Looking at Melina's colorless statue, which I do now every time I visit Athens, makes me question why anyone has ever made a statue of someone who has died—it seems to me incongruous, almost an affront. It seems an insult to Melina to have created her image, immobile, to be looked at. Melina was never simply looked at. She always looked back.

—

She and I

—

After Natalia Ginzburg

We met on the rocks next to the rotting piles of an old marina on the day of our 1995 school trip. I was in eleventh grade and she a year younger. Erika Voelzer was already standing by the water when I reached the shore. Ten minutes after the teachers had shouted, "Be back at three!" as we students poured out of a bus, I had had enough of exploring the town. Cyprus had only four cities not under occupation, and I had seen all of them already. Only by the water, with boats pulling in and leaving, could I hope to find anything new. I had expected to be alone.

It was April, and hot, with a ten o'clock sun glaring off the sea. Before we had properly introduced ourselves, we had our shoes off, our trousers rolled to the knee. We splashed for a bit, laughed, then rested on the damp rocks close to the creaking wood of the pier. We talked while the sun made our hair so hot we could smell it. Fishing boats knocked against each other with that hollow, patient, small-harbor sound. We talked about books a little, but mostly we looked at the light dancing on the water. We looked at the water, which spread out and ended in confusion, mist, and sky.

Our classmates, we knew, were shopping in packs. Hers in the tenth grade, mine in the eleventh, they bored us quickly. We'd each attended the Limassol Grammar School for the last four years but never met. I had read an essay of Erika's in our yearbook. The writer had claimed she loved to write. I had laughed because I was sure nobody else in my school could apprehend the secrets that I knew during the nights I spent with pencils and dim light. I was wrong. I write well; she writes better. I confuse myself with my own explanations of books; she makes things at once simple and deep. By the time I was a senior, we would compete for a poetry prize and never say, "I hope it's I rather than you who wins." There was a boy in my class who said his poem was brilliant and we believed him, so we had little hope anyway. It seemed fitting, though, when our English teacher passed by in the yard and said in passing, as if our victory was to be assumed, that she hoped we didn't mind sharing first prize.

She got a Fulbright for college because she is Cypriot; I got financial aid because I am American. So we both ended up students in the United States. My mother sent letters requesting applications for me, and when they arrived, she merely pointed to the directions and the lines on which I needed to sign. Erika did it all herself, explaining patiently to her parents the financial details required by the scholarship application. I started in physics; she knew it had to be English. I switched to English in my sophomore year. She switched to physics in her sophomore year. We spoke little during college. She went to the West Coast; I stayed in the East. I visited her in Santa Cruz; she never came to Ithaca. We both graduated as English majors.

Back in the last two years of high school, she studied physics, chemistry, applied math, Greek, and English literature. I had taken the same subjects a year before. She used my books. She got As in four subjects and a C in English. I got the same. I wrote poems during math class, mostly poems of rage addressed to a supercilious teacher who made jokes tinged with an irony that sounded hurtful, pathetic, or both. She lost patience with the supercilious math teacher earlier in the year than I had, so while my angry poems cover chapter-eight diagrams of three-dimensional geometry, solid cones, frustums of cones, cylinders, and blocks, she wrote hers in chapter five, in the white space between fists swinging stones and the equations that calculate centripetal force.

I am intelligent but she is far more so; she finds simple solutions to the most complex of problems. I write interesting things once in a while but must labor to edit out confusion; she writes the deepest things and they are easy to understand. I started off as a teacher in one school or another, changing every year, looking for a match; I went back to school myself and seem to be making a fresh start. She graduated university and stopped writing entirely; only I get to hear her insights. She started tutoring, though intermittently; I tutored all my private students every week and kept up with their progress. She takes jobs and drops them again, a temp here and there because nothing is interesting enough, nothing is good enough. I have taken jobs and stuck with them a long time, perhaps even after I should have gone.

In school, we spent little effort on makeup and clothes. But now, when we go out, she looks perfect and I look plain. I wear eye shadow and garner compliments—sometimes. At least the effort is noticed. She wears eye shadow in ways that make it look like part of her face, an uncanny yet natural loveliness. In fact, when a summer job training session once required everyone to go into work wearing makeup, she was sent home, since the trainer refused to believe that her perfectly made-up face was anything more than her own perfect face. They didn't notice the subtle mascara. Did you know that one must wear mascara in addition to all other makeup? She says this is obvious, common knowledge, and I should already have known. I say she should publish a rulebook and after that complain.

For Erika was born with taste. I have developed some competence, but only thanks to many consultations with the natural. She wears jeans and a simple turquoise top and turns heads. She is in fashion, or rather ahead of it, at every moment, because she gets the magazines when they come out. But she is never ostentatious; she didn't wear the plaid thigh-length skirts when they came out and everyone wore them all at once, like a uniform. She did not wear the cheesy plastic earrings when the eighties came back. Light on the plastic, even when it is fashionable, she advises. I secretly question the entire point of fashion. I would prefer to go on wearing the turtleneck I bought as a twelve-year-old because it is comfortable, has only one barely noticeable hole, and matches almost all of my other clothes. I was once told by my boss at a small school where I taught English to spruce things up a bit, to look a little less like a gypsy. I started with hand-me-downs from Erika, which were the last year's fashion, but *some* year's fashion at least. I will wear whatever bargain I find. She devises outfits; to construct them she will hunt for a specific item in each store in two cities. When something is on sale, she'll buy it only after figuring out how it will fit with her existing wardrobe.

Each season there's another rule, another self-evident

principle violated left and right by my own tribe of fashion-ignorati. Capris with high heels, Bermuda-length with low heels, or is it the other way around? If your calves are thick, wear only narrow heels. If they are scrawny, do platforms. More rules Erika expects everyone to know.

"Accessorizing is key," she says. She chooses the handbag, jewelry, and hair clips with so much attention it seems she never thought about them. I cannot accessorize. When I once told her I couldn't balance an equation with so many variables, shoes and trousers and top plus the jewelry—earrings, necklace, and a ring—she said, "Sure, that would be a lot for you; forget about coordinating all that. Wear silver." For years, I wore silver earrings, bracelets, and rings: the fashion-protégée-of-Erika signature. A simple rule I could follow.

As for food, like all the girls in our city of our generation, she and I have an obsession with thin. I run, she uses the gym. I eat fat free, she counts carbs. She uses olive oil, I use the spray for a fat-free sauté. We both consume inordinate amounts of aspartame. She has sugar in her morning coffee because she needs solid food. I don't. I am fearful and have been known to starve myself slowly without ever skipping a meal; she will eat and enjoy and then diet so methodically it scares me.

On faith: She thinks all religions are dumb. I go to church each Sunday. But. When I am at her house, she always remembers to ask while stirring coffee for me—"Is today a fasting day?" She always has some beans or bread for me. She says religions are pointless, but takes better care of friends than I, the religious person, ever do.

I finger the telephone and plan what I will say; she says just call and words will come; I say they won't, although they will for you.

On the beach, Erika and I used to toast our skin into
the color we liked, light brown, the genes from her father's
German side evincing something a little ruddier than my
olive tint but still close enough that we looked like sisters.
Once in a while we rubbed on sunscreen, but usually she
or I just toted it as a sort of token of our judicious bent, our
understanding of the principle by which one prevents skin
cancer. But we baked anyway, unprotected and chic, and I
sucked up can upon can of aspartame-laced colas while she
extinguished cigarettes in the sand. Before leaving, we kicked
sand over the crinkled cigarettes and bent soda-can rings.

Sometimes I would ask her if she noticed how the water
glistened, how gold seemed to be dancing on the bay. And
she would say, "Joanna, that is just sunlight, hand me my
sunglasses in fact because it's making me dizzy." Then
I used to run out like a child looking for mermaids and
pretend she was my mother; when I swam quickly, I hoped
she would notice, and when I disappeared behind the wave
breaker, I hoped she would worry.

When the sand was all brushed off we'd go for coffee,
our reward for enduring sunlight so long, and also for my
ambition in swimming out to the rocks. Our favorite café
was Flo-Café because of its leather couches on the beach.
We would sit under an umbrella and hope the iced coffee
came quickly, as if there were a reason to hurry after three
or four hours lying on the sand. Often, we met the waiters,
who would wonder why we spoke both Greek and English
like natives and considered us a pair. They asked for our
stories, as if the doubleness of the mystery confirmed its
truth. We speak the same, it's true, but she lived in Cyprus
all her life; I was born abroad.

At a club she dances, and I dance too, but everybody
watches her; I watch her. When she dances even the beer

can in her hand glistens sexy, green, sweating, the script of the brand name curling beneath her thumb. Erika dances and everyone watches, if not openly, like I do, then from the corner of an eye or of the club. The men move closer with a finger or an eyelid twitching; they hope to dance in front of her or next to her, just close enough.

Men slide off me like too much rainwater, like magnets off aluminum. She is hot, as the boys so love to say, blowing the word out of a throat on fire; she is attractive, as the girls say. I know the corners of her beauty, the precise proportionality of torso and thigh, the perfected arch of her eyebrows, and the endless tempest in her eyes. If her looks were less magnificent, I might be jealous, and wonder—why her over me?

As things stand, though, I laugh, and I love her; we can sit at a café, she and I, and let the men come and admire; they try to be unobvious, discreet; we laugh. When men come up, a little shy, and oh-so-eager, they look at me—less of a challenge—and I smile and talk a little until I am bored and then they turn to her. She makes men's eyes widen and their cheeks stretch to the edges of their faces in smiles. I love to watch the men, watch them start to melt away and fish around for things to say. I laugh a little because the voices of the huskiest and tallest men tend to weaken most when they get a little bit of her attention; she humors them a while, and I humor her.

All this happens before the men know she likes to watch football. She enjoys football so much she watches every game, and called in sick at work several times during the most recent World Cup. When the men learn this, they often turn away, as one turns, stunned, from a vision or a miracle.

We talk about the future, then, the only things waiting for us. She says do not as I do, find yourself a husband, settle down; I say do as I do, go back to school or find better employment—as if we are teaching one another to give up the simple, slightly happy limbos of celibacy or no career. This, the meager advice of our love, might slow down the spiraling orbit of a silent, nameless devastation that, sometimes, when we lie together in the sand, hip by sweat-glistening hip, we apprehend while laughing at the men, who steal glances from behind their tinted glasses—who steal glances at the empty spaces between our breasts.

—

Ithacas

—

Wise as you've become, and full of experience,
You will have understood what Ithacas mean.

—C. P. Cavafy

I was born with nostalgia in my blood. Immigrants from all parts of the world tell stories of their old countries' perfection, but Diaspora Greeks hold onto their homeland with a special tenacity. You can't live very long in Greece without hearing songs of the bitter bread and hard, cold beds of *xenitiá* (ξενιτιά), which means exile, or being far away from Greece. When I had learned enough Greek to understand these songs, I wondered at the pleasure Greeks seemed to take in singing about exile's pain. Like the bite of retsina in their wine, like the moan of bagpipes in their music, longing for an Ithaca from the distance of Calypso's island still moves the Greeks to sing. And while Odysseus, archetype and father of all homeward wanderers, finally got home and stayed, most Greek émigrés take up residence abroad, making xenitiá, and distance from Ithaca, their fate. For Greece is poor, its soils are barren, and its industry unable to turn a profit. Greek immigrants in America chink glasses of whiskey and ouzo and remember mother Greece, the sun-soaked land surrounded by the sparkling Aegean, Mediterranean, Adriatic, and Ionian seas.

I was born in America, the world's youngest empire. My earliest memory takes place in one of its states, during a visit my maternal grandfather paid to my house in Queens. I was eighteen months old, and so I remember his knee at about my eye level, and his shoe resting on it. In the fireplace, a blaze. In my memory, my grandfather's shoe is so well shined it reflects the flames, which flicker against the black surface, orange tongues lapping at the toe. I remember the incline of his trousered shin and the brown frame of an armchair, but most of all the orange flames against the shoe.

Such flames would appear before me again, much later, in a museum-screen reproduction of fire raging against the already-charred ruins of Smyrna's Greek and Armenian quarters. It was a camera trick, footage of fire superimposed on the photographs of the razed neighborhoods of Smyrna—photographs preserved since mid-September 1922, when the fire drove hundreds of thousands toward the sea. As their city became a charnel house, they waited, as Hemingway described in "On the Quai at Smyrna," to become either refugees or ash. The museum itself, situated inside the iconic Thessaloníki landmark, is now called the White Tower. It was called the Red Tower until about a hundred years ago because it was a prison, and the site of so many bloody executions.

At the time of my earliest memory, of course, I knew nothing of executions, or empires, or nations, or modernity, or wars—nothing of ship manifests or Ellis Island, or of grandfathers, for that matter, or fires. That I remember the flames reflected in my *Pappoú* Spyros's shoe at all is a result of the many times I recalled it, reassembled the scattered members of the moment in remembrance, and created the memory anew. A memory of embers.

At times I have had what feel like memories of my grandfather wearing a fez and divorcing my grandmother. I have felt like I had memories of my mother, in middle school, taking the subway to visit him on weekends. And now, writing this history of my family and of the falling empires which gave rise to it, I am changing something, taking away from the accuracy of history even as I seek the truth about where I come from. I write without my father's training in history. I have only the archives—letters, journals, and the internet's vast stores. And I have my family's artifacts, and the words they have spoken.

Though they entered Ellis Island within six months of one another, my grandfathers wouldn't meet for fifty years. Constantínos Eleftheríou, my paternal grandfather, arrived at Ellis Island in August 1920, months before my other grandfather Spyros.

Constantínos Eleftheríou lived his pre-emigration life in Cyprus, a colony in transition from Ottoman to British rule. I possess Cóstas's *boúla*, which is a stamp, like the Papal bull. It says, "ASGÁTA" in horizontal capitals across the center, and in a circle, "CERTIFYING OFFICER * CYPRUS." The mayor retained the Ottoman title of *mukhtar* during British rule—which lasted from 1878 until around the time my father left. Cóstas took pride in being a British subject, and when I took a course in postcolonial theory, his affection for the Crown began to make sense to me. The British Empire always privileged a certain class of natives. The British gave people like my grandfather positions of authority over the peasants. They were sympathetic to the Crown because it gave them privilege, and thus they acted as sympathetic ambassadors of the empire to the subjugated natives. While the majority of Greek Cypriots hoped that in the twentieth century, Cyprus would follow the Ionian islands and be ceded by Britain to

Greece, my own grandfather was content with his position as
a British bureaucrat. He liked working for the Crown.

The ship's manifest that I found on the Ellis Island website
lists Constantínos's residence as *Asgáta, Mediterranean*, as
if the only way to designate the location of Asgáta (population: a few hundred) was to name the sea, which has no
government, no treaties transferring control from empire to
empire. Between 1878, when Cyprus became a protectorate
of Britain, and 1925, when it became a crown colony, the
political changes are difficult to parse. Here is the information listed for each grandfather (my grandmothers aren't in
the Ellis Island archive, since my paternal one, Agáthi, arrived
from Cyprus on her husband's second trip, after the 1954
closure of Ellis Island, and my maternal grandmother Joanna
was born in New York):

FIRST NAME:	Constantínos
LAST NAME:	Eleftheríou
ETHNICITY:	Great Britain, Greek
LAST PLACE OF RESIDENCE:	Asgáta, Mediterranean
DATE OF ARRIVAL:	Aug 11, 1920
AGE AT ARRIVAL:	19
GENDER: M	MARITAL STATUS: S
SHIP OF TRAVEL: *PANNONIA*	PORT OF DEPARTURE: Patras

FIRST NAME:	Spyros
LAST NAME:	Papadopoulos
ETHNICITY:	Turkey, Greek
LAST PLACE OF RESIDENCE:	Con/ple, Turkey
DATE OF ARRIVAL:	Jan 05, 1921
AGE AT ARRIVAL:	12
GENDER: M	MARITAL STATUS: S
SHIP OF TRAVEL: *KING ALEXANDER*	PORT OF DEPARTURE: Piraeus

Ethnicity is just as difficult for the officials to describe, apparently. I don't know what they mean when they print *Turkey, Greek* in the row labeled *ethnicity* on the record for my grandfather Spyros. The Cypriot identity card I got as a teenager has distinct boxes for ethnicity and citizenship. My ID card says *Cypriot* in the ethnicity box and *USA* in the one for citizenship.

During the early 1920s, the story goes that Cóstas worked in what my dad referred to as a "Pittsburgh screw factory" until he'd made enough cash to render himself an attractive alliance. Then, he wrote home to request Agáthi, the sixteen-year-old daughter of the landowner Cashanós, as his bride. Old Cashanós agreed, and by 1924 Agáthi was back in Cyprus and married to Agáthi. The couple merged their inheritances, and then The American and his father-in-law could stand upon the roof of the house they'd built and say to one another, "Look in whichever direction you like, you'll see land that's ours." Cóstas would farm much of the land himself, hire laborers to help during harvest time, and rent the rest to tenant farmers, villagers who lacked enough capital to buy land.

Because Cyprus was a crown colony when my father was born in 1939, his first passport, which my mother keeps, says *British Subject*. His next passports were all American. My first few passports were American, but later I provided proof that my father was born in Cyprus, and got a Cypriot passport that lists both my ethnicity and my nationality as Cypriot.

Spyros got work as a shoe-shine boy in Boston, became a violinist at the Boston Conservatory, opened a music school, and married Joanna, a Greek American girl born in New York City on the Lower East Side. When my brother Dino was a child, he discovered my mother's birth certificate, which lists her father's birthplace as Turkey, and to tease our mother he began to cry, "Mom's a Turk! Mom's a Turk!" She tried to explain the complicated history of Anatolia, but little Dino was more interested in teasing.

Turkish acquaintances who have heard my history have explained that from a Turkish perspective, it would make no sense to call a Christian Greek-speaker a Turk. Anyone Christian and descended from the Greek people that populated the Ottoman Empire since its beginnings are called *rum*. Rum continues to be the word they use for a Greek from outside the nation-state of Greece. The word is a Turkish pronunciation of what the Greeks called themselves for a long time—*romiós*—during the years when Greeks were governed by the Ottoman sultan, before their appeal to the western imagination (and political power) required they revert to the name that predated their history as Romans, and call themselves Hellenes. They tell me that I, too, am rum. My mother, my father, my paternal grandparents, my maternal grandfather, all rum. A Greek woman will still refer to herself, at times, as a *romiá*.

Turkish has a distinct word for people like my grandmother Joanna's parents. Greece, the young nation-state, is the birthplace of only two of my eight great-grandparents, who emigrated around 1900, and so they are the only two whom a Turk would call *Yunán*, a name that comes from the ancient tribe of Ionians. Greece in Turkish is *Yunanistán*. Just say it—*Yunanistán*—what a different ring from *Hellas* and *Greece*.

As a child, I attended the parochial school attached to St. Nicholas Church on Northern Boulevard in Flushing, Queens. Greek lessons were daily, with Greek history on Tuesdays, religion on Fridays, and language on the other days. The restaurant owners whose profits kept our St. Nicholas day school open spent summers with their children, my classmates, in their Greek towns of origin, where they swam in the morning, slept through the sultry afternoons, and reveled in the breezy nights with music and good wine. Then they went back to America and told everyone that Greece was paradise, that they would live there if only they could. For the years I attended St. Nicholas, from pre-K until we left at last after I had finished fourth grade, mine was the only hand that didn't rise when teachers asked who'd be going to Greece that summer. My parents taught high school and couldn't afford yearly trips. Plus, they were saving up for what my father, unlike all his family and friends and against their advice, was determined to achieve: *permanent* return to his own island, Cyprus, his Ithaca.

My mother began teaching me Greek when I was three. In my memory of that moment, Georgia looks down at me and says, "Joanna, you're three years old now. You're old enough to begin learning Greek." We might have sat down on the pebble-and-cement stoop, a mild New York wind tousling her fine, still-brown hair, and a susurrus coming from the fir trees that shielded us from our neighbors' view. Smiling behind thick, plastic-rimmed glasses, my mother probably started with the body. I imagine little Joanna tapping on her baby nose and saying *míti*, tracing a ring around her mouth and saying *stóma*, tugging at her ears and saying *aftiá*. Wagging a three-year-old foot and saying, *pódi*.

With my tiny handful of Greek words, I was sent to Greek-immersion kindergarten at St. Demetrios in Jamaica, Queens, just before I turned five. I suspect my parents figured my limber young brain would adjust soon enough, for no one prepared me for an all-Greek classroom. I sat on the first day at a low circular table with children I didn't know and trembled. *Kyría* (Mrs.) Cósta, in a tailored suit, spoke entirely in Greek. Thirty-four years later, I see her before me, powerful, unintelligible, and frightening.

"Why are you crying?" a second teacher asked, having noticed my tears. She was shorter and wore plainer clothes than Kyría Cósta, and spoke English, so she reminded me of my mother.

"Because the teacher is speaking Greek and I can't understand," I whimpered.

"Am I speaking Greek?" the plainly dressed teacher asked again.

"No," I said. I cried harder because I heard the question as a jeer at my silliness for missing the obvious fact that this second teacher was speaking English.

On top of feeling excluded because I didn't know enough Greek, I was excluded from dance. Kids fluent in Greek learned the *kalamatianó*, joining hands and moving in a large circle to a twelve-step rhythm whose quick and bouncy circular procession evoked my envy.

The Greek-proficient kindergartners danced to a song whose onomatopoeic *droung* is repeated six times, paired with the phrase "*ta vrahiólia tis vrontoún*," "her bracelets thunder." Much later, I discovered that the song recounts the plight of a girl who sets out to fetch water and falls into a well. To call attention, she shouts and violently shakes her bracelets—*droung*. To this sound, the girls got to shake bracelets and call out, and I'm glad I didn't have enough Greek then to understand this nightmare-producing scenario: the lyrics leave us with this scene, the bangle-banging girl in the dark well-shaft, drenched but not drowned, her rescuer on the way, but late. He is promising to marry her once he's retrieved her, and in one version, he casts a "golden rope" to haul her up "by her belt." I knew none of this, and only watched, coveting bracelets.

>>•<<

By first grade, I had left St. Demetrios in Jamaica and was enrolled in St. Nicholas, the Greek American parochial school closer to our house in Flushing. My daily Greek class assumed its pattern: religion on Fridays (gospels, saints' lives, early Christian persecutions, Byzantine emperors, 1054 mutual excommunication of Patriarch and Pope, the seven sacraments) and on Tuesdays, history (Spartan customs, 1821 revolution, Olympian gods). A paper program from an Independence Day performance in March 1985 declares, "Hail, Hail, Liberty," on its cover, and that line from the Greek national anthem is underscored by images of a saber and a meander, along with school's full name: The School of William Spyropoulos of Saint Nicholas of the Greek Ortho-dox Church. The Greek-speaking Christian subjects of the Ottoman Empire started their revolution on Annunciation Day, and inside the program an icon of Mary Mother of God faces drawings of the Greek and American flags. Beneath the flags, both "Long Live Greece!" and "God Bless America!" are printed.

At St. Nicholas, the American and Greek flags stood at each end of the stage in the school's lunchroom-gym-audito-rium-ballroom (for school assemblies, the basketball appa-ratus was removed, and the big round lunch tables snapped flat and tucked behind giant drapes). Since no Cypriot flag ever appeared, I didn't quite understand that Cyprus was a separate country until I went there. It was always Greece and the USA. Two flags, I suppose, already took up too much space.

In the school plays that marked Greek Independence Day celebrations, the tallest boys got to be Ottoman pashas and emissaries of the sultan. Lavishly turbaned, fake-bearded, with plastic sabers in their red satin belts, they would swagger on stage to deliver their threats to the Greeks. The Greeks, in turn, were played by the kids who'd learned Greek best, dressed up as nineteenth-century soldiers and symbols of Greek authority-resisting pride. The name for these particular freedom fighters is *tsoliá* (τσολιά). Shod in red wooden clogs with large pom-poms on each pointed toe, and sporting thick, off-white woolen tights, they climbed imaginary mountains in their bright white skirts (picture a kilt, only shorter, fluffier, almost a masculine tutu). Over buttonless, flowing white shirts, they wore royal blue vests embroidered with gold braids, with long rectangles of matching fabric attached loosely at the shoulder to make swinging, oblong wings. These were the Greek heroes, the mountain rebels, who on every holiday said no to the foreigners, who told the turbaned Turks that they could not have Greek land, could not have Greek women—the females a symbol for home, for Greece itself, for the sacred earth to which we trace our lives.

The scene I remember best was the reenactment of a time when it seems the "no" of the *tsoliáthes* (τσολιάδες) failed to protect Greek women from the hands of the Turks, so that they had to protect themselves. And so they did, we learned, when in mid-December 1803, the enemy began to close in on a place where a group of women were hiding with their infants, and those women took their children in their arms and ran toward a bluff. Before their pursuers could catch and dishonor them (we never asked our teachers what this meant), the women tightened their kerchiefs, straightened

their dresses, and broke into song, dancing in loops toward
the cliff. Tracing complicated footwork over the snow, dead
grass, and rock, they took their last steps—still free, still
honorable, still Greek—and one by one they jumped, singing
still. Farewell to you, oh poor, suffering world, farewell to
you, sweet life. The music was at once woeful and trium-
phant, terrible in its sweetness, a keening that is as broken
as it is proud.

> Οι Σουλιώτισσες δεν μάθαν
> για να ζούνε μοναχά,
> ξέρουνε κα να πεθαίνουν
> να μην στέργουν την σκλαβιά.

> (Souliot women have not only
> learned to live
> They've learned to die.
> They'll die before they'll be enslaved.)

Our teachers, of course, never explained that the women
were rejoicing because they'd managed, just barely, to escape
their enemies' raging lusts by choosing suicide. The teachers
simply ordered us to bring dolls to school and clutch them
to our chests as we jumped off the stage onto a heap of mats
below. It was fun, jumping from the stage in long dresses
and headscarves decorated with fake gold coins. Although
we didn't understand much about what we were doing, I
think we did get the sense that this mysterious dance, like the
strange costumes and the language that was so hard to speak
without mistakes, was telling us something about where
we came from, and what made us distinct from the public-
school kids we played hide-and-go-seek with on our streets.

While the grownups made it clear that our Greekness
made us special, during my childhood the Greek aspect of

my identity still felt mostly like a chore. To me, Greekness was difficult spelling tests, unintelligible aunts, and distressed efforts to wrap my child's mouth around *ímeh ellinoamerikanópoulo* (I'm a little Greek American). In my Greek American parochial school, I was tested on my ability to pronounce that ten-syllable word. But it was the characters of Beverly Cleary, Laura Ingalls Wilder, and Lucy Maud Montgomery that helped me construct a sense of self. I was Ramona, then Laura, and finally Anne, the loquacious and romantic adventurer with a hankering for a bosom friend.

Though the *Little House* books take place in America, it was nevertheless Laura Ingalls's story that caused going to Cyprus to feel like an arrival on a prairie of my own at last. I'd read all the books up until Laura's marriage by the time we moved in the summer of 1988. At the time, I was a nine-year-old girl who felt that I was meant to be like Laura. I belonged in a place with rock and wild grass between our house and the faraway neighbors. Cyprus felt like a long-awaited release from the cement and fences of my urban childhood. And despite the entire institutions dedicated to making me feel Greek, Laura Ingalls persisted as *the* fictional character who allowed me to imagine who I was. I read *Swiss Family Robinson*, and when my family swam on Cypriot beaches, I would play at being shipwrecked. But neither that novel nor any of the other ones I read in fifth, sixth, seventh, or eighth grade offered a character that rivaled Laura.

It wasn't until I read *Blood-Soaked Earth* (Ματωμένα Χώματα) in ninth grade that Laura was replaced by that novel's protagonist, Manólis Axiótis. *Blood-Soaked Earth* was the first novel I completed in Greek. Up until the end of eighth grade, I'd insisted that I didn't know enough Greek to be in a class with native Greek speakers. But after getting full credit on every test in the Greek as a Second Language class,

I wasn't permitted to stay. I started ninth-grade Greek with the native speakers, at once terrified and proud. I failed my first test and just managed to scrape by with a C on my report card for the first term, but my parents (in their wisdom) encouraged me to stick with the difficult Greek class in spite of the significant dent it made in my grade point average.

The novel that the native speakers' Greek class had been assigned proved so difficult that my mother offered to read ahead of me and look up the words she didn't know. She wrote the English translation in the margins for me. Our Greek was at about the same level at that time. *Blood-Soaked Earth* takes place in Asia Minor, around the time my mother's father Spyros was a boy. On top of the difficult Greek vocabulary which she was able to put into the margin for me, there were words neither of my parents could help me with, Turkish words and Greek words particular to the idiom of early twentieth-century Greeks who lived in the Ottoman-Empire-about-to-become-Turkey. In spite of how hard the language was, the novel nevertheless captured my fourteen-year-old mind, and in doing so changed forever the landscape of my imagination. Manólis describes the way Greeks and Turks lived in peace in his village in the Ottoman countryside when he was growing up. When the Ottoman Empire enters the First World War, Manólis is drafted into the Ottoman military. Sent to a labor battalion to construct roads and railroads, Manólis hears about what is happening to the Armenians and decides to take his chances as a deserter. I learned the Greek word for nipple from this novel because I read, at age fourteen, Manólis relating the news that Turkish soldiers were entering the homes of Greek and Armenian civilians, killing the men and raping the women, then cutting off their breasts and making worry beads out of the severed nipples. I realized many years later that when the Greek army invaded Anatolia and was sent into retreat in humiliated disarray, they surely committed atrocities of their own, and no one taught us about those.

After his escape from the Ottoman military, Manólis remains on the run for many chapters. He's caught, imprisoned, and punished for deserting. Young men around him are dying of starvation, exhaustion, and disease. Manólis breaks out of jail and runs toward Turkey's Aegean coast. World War I ends with the Ottoman Empire on the losing side, but the Greeks and Turks keep on fighting. At some point Manólis joins the Greek army and fights against the army he's recently deserted. Then the Greeks lose the Greco-Turkish war. Eventually, the Empire becomes the nation of Turkey, and in 1923, one and a half million Greeks are expelled. In the last chapter, Manólis jumps into the sea with an inflated sheepskin as a life preserver. The novel ends with Manólis seeking a new home on one of the Greek islands, which won't take him, because they are all filled with too many refugees.

By identifying, at fourteen, with the teenage Manólis Axiótis, I began to develop a sense of my own Greekness as more expansive and interesting than difficult spelling tests, unintelligible aunts, difficult dances, school plays, and Greek Independence Day parades. While living in Cyprus rendered me capable of understanding the Greek my relatives spoke, and reading novels in Greek turned me into a confident speller, my identification with teenage Manólis gave me a new sense of myself as a person with roots in mass expulsions. I had not suffered the hardships endured by American pioneers or by Ottoman Greeks or by the Armenians, but these were the books I read, and so these were the books that forged my identity. I imagined my own life according to these books' patterns.

My education in Greek, begun in New York and continued in Cyprus, enabled me to read the Greek novels that I would soon love. I earned a B during the second term in ninth grade in the native speakers' class. In the third, we studied Cavafy's poems. We read "The First Step," which gave me lasting insight into the problem of making art. We read "27 June 1906, 2 P.M." and I wondered at how a male poet could describe another male body as beautiful, as if he had looked at it with desire: "*to ephebekón oréa kamoméno sóma*" ("the young, beautifully shaped body," "το εφηβικόν ωραία καμωμένο σώμα"). By spring, I'd stopped asking my parents for help with Greek and started to do well on exams. I wore out my already-worn-out Greek-English dictionary even further.

In tenth grade, my Greek class read the short story collection *Hope Wanted* by Antónis Samarákis and Solomós's *Besieged and Free*; in eleventh, Myrivílis's *Mermaid Madonna* and Karkavítsas's *Words from the Prow*; in twelfth, Tachtsís's *The Third Wedding* and Papadiamántis's *The Murderess*. Each of these books in its own way moved me more powerfully than the Shakespeare, Hardy, James, Desai, Lawrence, Austen, and Brontës that I had read in English class (except maybe the Brontës).

Reading, above all, *The Mermaid Madonna* in my Cypriot village felt like someone put my own self into language. The novel captured my love of Greek music, of folktales, and of the sea. It takes place on Lésbos, a few years after *Blood-Soaked Earth* is set, among refugees escaping the same troubles that enmeshed Manólis Axiótis and expelled my grandfather Spyros. I was sixteen when I read *The Mermaid Madonna*, newly weaned from my Greek-English dictionary. At last, I knew enough words to figure out what was happening from the context, as I had always done with books in English. My fledgling Greek may have prevented me (I can't remember) from realizing that the protagonist's adoptive father raped her, or that the fellow villagers, when they learned of it, called for the irons to be heated so they could burn with them the rapist's testicles. I understood only, I think, that there was a girl in this story who had her own boat and who got to go fishing alone. Though I missed a lot of the nuances, the novel gave me a language for joy, for longing, and for loss, and gave me Smaragdí, the only heroine in literature as indifferent as I was to men. The novel's ending permits Smaragdí to remain unmarried. I wrote a paper about *The Mermaid Madonna* during graduate school, but apart from that, I've kept the novel's throbbing power silent inside me for decades.

My education suspended me between identity poles, and asked me to find a mirror for myself by choosing from among Laura Ingalls, Jane Eyre, Ursula Brangwen, Cathy Earnshaw, Manólis Axiótis, and Smaragdí. It provided me with nothing to legitimize a Greek American cultural allegiance. None of these models for myself fit—I was no more the green-eyed, orphaned changeling Smaragdí than I was Jane Eyre, English, Protestant, and poor, walking across rainy moors, or Laura Ingalls, the pioneer, sowing corn on a Kansas prairie.

My identity became a hodgepodge of these figures. I sometimes catch myself romanticizing the experiences of my former Greek American classmates, who have had stable, constant cultural reference points. They send their own children to St. Nicholas, and those children perform their Greek identity in the way we did thirty years ago. The music they listen to doesn't accuse American foreign intervention-ism of interfering with Greek sovereignty. They don't have to choose.

Members of my New York family send me pictures from

the Greek Independence Day parade. Kids dressed as *tsoliáthes* or in Greek parochial school uniforms march down Manhattan's Fifth Avenue. But I feel estranged from this culture, an outsider again. It is not only that the patriotism of Greek America feels a bit provincial and naïve after one has gone to actually live in the idealized homeland, but also this: once I left for Cyprus, the anti-Americanism of Greek leftists made me ashamed of the way Greek Americans express allegiance to both nations. It's taken decades to begin winding my Americanness back into my identity. I had trouble making peace with the birthplace I'd left.

When we first flew to Cyprus, my parents rented us a furnished beach apartment. The next day, we drove thirty minutes up into the Troodos mountains, where my father's best friend was building us a house. Later, I would find in my father's journals many descriptions of his adventures with this best friend. Ándros's name comes up in every second or third entry. Ándros and Andréas went to the cinema together and to church together, played backgammon and ate ice cream, cheered each other up when they stayed home with colds. Once, on the first day of Lent, 1959, my father records a school trip up to this very place, Saittás next to Moniátis, where my father would eventually buy land to fulfill his youthful dream of building a house here.

On the lot in Saittás where the nearly finished house should have stood, our family found only cement foundations in the square shapes of rooms, with rusty steel rods poking out at each corner. A few yards down the mountain from the squares, there rose a long wall, also of cement, also with rusty rods poking out.

"It's a retaining wall, and costs a lot," my father explained to my mother when she asked where all our money had gone. Dino and I threw pine cones at each other and scampered up the slope and lay back on the ground, which was soft with its blanket of needles.

Twenty years later, Ándros was in court, declaring bankruptcy.

For years, my father waited for the money Ándros had gambled away. He said it was taking a long time because the architect had stolen much more money from others, and had to pay them back first. In the end, my parents bought a small, already-built house in a mountain holiday homes complex near the plot. He wore his best friend's broken promise like a badge that symbolized the betrayal he felt Cyprus had committed against him.

"But you're in Cyprus," my mother argued. I don't remember how he defended his inability to be happy. My father had believed in Cyprus as a land without a flaw, and as long as he had been in America, he had kept believing in that paradise. Not too cold and not too hot, he had claimed. Even once we all moved to Cyprus, the cool winters would erase his memory of extreme summer heat, and he would plant American grass, as though diligent watering would make it grow as thick as it did in New York. It never took.

I could not see, then, that the half-modernized, half-backward Asgáta of the nineties was a mockery of the paradise nostalgia had created in his mind. I didn't understand that he had idealized the mountains because he had gone there on Boy Scout trips, and moving us there was his attempt to recover the excitement of childhood sleepovers with his friends.

It was much later that I learned how my father saved his father, the Anglophile mayor, from being killed by guerrilla

fighters seeking to overthrow British rule. My father hid
his father's *boúla* (stamp) and other official government
objects, and when his father searched for them, suggested
that perhaps this was a warning that they would do to him
what they had done to the mayor of nearby Tóchni (assassinate him) if Cóstas did not resign. My grandfather
resigned, and my father believed in the guerilla fighters'
message: that better days for Cyprus awaited once that
awful war was done.

Nostalgia comes from two Greek words: *nóstos*, homecom-
ing, and *álgos*, which means pain. The word nostalgia usually refers to the traveler's longing for home—that familiar
strain. The traveler's sweet homeward urge is, however, just
one of two distinct kinds of pain that the word nostalgia can
express. We mourn the loneliness of waiting to get home, but
say nothing of what happens if nóstos is achieved. After we
find ourselves home, we expect a sudden bliss. But real places
disappoint. Upon arrival, we feel not bliss but álgos once
again, and this is a different ache, an ache that isn't sung.

It is because of this other álgos, this nóstos-induced pain,
that for my family, the excited joy of reaching a Greek land
was short-lived. People who had gone back for vacations
had kept up with the ways Greece and Cyprus were rapidly
changing. My father, however, had stayed in America saving
up money for his return. Then, after an absence of almost
thirty years, he sought work, built a house, and struggled
to make friends. When he left in 1959, only the cities had
electricity, and only in the evening. When he moved back in
1988, Cyprus had become a major tourist destination with
discotheque signs that flashed all night. He remembered

honest people, who spoke simply, but he found shrewd businessmen and a people who'd been through so much violence
they were suspicious, guarded. He planted fruit trees, and
cucumbers and tomatoes like he had in New York. But the
plants died without pesticides. Every time I asked about the
chickens and the goat he'd promised me, he said "next year."
Eventually, he admitted that the animals he'd once raised
happily seemed too messy, too much work. Because everyone
else had at least one relative with a coop, the local grocery
store never sold eggs.

My father remembered rich, clean earth, but weeds had
covered his parents' untilled fields. Entire orchards had disappeared. In the absence of poison, rodents had eaten into
the hearts of all the carob trees. After years of reflection,
I've come to suspect that once he'd made the move, and
we had arrived in the longed-for land that nostalgia had
rendered perfect in his imagination, he stopped longing,
and he stopped hoping, and for this reason he had little joy
after that.

No one called us immigrants when we left New York for
Cyprus. No one called us ex-pats. Ex-pats can complain
about the provincialism of local bureaucracy and remember fondly the efficiency of their homelands. Native Greeks
and Cypriots use the name *epanapatrizómeni* (repatriates,
επαναπατριζόμενοι) to refer to people who spend decades
abroad and then return. I, however, prefer to call us *de-ex-
pats* because we left the homeland for a new land, and then
left that one behind too—a double exile. Before he convinced
my mother to move back again with him to Cyprus for what
would become the final time, my father whispered to me that

if my mother was too fed up with moving, he would build himself a tiny house and live alone.

I nodded yes—and hid what I knew about nostalgia, what Cavafy had taught me some fifteen years earlier about what Ithacas mean. In "Ithaki," which my class read in eleventh grade, Cavafy admonishes readers to demand nothing of their destination. The destination's gift is the very journey. You desire the destination, and that desire makes you go, go, go. The going produces pain and the pain becomes your teacher. The going leads to chance encounters, which make you wise. Once home, the yearning settles. Once the object of desire is accomplished, the going is done.

And so you go—put out to sea again. In Athens, Cyprus, and the immigrant parts of New York City, old men haunt the watersides. In fishermen's caps, long mustaches, and glasses, they clutch newspapers rolled up like telescopes. They walk up and down and look at the boats, beyond the boats at the waves, and up at the sky. My father also wandered alone toward the shore. I, too, am always looking for water, large bodies of it, and the horizon.

I went to college in Ithaca—not the Ionian island, the city in upstate New York. The unending precipitation and relentless cloud cover, low, gray, and ugly, hid even that dull strip of Cayuga Lake that, on clear days, served me for a glimpse of water to soothe the absence of my Mediterranean. All the Cornell Greeks used to gather on weekends and complain. Besotted with yearning for return, at a place a little deeper than romance, the Greeks drank too much and danced together and complained about the absence of light and about this gray prison-city Ithaca, its people so cheerful and its hills so low. We complained beautifully, ending the nights at four in the morning with the notes of nostalgia on a guitar. The old songs, the rebetika of refugees from Asia Minor, brought together undergrads, grads, and professors, who all desired their own memory of Greece.

The Greeks sang of the sea and of the moonlight, of their country's continuing fall from glory. Give the Greek an empty chair, a tumbler full of alcohol or air, and he will dance the *zeimbékiko*, the solitary dance of the Byzantine border-lords. He tumbles into each next step, tripping, bending, falling, rising just before he hits the floor. Around him in a circle, we clap and bend our necks not in worship but in love, and the dancer swings his leg circles over a stranger's neck.

In the summer of 2010, I had just been admitted to a graduate program that came with a nine-month teaching appointment in America and an all-expenses-paid trip to Greece each summer. I'd work for the study abroad program for a month, then fly cheaply to Cyprus. "I'll have the best of both worlds," I told my Cypriot friends and family. "A salary from America and all summer to read and write by the beach." In a way, it's still a compromise that leaves me where my father spent his life, on the edge of two worlds. In another, it's a way of at once claiming both countries and none. In one of my favorite songs, songwriter Manólis Rasoúlis says that the heart is the sweetest homeland, and its land is made of pain and joy.

The heart may be the sweetest homeland, and Greece, as Rasoúlis writes, may have taught generations of emigrants to breathe and to die no matter what land they find themselves on. But even as I spend winter after winter in America, the Cyprus of carob, terebinth, and cyclamen pulls me. I feel that

I know who I am through this yearning—for the churning of seas, the light of the sun, the slope of a rock, the lift of a wave. I love to run in the heat of an American day and watch sunlight sparkle on water that makes me ache even harder for Cyprus—where I cannot stay. While I run, sweat runs down my face as it does when I run in the sun-parched hills close to my home. I love to smell ocean; even in America, I always find water to run beside, to smell the salt and the dying fish as I remember mountains sloping into the sea. I live the new Greek poetry and the old, old stories—I live my myth and my story—as I run by the shore of an Atlantic inlet that smells to me like the wide Mediterranean Sea.

The Temple of Zeus

The lack of concern for the erotic root and satisfactions of our work is felt in our disaffection from so much of what we do.

—Audre Lorde, "Uses of the Erotic"

The Temple of Zeus is a little independent café tucked in the basement of Goldwin Smith Hall at Cornell, where Vladimir Nabokov held office hours and Strunk met White before they produced their famous manual. When I served A. R. Ammons coffee there, and his pale hand shook its way toward mine, I felt ashamed, as if poets shouldn't pay. Although I hadn't yet read his work, I'd learned of Ammons's fame from my other professors. In a fake southern accent, they'd repeated his storied line, "I made half a million dollars just from poetry!" I think they were a little jealous and a little proud that Ammons had the gall to bring up profit. Even more taboo, the poet's exuberance implied that art had, on top of money, brought him pleasure, too.

Before Goldwin Smith Hall housed prizewinning poets, the space was used to make cheese. The *Cornell Daily Sun* reported in 1893 that the "Agricultural Building now in course of erection" on the quad would be "devoted to instruction in dairy husbandry." A cheese room and a creamery as well as a laboratory would afford students hands-on learning in agricultural science. By the time I arrived on campus in 1997, the agriculture school had become a college in its own right on a green expanse a mile away, and Goldwin Smith Hall, built around the structure once intended for cheese, now held classes in philosophy, classics, comparative literature, English, and history of art.

Built in the beaux arts style, with foundations of Medina sandstone and windowsills of Indiana limestone, the newer structure boasted four grand columns at the entrance. A triangle above the columns made the building look grand, like a museum. The Goldwin Smith Hall I entered as a freshman retained no trace of the building's dairy days. Gone were the vats and lactometers, the curd knives and rennet testers. What remained were lecterns, high-ceilinged atriums, and offices for professors, admissions officers, and deans. All of these were beautified by bright white statues of ancient orators and gods.

Back in its early days, The Temple of Zeus housed an actual statue of its divine namesake. Plaster casts had gone out of fashion as instructional tools by the 1960s, and Cornell's vast collection of statues had been hidden away in a storage room. In 1964, because of ongoing harassment, students demanded an egalitarian, neutral space to meet with their professors, and staff members responded by setting up a coffee shop in that storage room. The most striking of them all, Zeus's statue gave its name to the makeshift shop, which at first sold only low-grade coffee and whatever doughnuts were left over from the breakfasts served to ROTC kids at dawn. Later that decade, students would resort to an armed takeover of a Cornell building to make the university take a stand against harassment perpetrated by white students.

By the time I arrived in 1997, the political tensions of the sixties had become invisible (at least to me), the café had expanded its menu and moved out of that storage space, and the plaster cast of Zeus had found his way back to a position of dignity. But Zeus the café retained its name and its basement home (just a bigger space), and it still displayed some ancient casts. They were friezes on the walls, and I remember looking at them, though I don't remember exactly which ones were hanging back then, in Zeus. None of them came from an actual Greek Temple of Zeus. I've seen two of these (or at least their ruins), one in Olympia and one behind a wire fence in the very heart of Athens, near the National Garden and the Syntagma, where all the protests happen. The friezes I gazed at as a Cornell student worker may have been casts of the Parthenon Marbles. Those depict men on horseback, the legs of the horses raised and indicating speed. They may equally have been friezes from the Temple of Apollo Epikourios at Bassae, an hour's drive northwest of my great-grandmother's birthplace near Sparta.

In these, we see bodies of men and of centaurs, guests at a royal wedding in central Greece. The centaurs—famously, the half-beasts who were easily inebriated—get wasted fast, and so they become feral and ready to rape. The centaurs start mounting boys and young women, including the royal bride. The groom-king and his friends fight off the half-men who cannot or will not restrain desire. Then, the beasts beat back the humans with broken jugs and table legs. On the friezes, the men and the beasts appear frozen in mid-jump. The art on the wall had captured movement and held it, so that when I turned around, I felt the ancients would take up their battle once again, right there in our basement café in upstate New York. The casts were so good, I hardly realized they were copies. I didn't learn until much later just how very

many casts had long ago been made and distributed throughout the New World, while the original statues remained in
Greece or in museums in Britain or France.

When I walked to Zeus with Vasilikí and my other Greek
friends, they called me "priestess" and jokingly wished me "a
good sacrifice." They called my workplace the *témenos*, an
old word that means temple and evokes the kitsch tokens of
antiquity sold at the foot of the Acropolis: Mount Olympus
bottle openers, Socrates sandals, Hercules magnets, and miniature busts of Plato with pen holders glued onto the back.
None of us understood, then, the history of the plaster cast
that had given Zeus its name, or that plaster casts had been
called "the perfect textbook in 3D." We didn't understand
that Americans and northern Europeans who weren't rich
enough to tour Italy, Greece, or Turkey gained access to
knowledge of ancient sculpture via plaster casts. We furthermore didn't understand that many originals had been lost
sometime after the casts were made, in wars or other disasters, so that copies like those displayed in Goldwin Smith
Hall now preserved the only lasting trace of a ruin.

I loved working at The Temple of Zeus. When I entered the
kitchen to retrieve an apron and a register key, crates of shining eggplant, zucchini, and green pepper welcomed me to
work. With tiny patches of earth stuck to their skin, the vegetables awaited chopping, along with fresh, sandy spinach.
Crates full of milk came from Cornell Dairies. I had worked
at Cornell Dining briefly, where everything was packaged
and frozen, all corn syrup and salt. At Zeus the vegetables
still smelled like they'd actually come from the ground. As if
that weren't enough, the dining hall had only paid minimum

wage, but Zeus paid us work-study kids $6.25 an hour. By my senior year, this was still a dollar and ten cents higher than New York minimum wage. I felt lucky to have the job.

Zeus opened its wide double doors at seven thirty, and the earliest work-study shift began at eight. So whenever I traipsed over the snow from my dorm in the early morning, I would find the café already fragrant with coffee and simmering chai. The full-time staff in charge of opening, Nyima and Chocklay, had come to Ithaca from Tibet. Every day, they worked a seven-hour shift at Zeus and then went to work the dinner shift at Moosewood, a vegetarian restaurant downtown. Both were shorter than my five feet four inches, but Nyima was stronger than three of me, his wiry frame cabled with muscles under his smooth, tan-even-in-winter skin. Whenever I arrived, Nyima would be decked in his white apron and a baseball cap on backwards. He wore wide, untied skater sneakers, dark T-shirts, and low-slung, baggy jeans, and I had no idea whether he was my age or twice it. He whisked cases of Snapple and Arizona iced tea up the stairs and carried big crates of vegetables that I could barely slide along the ground. We spoke mostly in smiles, for his accent was too unfamiliar to me, my ear used to English affected only with the vowels and consonants of Greek.

For my whole first year at Zeus, I thought Nyima and Chocklay were married, their easy conversations, affectionate banter, and comfort in each other's space giving me the impression of an intimate, conjugal connection. Once I arrived and took over the register, they would sit down together and breakfast on dishes of rice topped with cooked vegetables, sauces, eggs, and meat. Chocklay had a round face that always seemed to be smiling—even when we talked about our countries and their respective occupations. She explained to me how China had invaded and occupied Tibet, just as Turkey had Cyprus. She, unlike my college peers, seemed to understand why I felt so affected by the occupation of a land I'd never seen, at a moment four years before I was born. In the picture on Zeus's website today, more than twenty years on, Chocklay is featured just as I remember her, wearing a skirt that reaches just below the apron's hem and pink leggings beneath her skirt to match her pink running shoes and socks.

As soon as Nyima and Chocklay had eaten, they would hurry back to work. Nyima restocked sodas, iced tea, bottled water, candy bars, potato chips, sushi boxes, and steamed rolls. Chocklay peeled the purple skin from eggplants to reveal their pale-green insides, sliced zucchini, and diced carrots into cubes bright as children's toys. Then, she chopped stale bread for croutons and stirred the soups while Nyima weighed precise portions of ham and turkey for sandwiches on a scale that looked like it belonged in a pharmacy.

I never saw Chocklay use a recipe or a measuring cup while she cooked, from scratch, the two soups we served fresh every day. Her soups ranged from Armenian lentil to cauliflower curry, Crema Andaluz, Hungarian mushroom, Lebanese vegetable, and East African stew, and they all tasted delicious. With her eyes alone, she measured out onion, garlic, cumin, lemon, cilantro, and saffron. She applied a big industrial can opener to giant cans of beans and added them to the onions and garlic already sizzling in the tall pots on our big but not very industrial stove. She emptied cans of diced tomatoes, too, and used the wide carving knife to guide into the pot the fresh carrots and green peppers she had just chopped. I felt protected, in her kitchen, from a world outside it that I did not understand.

Once, I was worried about finishing a paper, and Chocklay asked me why I worked so many hours. I remember distinctly her critique when I was ladling soup for customers while an unfinished paper awaited. "You have your whole life to work," she said. Most of the other work-study kids pulled even fewer shifts than my twelve hours a week. Generous with its financial aid packages, Cornell wasn't like the city schools I would become familiar with later. There, I'd meet kids who hadn't gotten the enormous grants that Cornell offered to students with need, and so they would work multiple jobs just like Chocklay did and take classes between shifts. I didn't have money, but Cornell gave me so much that I could study full time. A lot of Cornell kids had money, and I would understand one day that this made it harder for me to connect outside this haven of labor, fresh vegetables, and cash. Since Zeus was independent of the university dining system, rich students could not wield the power of their parents' vast bank accounts via identity cards loaded up with Big Red Bucks.

I didn't ask Chocklay about her life, so I learned only decades after I last saw her that in Tibet, she had owned her own restaurant. Because I didn't try very hard to talk to my coworkers, I will never know this for sure, but I sensed that Chocklay recognized what no teacher or administrator or counselor ever did: that my classmates' money made me feel alienated from them, while my overseas adolescence compounded the problem. My American citizenship deprived me of international student status, and so, though I too lacked American pop-cultural references and a grasp of American youth culture, I did not get to benefit from the cultural translating that went on in activities held for all the other eighteen-year-olds who had spent their adolescence abroad. I heard myself referred to by an American classmate as someone nice enough, but weird, since I was "always talking about politics." I'd thought I had been making small talk.

Fortunately, the other Greek kids understood me, especially Vasilikí, but I saw her infrequently, so busy was she with her premed courses and labor of her own in some sort of windowless lab observing fungus.

In contrast to the lone keg party I attended, where my effort to have fun with fellow Americans began and ended, at Zeus, I always knew what to say. I confidently fielded questions about ingredients and allergens, and expertly described our "BLTease" tofu sandwich. I fed the professors, the keepers of knowledge. Best of all, at work, I *made* things. And I had a routine.

When I arrived for an 8 a.m. shift, there would already be a small breakfast crowd. A group of five or six men whom a coworker dubbed "the old boys' club" sat near the windows at three narrow tables pushed together, and held animated, even boisterous conversations over morning newspapers and doughnuts until around nine. Then came the currently employed people, the nine-to-five deans and admissions folks. I was struck by how easily I could tell which were the nonacademic folk. Two registrar secretaries always came in together with their eighties-style haircuts and turtlenecks, acid-washed mom jeans and chunky white sneakers. They shared my own partiality to pumpkin cream cheese muffins.

The construction workers would enter together a little after that. They seemed to emerge from a different world, entering in dark denim bearing the grease marks of machines. I remember them as red-faced from the cold, always with stubbly, reddish goatees, their fluorescent work vests bright against the backdrop of the classicists' tweed. I envied their calloused, cement-flecked hands. I loved their direct talk, their jingling keys, the splashes of mud on their clothes, and the clothes themselves: big camel-colored jumpsuits or overalls with sweatshirts tucked inside. These men needed no jackets against the snow. I loved the wide vowels of their upstate-New-York accents, the rumble of their curt requests, their work boots, and the slow thud of their steps. As I pushed the button to eject the register and make change, I wished for their ability to build, to fix electrical problems, to change landscapes, and to make sidewalks where before there had only been dirt.

After the 9 a.m. breakfast crowd would come the ten o'clock coffee topper-uppers, people who'd had breakfast at home and were coming down for a second coffee to tide them over for the hour or so until lunch. Jonathan Culler would descend and acquire a refill of coffee—well, half a cup, as I distinctly remember the large, empty inch beneath the navy rim of his ceramic mug. I formulated a rather erroneous opinion of literary theory, because during undergrad all I learned about it was that Culler was in part responsible for the class that taught it. Culler's demeanor suggested that his was an arduous and mirthless form of work. Literary theory must therefore rob literature of its ineffable qualities, the mystery and the truth that lead to joy. These deductions seemed logical because I was nineteen. Mostly, I was mad he didn't look me in the eye. It wounded me, that disregard, because I deduced that this man saw that I punched buttons on a register, wiped up spills, and ladled soup for a living, and so decided he didn't owe me respect.

I eventually studied structuralism in an anthropology course during my senior year, but it wouldn't be until graduate school that I grasped what theory folks like Culler had invented. I would see that theory deepened my appreciation of literature rather than drying it out. I would further recognize that as chair of a large department, Culler had more on his mind than coffee. At the time, though, all I gleaned from this lone representative of theory was that he possessed an unfriendly mind, which differed in some profound and fundamental way from the mind of Ammons, the content and genial poet. Archie looked me in the eye and he smiled.

Later in the morning, in my memory, would come the beautiful one who always glowed, smiled at me with even greater radiance and warmth than Archie—like she meant it and could really see me—and she bought her cookie or bagel and coffee with joy, without apology. The beautiful one gave me courage for the lunch shift. I would notice her entrance from the corner of my eye while serving others, because she had her own particular walk, one that made me think her glorious hips were more used to dancing, indeed would always rather dance than walk, so that her entrance into the café seemed to be accompanied by music. She attended to fashion, too, an oddity at Cornell, and wore new, well-fitting jeans with handsome belts and either dress shirts or sweaters in joyful colors that looked good with whatever chic red or orange shade her hair was freshly dyed. And she wore lipstick. I didn't know her name until decades later, while flipping through an anthology of English literature. I was searching for a Hemingway story and noticed her face beaming out at me from the page where her story "The Moths" appeared. She is, the bio notes, among the great writers of our time.

After the midmorning customers, there would be maybe a fifteen-minute breather before the lunch rush. The hungry academics would begin to trickle in at eleven, when the kitchen opened, and more student workers would arrive. One would open a second register and the other would don an apron to serve soup, salads, and sandwiches.

While the people in the long soup and salad lines would gaze up at the menu board above and think about their choice, those in the cashier's line, which wrapped around the counter toward the door, had food in front of them. They rattled change, or sighed, or chatted with their neighbors about how eager they were to pay and eat and get back to their offices. Most seemed hunched below an invisible but weighty pile of work. I would try to sneak smiles at them. Receiving my patrons at the register, and handing them their change, was often an effective way to satisfy my urge to be helpful, since it involved a comforting little pep talk for the day (most would report feeling tired, inadequate, or worried about productivity). Graduate students near graduation would confess to shirking their TA duties because they were on the market. They would apologize for using twenty-dollar bills to pay for refills, and I would tell them it was all right, that big bills were not a problem, as each morning I enjoyed going on excursions to the bank with an oversized pencil case filled with a few hundred dollars to make into change.

No matter how gently I tried to soothe them, though, the patrons remained embarrassed by need. Where there are bodies, there is need. Bodies need soup, cough drops, sand-wiches, milk, croissants, iced tea, napkins, and sodas, but also a person to clean up their spills, to read them the in-gredient lists when they forget their glasses, and to reassure them that helping themselves to the very last everything bagel is really okay. The patrons of Zeus, mostly upper middle class, didn't want to put someone else out. They didn't want to impose. They were apologetic not merely for indulging and making messes, but also for needing food at all. Only a need for coffee came without shame, I noticed. Coffee, after all, isn't for the body. It is for the mind.

From the corner where the cookies lay, Cornell's great writers and scholars would sneak glances toward my ca-shier's perch, requesting absolution before they committed their sin. They fawned over cheese Danishes, especially ones with dollops of raspberry jelly on top. When they arrived too early, before the doughnuts, they stared at the clear plastic display case as though desire alone could make breakfast appear. When they pumped an air-pot's last drop, and the coffee gurgled because it was spent, they lifted it up high to display the offending weightlessness of the emptied pot.

When a napkin holder emptied, they called, "Out of napkins!" When the last paper cup had been taken, they stood before the dispenser, puzzled. When sugar jars emptied, they looked around, despondent, as though ship-wrecked and washed up on foreign land. When the soup was gone, they were sad. When only white rolls remained in a bin that had contained basil-parmesan and cranberry-walnut ones, they went on sifting for many minutes through the bleached wheat. One never knows what miracles might result from an intense enough desire. When asked if they wanted blue cheese on their salads, some grimaced, asked how anyone could eat mold. Others nodded with vigor, asked how anyone eats salad at all without the stuff.

When they spilled their soups and dropped oily leaves from their salads, dripped juices and teas on my just-cleaned floor, they looked at me in shame and apology as I leapt for a mop or for paper towels and rags, and they reached out to help with the mess. Despite their enormous intellects, my patrons could not imagine how very happy I was to clean it up, how I did not want them to help me; more keenly than my seat in their Ivy League classes, I felt this privilege, this fetching of fresh coffee and this cleaning of spills. They did not understand that by serving them, I felt freed from the debt I owed them for teaching me.

As they aged, America's great thinkers wore ever more comfortable shoes. The body changes its method of preoccupation. Young bodies demand decoration, and their owners work to keep them thin. Old ones demand comfort, articles that ease the aches of age. Women's makeup faded and men's neckties, watches, rings, briefcases, earrings, and fancy hairdos tapered off. The oldest clientele took into their beautiful hands the richest of foods: deep-fried honey crullers, pain au chocolat, scones. Cupped in their liver-spotted, purple-veined, wrinkle-mapped hands, they bore the sweet things of this world, and they set them down with gladness, in jovial embrace of their sweet pending pleasure, and they counted out for me, these meticulous elderly, the exact change. It was good to see them, the old, no longer afraid of an appetite. I wanted to see people unafraid of their appetite for literature, too, of an erotic appetite for knowledge. I wanted to tell them that a well-made sandwich, with its lettuce peeking out from under its bread just so, is an occasion for joy. And I was glad, so glad, to take care of them this way.

One day, much later, I would see that this part of my job was also what was satisfying about being a professor: being able to satisfy hunger, to lessen a student's suffering, ever so slightly. I would be reading Anne Carson and feel that I had at last found words for the reason why sweeping around the feet of the discoursing professors and their students gave me such joy: "In any act of thinking, the mind must reach across this space between known and unknown, linking one to the other but also keeping visible to difference. It is an erotic space."

I remember the day when A. R. Ammons died, and my professors expressed their love for the man and their desire for him to be on earth still. I felt, then, or glimpsed, what I believed the literary life was supposed to be, and what learning could feel like. My writing teacher handed out copies of "The City Limits," and began class with Archie's words: "When you consider the radiance that it does not withhold / itself but pours its abundance without selection into every / nook." She was undone by the loss, and I trusted her from that moment.

Roger Gilbert wrote an essay for one of the school papers, and I've never forgotten the last line: "You know a poem from the burn." Gilbert also once wrote an article with the word *bromance* in the title, about Ammons and Harold Bloom. He was the poet whose "In View of the Fact" says his "wife is baking for a funeral," and that "until we die we will remember every / single thing, recall every word, love every / loss." In those lines was what I wanted, and I couldn't get it in classrooms.

Mathematicians, led by Graeme Bailey, who spoke to my Mind and Memory course about the creativity demanded by math, and many linguists, anthropologists, and architecture professors would arrive at the start of the lunch rush and sit in large groups at several tables pushed together. It was a noisy time, a time to move fast and mop up spills as fast as I could and then run back to the register and ring up more food. While one customer fumbled for more money, I would calculate the next one's change because I could tell from each face whether they had exact change or a twenty. Time flew as quickly during the lunch rush as it did during exams, and before we could feel tired the professoriate had been fed and we were left to clean up the mess.

As soon as the cashier line shortened, the second register would close. Unless I absolutely had to read some last pages for class, I always asked the other student to stay and sit while I swept. Sweeping was joy. I liked to sneak up to the still-lunching clients and listen to their thoughts about books, original thoughts like the ones I longed to have. I swept close to their feet without disturbing them too badly, and I helped those who fumbled as they attempted to bus all their trash with one hand and lift their books or briefcases with the other. I loved to pick up their plates, whisk away crumbs and croutons left behind, bits of lettuce flown off the plate and dressing trickled onto the table.

And after sweeping, the daily ritual of trash. I would remove full trash bags and line the bins with new bags, then bring the dolly over and heap the not-yet-smelly waste onto it and trundle out. Oh, the joy of that garbage dolly's rumpus! What a racket its old wheels made on the bumpy tile floor, how I loved to make noise and disturb the somber deans and their form-filling bureaucratic assistants with the food scraps their own bodies, their earthy appetites, had left for me. This, this is your waste, I thought, and let us not forget, just because we wear ties and have doctorates, that this is man. Compost to compost. I loved to get out of doors hot from the exertion of pushing trash—I wore a jacket only if it dipped below twenty degrees, for it took just a minute to push the trash to the dumpster and lift each bag up, spinning it into the air and listening for the plastic-on-plastic swish of its landing. I loved the sensation of cold against my warm body, like diving from July heat into a chilly ocean, a taste of summer in the deep, cold Cornell semester.

On the way back inside, I would sneak peeks into their offices, dark rooms with exotic rugs, plush but aged couches, bookshelves which loom, in my memory of them, much higher than any ladder would ever reach. Some of the plaster casts had found their way out of storage and into professors' offices, so that some faculty still kept company with gods. I eavesdropped on conversations and desired entry into their world, but was satisfied with, at least, the chance to push along their trash. It was as if this service, this dutiful feeding of the teachers, might help me find out their secrets with better success than the dizzying time I spent reading their sentences and listening to lectures that kept me wondering, kept me hungry for their language, their insight into the poems and stories that to me still felt under lock and key.

I knew nothing of what they wrote. For instance, there was a tiny man with snow-white hair parted like a little boy's, and he used to buy a cup of soup and bread roll, preferably wheat, every day a little before noon. I never spoke to him, but learned recently that he had been born in Bavaria and was writing about surviving *Kristallnacht*. I didn't know what a literary journal was either, so I didn't know what *EPOCH* was when I passed by the room with the long table around which graduate students were silently, perennially hunched.

Though ignorant of their writing, I loved listening to my professors' lectures. I loved the way their arguments could twirl and swoop and soar. Gordon Teskey, my advisor who left me for Harvard, made that bright lecture hall in the chemistry building seem like a stage for *Antony and Cleopatra*; he described the Globe to make me feel I was there, he said the words *dissemination* (was this something lewd?) and *grammatology* but not Derrida, leaving me intrigued. Winthrop Wetherbee illuminated *Beowulf*'s adventures and spoke those strange medieval names, *Hrothgar* and *Grendel*, with magnificence and poise. But scribbling scraps of these performances into my notebooks left me feeling on the outside of knowledge. My papers and their comments on them always seemed like a farce, like writing them was only pretending to participate in what they did. But the ritual give-and-take of food was a space that made me feel different, close to the insides of the intellectual labor, and to the secret rooms of thought.

I lacked keys to the intellectual world, but I did have the key to my cash register, and the key to the storage closet upstairs, which was my other adventure, my treat after the lunch rush. The cups and spoons and forks were stored in a closet up on the fourth floor, which had space for only a few professors' offices and our little closet, so that going up there was a trip to a secret place, like some Narnia. I would steel myself to fight for the right to go, but of course I never had to, because no one else got quite as excited as I did about going upstairs.

At two or two thirty Chocklay and Nyima would leave for Moosewood, and Zeus would settle into its afternoon trickle. We had no dinner rush, as the professors would go home to their husbands and wives, but a few students would come in. Some rehearsed plays in Kaufmann Auditorium while others studied in empty classrooms. I would tidy up the café with an attentiveness and care I've never applied to any of my own houses, and then I would sit and read in my resting, neatened Temple. Goldwin Smith Hall smelled of steam and wood and the machines that wax the floors. Outside, the snow swirled down, but inside, the building seethed with heat.

Tom Walls, our manager, would also bid goodbye sometime after the lunch shift ended. Tom would talk to me about my classes when he emerged from the office where he balanced Zeus's books. The first time I heard the word *Midwest*, he was telling me where he was from, and I thought it really was the middle of the West—Utah or Nevada. He was thin, of medium height, pale and blue-eyed with dirty-blond hair (the kind that hides gray), and a whistler. He tried to make me believe mistakes were OK, and taught me the phrase *water under the bridge* (there are many bridges over the various Ithaca gorges, and when he used it to tell me not to beat myself up about a mistake, I may have pictured one specific bridge: there was one that had spiky, suicide-inhibiting bars).

After I closed the café doors at six, I would pour out the stale coffee with sadness, and before I poured it out I would drink as much as I possibly could, a habit which has resulted today in a caffeine tolerance of enormous proportions. My greatest delight of all followed this. It was the aerobic workout of lifting the black wooden chairs onto the tables. I would put on music with a speedy tempo and begin to lift the wooden chairs. I remember how heavy they were when I lifted them swiftly, twirled them to get the seat onto the tables in one smooth motion; how I had to take off my turtleneck halfway through lifting; how proud I was of my physical prowess; how much it mattered to me (though I would never tell) that the nighttime customers, the few professors who had no kids and worked late, would walk by Zeus and see me and know that I, a girl, could do this work. I needed for them to see the sculpted bulbs of my shoulder muscles, to see the strength needed in addition to the gentle care with which I asked for salad orders, saran-wrapped takeaway, and ladled soup. I wanted them to know with what devotion I served, and that I expressed devotion with both my body and my mind. I loved this work with an intensity that matched the seriousness of scholarship, of mining texts for truth.

Yes, at Zeus I found something I deeply desired from my undergraduate education: scholar as body, as lover, the subtle notes about desire left by the ancients for us, *paideia*. I am starting to read Marcuse, to think about alienated labor and Eros. I think there is a way to work through these problems, ways better than rumbling a garbage trolley through hallways that treat students like customers. Perhaps I just wanted to feel safe.

Safe I was not, though I didn't know why or how. Like

many female freshmen, I received attention from an older male professor and believed that the pursuit of learning required me to reciprocate that attention. He took me off campus in his beat-up van, and we drank coffee at night in some kind of old diner whose location I did not know at the time and have not figured out since. He gave me copies of his own books as gifts. We only really talked about books, and nothing terrible happened, although had I not begun to refuse his offers he may have behaved toward me in the manner of drunk centaurs. When I began to pull away, he called my behavior "hostile," but agreed to leave me alone. Many distressing moments like these arose with men (mostly much younger than the professor) who argued that my friendliness toward them should turn erotic. It took years before I resigned myself to the truth that men would only on very rare occasions value my friendship. It was hard to be a person so full of love, learning new ways of seeing and learning about art in ways that made my heart burst, and then find myself cursed, also, in the name of love. I didn't know that this is the way of the world—that Eros makes life beautiful, and makes it hurt.

The stability of manual labor at Zeus helped me get through this period. It's hard for all young people, and most college students have to endure this sad fact: even as my entire life was devoted to hearing and reading, day in and day out, knowledge and truth, the most important truths went unspoken. I had to discover them alone, by watching and aching. Labor made it easier to bear that loneliness and the dizzying paradoxes of the world. Even as I settled into a life of teaching for a living, and as a graduate student gave up on the possibility of making a decent living as a laborer, I made up opportunities to do physical work. I donated labor to a yearly grad school auction, and spent hours raking leaves or preparing multiple fresh dishes for department potlucks. There is a sacred quality in physical donations, and a deliciousness—one that is safe. Manual labor, too, let me hold onto some of what capitalism was taking away from me, and let me reclaim my body even as I entered deeper into an academy that forces people to be only brain.

As a graduate student, I also learned to better manage the slippage between love and careerism, and to endure the paradox of being a student eating lunch with a professor in a place like Zeus, wondering with each bite what I wanted from the person before me, the path to enlightenment or a reference letter.

I could never have guessed, when I served at Zeus, that I would eventually become a professor myself, with an office of my own for students to sit in and tell me that writing is hard. I don't tell my students I despair over the impossibility of attaining, in intellectual work, the certainty of a well-swept floor. I tell them we are lucky. We can masquerade as people slogging away to get three credits—as people performing the self-abnegating practice of work—while all the while our class is a secret, communal, and subversive celebration of what we most love. We don't have to tell anyone quite how much pleasure we taste when together we read poetry. I know that teenagers enjoy a revolution.

The other day, I turned from a text by Jonathan Culler to a video of the man. The face that had seemed to me so distant and so uninterested in the world was there on the screen, and it became suddenly animated. When the great scholar read a Baudelaire poem out loud before the cameras, he started hopping up and down with excitement, as if the poem's energy might propel him into flight. You should hear his French—the beauty of it—and the clarity of his arguments. By now, having been through graduate school twice,

I know enough to make sense of a Cornell professor's lecture, and I recognize the names he drops: Maurice Blanchot, Benedetto Croce, Virginia Jackson, Northrop Frye, and Rei Terrada. Culler displayed the very physical passion that I suspected he—and along with him, theory—lacked.

Now in my forties, I have begun at last to understand the root of my young self's suffering. Alone, I sought community and a language for the eroticism and alienation and desire I felt. And I had no such language, then. But at Zeus, beneath the friezes from a time before Greek culture was straightened by Christianity and the Victorian Pan-European cleanup of what art meant, I could listen and bide my time until a day when I, too, found a language with which to speak.

The Other Side

The word *fierce* does not do justice to the Cyprus sun's violent heat. Rays bounce off every surface in blinding white glares, and the landscape looks like a parched yellow expanse that will never again foster life. Come April, green carob trees turn gray and olive trees turn grayer as dust settles on the leaves until October, when it rains. In between, there come days every two weeks or so when a cloud makes a hole in the blue canopy above. This was not one of those days. It was a day for the beach, for sunscreen and a good umbrella. At least not too many cars were on the highway. In August, most Cypriots take a week or two off for a vacation on one of the Greek islands. I'd already been to Crete, Corfu, Tinos, and Paros. That year, though, Christine had come to visit from England, and she'd be staying with me in my parents' house in Asgáta. Instead of visiting other islands, we'd be driving over the Green Line to the *katehómena*, the part of Cyprus that had been occupied by Turkish troops for thirty years at that point.

Christine and I got into the car as early as we could. We'd gone out the night before, and it was well after nine by the time we were dressed and packed. My Mitsubishi Mirage was a furnace. The steering wheel singed my hands. After a minute on the road I was blinded and fished for my sun-glasses among the junk I keep in the little receptacles between the two front seats. Christine handed them to me and they relieved what they could.

Since the 1974 invasion, almost no one had crossed the dividing line without being jailed or killed—until April 2003, when Rauf Denktash, the Turkish Cypriot leader, surprised everyone by agreeing to open a checkpoint to allow Greek Cypriots to visit the North, and Turkish Cypriots the south. After twenty-nine years confined to the southern half of the island, Greeks who'd fled during the war and left every-thing behind would be allowed to tour the occupied north, get a glimpse of their homes. They were required to leave before midnight. Many were scared, others excited by the change. Almost no one could believe it. Politically, we'd still be a nation under occupation, but in terms of human rights breaches, one essential freedom, the freedom of movement, had been suddenly restored. Our protest songs and petitions would have to change.

In spite of everyone's misgivings about Denktash's motives, thousands queued up at the border. By sundown on the first day, fourteen thousand people had gone across. By the seventh day, twenty-five thousand Turkish Cypriots had come from the North to see homes and friends they'd left in the south, and to obtain a legal passport from the Republic of Cyprus. Another one hundred thousand Greek Cypriots had made the trip to the North. That was more than one in every eight Cypriots. On television, I watched cars form a line twelve kilometers long. The cameras caught people stretching awake after spending the night in their cars to be sure they were among those who got across. No one knew when Denktash would close the checkpoint again.

I figured it would close in a few days, when the queue of

cars stretched on even longer, and thousands would head back to their quick-built refugee houses without seeing their birthplaces. I figured it couldn't turn out well because nothing had ever been well on this island as long as I had been alive. While I was composing college application essays in 1996, three men had attempted to cross the Green Line; one had wandered into the buffer zone while gathering snails to eat; all three were killed.

Like most of those born after 1974, I felt frustrated that I had never seen the other half of my island, my father's island, our island, but I didn't know if I wanted to be among those who actually went and visited the *katehómena*. Without actively choosing not to, I never went.

Then Christine called from England to say she was coming to visit me in Cyprus. My parents' house had plenty of space. Christine and I were both twenty-three. We had met during our university years, while I was on study abroad in the English Midlands. Christine gave me a tour of Sheffield and Leicester before I left her country, and I invited her to mine. Before Christine took me up on that invitation, we backpacked through Europe together. After she finished her master's in medieval history and I got my bachelor's degree, we rewarded ourselves with a trip from London to Istanbul by boat and train. I gathered $500 I'd saved while making sandwiches at The Temple of Zeus, spent half on a thirty-day Eurail ticket, and stretched the other half across food, campsites, and hostels. We toured Dover, Calais, Paris, Frankfurt, Prague, Budapest, Timisoara, Vienna, Rome, Athens—then, exhausted, we parted. She flew to England and I to Cyprus. We never made it to Turkey. I was secretly relieved when she asked if I'd like to truncate the adventure, both because I missed my own comfy bed and because I was, I admit, scared by the idea of *being* in Turkey—I was brought up to perceive them as the eternal enemy; how would I explain myself entering their country as a guest? When you're taught to despise the neighbors, do you pay them a visit?

The problem was the same for the occupied territory of Cyprus. Most Greek Cypriots felt that crossing the Green Line was a betrayal. "Don't make the occupying forces look good for letting us back in," they said. "Ignore the bait and stay your ground—it's our thirst to see the North that keeps us fighting." When Christine asked me to take her, though, this favor balanced out the possibility of such selling out. For a Cypriot, an act of hospitality is an act of patriotism.

Friends my age discussed the matter little. In fact, most said going to the North would be fine. Only, there are good beaches in Pafos and Polis, great times in Limassol, and a cosmopolitan clubbing scene on our side of Nicosia. So why go to the trouble?

We, the youth who never saw the land, were taught that we must love the beauty of that stolen part of our homeland and wait restlessly for the moment of return. After commercial breaks, the public broadcasting station airs pictures of occupied landmarks with mournful patriotic music and the caption "I Don't Forget." Elsewhere, the motto appeared on images of the island that had manipulated to make the northern half drip blood, or the Karpass peninsula look like the barrel of a gun. Throughout elementary school, children received free notebooks for every subject with the same "I Don't Forget" motto and a picture of an occupied northern town on the cover. When a child empties her schoolbag, out tumbles a small pile of open wounds.

Along the boulevard that runs parallel to the southern coast in Limassol, the city council put up signs that read, "← WAY BACK," with an arrow pointing north. Christine always thought they were the oddest things. The way back *where?* I couldn't answer her, but guessed that since the sign pointed north, it must be political, indicating a way back to Kyrenia, Famagusta, Morfou, and other occupied cities—a way back out of exile.

Until my trip, I felt a strange sort of yearning for the *kate-hómena* that didn't come from my own mind or experiences, but from somewhere deeper than me. It came from elementary school when I recited poems about our nation's suffering and our aching loss. From my father, who taught me to love what's right, I learned to denounce the wrongs my country has suffered and to wait for justice in patient but not passive resistance. He taught me to lament our Greek nation's fall from its old glory.

And yet, for all he had taught me of the beauty of Northern Cyprus, and for all his sighs over its loss, my father simply would not go. Time and again, he'd refuse to go "until there's a just political solution." Every New Year's, all my relatives would raise their glasses in a toast to "Freedom for Cyprus." The freedom always beckoned, imminent in the fury of peace talks and negotiations that have dominated the headlines as long as I have watched Cypriot news. Every year, there has been a critical week in which the reporters have assured us a solution will be found in the next month. No one seems to worry about this question though: If we go back, where will the Turks go?

For as long as I can remember, my dad would tell me about the beauties of Kyrenia and Famagusta. "They took the best parts of Cyprus. The most developed—a huge luxury hotel complex had just been built in Famagusta when they invaded. They took Apostolos Andréas." That's a monastery built on the tip of the long cape that juts northeast into the Mediterranean. It was dedicated to the Apostle Andrew, who stopped there after leaving Jerusalem, and since then it has always been an important place of pilgrimage. When we need help from God, we ask a saint to intercede, and we make a *táma*, or promise, that if the need (usually for healing) is fulfilled, we'll bring an offering to the place where the saint is venerated. A *táma* to Mary the Mother of God usually brings pilgrims to the island of Tinos, where there is an ancient icon of her. A *táma* to the Apostle Andrew brings pilgrims to Cyprus.

"Of all the peoples you could have as a neighbor, the Greeks got stuck with the Turks," my father used to say. Having a father who's a history teacher, a romantic idealist, and a patriot, you never have to ask about historical events or current politics. You get told, annoyingly and endlessly, until you're used to understanding what happened before you were born. As a teenager, I sought out my own sources and pieced together the story of Cyprus from Cypriot literature and music, and from long television programs which analyzed just how insidious and wrong the invasion had been. I shouted and marched in protests and cried to resistance songs. It took me a while, however, to start asking what was missing from the puzzle, what the stories I heard were leaving out, and to think about what had really brought the troops that morning in July. And what had brought Turks to a Greek island centuries before that?

Although my father left Cyprus in 1959, and was in New York during the invasion, he described the events as if he had been there. Over Kyrenia and Morfou, paratroopers darkened the early morning sky that July 20, 1974. Tanks advanced, bombs fell, and people jumped out of bed and into their cars with blankets and food to ride out the storm— but when the gunfire died down and they headed home, they were stopped by soldiers in the center of Nicosia. After two days of fighting, the miniscule, traitor-ridden national guard was crushed. All of the Turkish Cypriots were obliged to leave for what would become, in 1983, a separate state which only the Republic of Turkey has recognized. Those who stayed were given the houses that had belonged to the Greek Cypriots who'd fled; some of them were given homes of Turkish Cypriots. Most were put up in tents until new homes could be built. Little violence has occurred since that short war—wounds of memory have replaced war wounds and death. Grenades go off in our minds when we remember our loss.

The Cyprus problem sounded like Northern Ireland to Christine, only our equivalent of the IRA only talks and shakes fists. Once, our EOKA (National Organization of Cypriot Liberation Fighters) did more than that—they kicked the English imperialists out in 1959, when the Republic of Cyprus came into being as an officially bilingual, bicommunal state with a Greek president and Turkish vice president. After they'd won the fight for independence, the guerrilla front mutated into EOKA-B, an underground Greek nationalist group that wanted to make Cyprus part of Greece. EOKA-B was funded and supported by the military junta that had seized power in Greece in a 1967 coup d'état. It tried to seize power in Cyprus by force on July 15, 1974, giving Turkey its excuse to intervene and take 36 percent of Cypriot territory. I learned that if any Greeks are to blame at all, they are the members of EOKA-B (which was funded by the Greek junta, who in turn had support from the Americans, who feared that Greece would go Communist like its Balkan neighbors). But if I examine how I imagine a peaceful Cyprus, I see I do little better than the nationalists. I don't know how to figure Turkish Cypriots and some hundred thousand recent migrants from Turkey into a post-partition Cyprus.

The Turkish Cypriots made up 18 percent of the Cypriot population before the invasion. A lot of Turkish Cypriots have gone to the UK now, though. In 1960, the leaders of the new state drafted a constitution that provided for the Turkish minority to hold positions in the government. The following fourteen years between British colonial occupation and the present Turkish occupation, when Turkish and Greek politicians shared power in a single government, are referred to on our side as the only time Cyprus has been free. Read a Turkish version of history, and you'll learn more about the tensions, endless haggling among politicians, murders in cold blood on the streets, so that Turkish Cypriots were forced into enclaves. The Greek Cypriot people, though, did not recognize that Turkish Cypriots were enduring systematic oppression. My friend Erika's mother was in the North at the time and recalls believing that Turkish girls remained in the enclaves out of bashfulness or modesty. She didn't realize that the minority had little political leverage, or that the Greek politicians newly in power might be making the Turkish Cypriots feel voiceless or unprotected. According to the Cypriot constitution, the president had to be Greek and the vice president Turkish. This system paralyzed the infant state and impeded necessary new laws. To this day, the eighty-member Parliament has a block of twenty-four empty seats waiting for the Turkish Cypriot members to come back.

As Christine and I thumbed through guidebooks deciding where to go, I kept my nervousness to myself. I told Christine I was glad to visit the North, but the counterarguments replayed in my mind. Besides the danger of growing national complacency, Greek travelers necessarily spend money in the North, and thus are complicit in financing the illegal regime. They make their enemies rich. I figured we'd avoid this problem by bringing sandwiches.

Christine unfolded a map and asked again where we should go. I thought about what I missed most, about what seemed most urgent to take the way back to. My mind a blur of inherited memory, I asked what interested her.

"I'd like to see this old abbey of Bellapais. I don't know, lots of things look interesting." She went on with the possibilities like we were tourists talking about islands.

"Kyrenia," I said. "Let's visit Kyrenia." The Pentadáktylos is a mountain range that shoots into the sky and rolls down to the sea with Kyrenia in its lap. I repeated the tales I'd heard of its charm to Christine. "The most beautiful little port . . . and not too far after Nicosia," I went on. A strange collage had formed in my mind out of all the pictures I'd seen on television and in books. I planned that trip like I was planning a journey back in time, like it could never happen. I had never felt it was a real place the way New York, London, Athens, a remote province in Poland even, are go-to-able.

The night before our trip, we drank at a pub with Erika, who had said several times that she'd like to come when I took Christine to the *katehómena*. She'd shown us some beautiful, nontouristy beaches north of Pafos the year before. Though her mother Ivi had been born in a village outside Kyrenia, the family hadn't yet made their trip back. We agreed that Erika would drive to my house, and then we'd go all together in my car. In the morning, she called to say she had changed her mind. "We'll go another time," she said.

Christine and I traveled alone together and had a calm drive north. When we finally got to the checkpoint, the line of cars was, as we'd hoped, not too long. I experienced the depressed anticipation you might feel at a police station, waiting to identify goods that had been stolen from your house while you were asleep. Getting there took longer than we had expected. I had heard so many news reports and seen so many people on TV waiting in their cars to get past the checkpoint, I never realized I didn't know exactly where the open checkpoint was. At first they'd opened Lydra road in the center of Nicosia, but due to the traffic jams, they made Lydra a pedestrians-only checkpoint. I stopped at a kiosk and bought a map of the occupied territory with both Greek and Turkish place names and asked the shop owner how to get across to the other side. He directed me toward the new checkpoint for cars, in the Nicosia suburb called Áyios Dométios. Finally, barrels painted blue and white signaled UN forces were near. A couple of soldiers with blue berets were sitting in the shade.

We joined the line of cars just before lunchtime. It moved slowly, and at times I turned the motor off. After half an hour or so, we had inched close enough to the makeshift offices for me to leave Christine in the car and see what I needed to do. Greek Cypriots were waiting in various lines in front of windows, behind which Turkish officials with stacks of forms were visible. It was hard to get someone to show me which forms I had to fill out and where I should stand. Most people seemed edgy, excited, or tired, and I said nothing to the few who cut in front of me in line. First off, we had to buy car insurance, as the regime in Northern Cyprus doesn't recognize insurance from the state of Cyprus. Nor would my Greek Cypriot insurance agency be willing to pay damages in the case of an accident. Legally, neither state exists for the other.

As I waited for my turn I could smell gyro—I guess the girl chewing that delicious sandwich of lamb and spices would call it *döner kebab*. Greeks and Turks eat the same foods by different names—our souvlaki is their *kebap*. Sometimes we even have the same word: *dolma*—stuffed grape leaves; *kiofte*—meatball; *karpuz*—watermelon. The clerk was courteous and quick. I handed her ten Cyprus pounds and my passport, driver's license, and car registration, and a few kebab bites later I had my insurance. Good for three consecutive days if anyone had the nerve for that much traveling. I prayed I wouldn't have to use the insurance, shuddering at the thought of getting into an accident in a part of the world where Greeks are more or less the enemy, little English and no Greek is spoken, and emergency health care is subject to the limitations of an international trade embargo. Since 1974, trading with a state created by military invasion has been against international law.

I continued to drive north. The bars of signal on my cell phone dropped off quickly, and in just a few minutes, I was cut off. Losing service unnerves me even when I'm at home with an alternative landline. Out there, I felt twice as anxious.

I concentrated on the view. The landscape, of course, changed little, since the Green Line follows no geographical boundary. Nonetheless, I expected some visible shift. The surrounding tall, dry rocky hills dotted with drought-shrunken pines all sang, "This is Cyprus!" to me—yet Cyprus is the Greek place where I live among friends.

The signs, in Turkish and English, first made me feel I was in a different place. License plates had a red stripe, too, signaling that this was Cyprus but not Greece. Those signs were all the communication I'd get, too. As I drove deeper in the occupied territory, I knew I wouldn't have the heart to speak to a Turk. I had intended to satisfy my curiosity and prove how progressive I was by initiating an open-minded dialogue. But now that I had reached the other side, I lost the will to speak.

Maybe I thought talking would make it harder to pretend I never visited the North, violated my people's mourning for their lost land. But right then, I thought none of this. I just couldn't believe I was allowed to keep driving. It had always been off-limits, impossible to proceed once you got halfway through Nicosia and confronted barrels, sandbags, barbed wire, and a guard holding a machine gun in his watchtower. Yet today, the rest of my nation, lost and longed for, spread before me. It just didn't feel real that the land should now spread and spread. The border, the Buffer Zone, and the Green Line were real to my mind, not this. Not the physical presence of my own self on this piece of the country, imagined and desired, but never ever touched. I drove on and emotions rose up. Tears welled up. At the privilege—to see that land at last—and a little hope—this country's wound had begun to heal, the violence had cooled and refugees' lives restarted, and now the refugees could come and look at their land. And at the pain. Because the division of Cyprus remains. The island is like a human bone that has been badly broken but that no doctor ever set, so that the bone has healed crooked, and we limp into our future to make ourselves a crippled history.

Christine looked out the window so calm and interested that she made me uncomfortable about my feelings. She was impressed and fascinated by the scenery. Granted, she opposes the Turkish occupation too, but she didn't have impassioned songs of love and betrayal in her head, and she didn't share my sense of personal loss of this land that I was at last laying eyes on. We didn't speak as I drove further northwards. I was almost angry because her placidness made me question how authentic my feelings could be.

And then the sign appeared: ridiculous, pathetic. We read it out loud in unison, having noticed it at the same time, and we laughed long and loud. "HOW HAPPY TO SAY I AM A TURK." Enormous letters: the phrase spanned both lanes of the highway above us. When I looked it up a year later and found it was actually a quote from Mustafa Kemal Atatürk, founder of the Turkish Republic, it felt less ludicrous. Apparently, schoolchildren had to recite daily: "I am a Turk, I am honest, I am hardworking, how happy I am to say I am a Turk." From five miles away, the words etched on Mount Ararat appear: "HAPPY IS HE WHO SAYS 'I AM A TURK.' " The entire mountain is happy to be Turkish.

We approached a traffic circle before we finished laughing. The map didn't show that kind of detail. "Oh no! Which way? How do you say Kyrenia in Turkish?" *Girne* sounded the closest, and it was the straight-ahead exit, which made sense. So we took the second exit and kept going north on a long highway toward the coast. On either side, flat land sprawled, empty. Just some warehouses or silos dotted the dead fields. And I remember a lot of fences that neither Christine nor I could think of a purpose for. I tried to ignore the real estate signs, all in English, advertising villas and apartments to European holidaymakers and pensioners.

Everyone was driving along the open highway at one hundred kilometers per hour: a line of well-spaced vehicles proceeded in safety, and I felt safer than I had on any road in all of Cyprus before. Christine agreed; she, too, a veteran passenger on Cypriot roads, had witnessed the tail-gating, speed-devil Greek Cypriots who traversed the narrow asphalt war zone that I learned to drive in. I'd never felt so safe. I added that the Turkish police must be so vicious no driver would risk going even to 101.

We were driving over the Pentadáktylos, named for its five peaks, which legend says were formed by the fingers of Digenís Akrítas when he grabbed hold of the mountain to give him leverage as he leapt across the sea from Cyprus into Asia Minor. The tale takes place at a time when the

Byzantines had lost Cyprus to Arab conquerors. Digenís's father was an Arab emir who carried off the daughter of a Byzantine general, fell in love with her, converted from Islam to Christianity, and raised their son to be the greatest protector the Byzantine Christian Empire ever knew. The name Digenís means "born of two races;" his story, in the *Legends of the Two-Blood Border Lord*, implies that mixed blood makes the strongest men. Having defeated countless dragons, bandits, and other enemies of the Empire, Digenís built a palace by the Euphrates where he died peacefully.

Here, driving across Digenís's cliffs with heroes' stories dying in my head, the whole excursion began to feel stupid and banal. You go to a place decked in legends and stories of yearning to return, and then you just drive. You look and observe; you are a tourist. I started to think that maybe this was the reason the border had been opened. Having traveled there, I became able to reconcile myself with the notion of the North as a new, other country. All the place names have been made to sound originally Turkish, and I felt the big red flags yelling at me: "Leave, you Greek, this land is ours now and you'd better get out and go home and cry on *your* side." I felt like an unintended and helpless spy. I had once thought I would always feel proud of being Greek, but up there, I envied Christine for being just an English tourist.

Before long, a sign for Áyios Ilariónas appeared. There were all sorts of warnings about the road being slippery in winter and "Do Not Take Pictures" signs, which implied some kind of military unit was nearby. The road curled round and round the mountain; we passed the army base (soldiers stood outside, but ignored us) and then the road got very steep and narrow and the view got better until we could see all of Nicosia and Kyrenia and the northern coast. The sense of Cyprus as an island first struck me, really, there—having seen only the southern coast until then, I could have been living on the edge of any continent. And then the castle towered above us.

I parked the Mirage near the gate and began exploring, picking up a brochure in English at the entrance (there were none in Greek; anyone else would think it obvious, but I was a little shocked). There were stables from the time it was a fort, and the ruins of a much older Byzantine church. Saint Ilaríonas himself chose the spot. After an ascetic life in Palestine teaching the monastic way and working many miracles, he left and sought to hide from the "praise of men." When he stopped in Cyprus on his way back to the Egyptian desert, he ended up choosing the rugged and remote terrain of the Pentadáktylos cliffs to pray alone with God until the end of his life. A church was built near his cave during Byzantine rule. When the Englishman Richard the Lionheart conquered Cyprus in 1191 and the Byzantines lost the island once and for all, successive waves of conquerors used the spot at some times as a fort and at others as a nobleman's summer retreat.

An overview of the island's history turns into a catalogue of successive foreign conquerors (Assyrian, Egyptian, Persian, Roman, French, Genovese, Mameluk, Venetian, Ottoman, British), who set up administrations but rarely penetrated the Greek cultural milieu. Egyptians, Phoenicians, and Hittites probably settled there around four thousand years ago, but when Achaean traders settled on Cyprus around 1400 BC, their culture took root. Mycenaean merchants followed a century later. Each of the modern cities was then a separate kingdom whose laws and literature indicate that a distinctly Greek culture developed on the island.

Western invaders left words in our dialect and a recognizably medieval European architecture. Only the Ottomans, who stayed the longest, from 1570 to 1878, and whose policy of Empire demanded the relocation of whole families to the new land, left behind a community. When the Ottomans gained control of Cyprus from the Venetians in 1571 (as recorded in *Othello*), they transferred 5,720 families from many parts of Asia Minor (Beysehir, Ankara, Konya, and others) to Greek villages in Rizokárpaso, Larnaca and Pafos, where earlier wars had wiped out most of the inhabitants.

Turkish Cypriots descended from those medieval transplants naturally have a different accent and cultural identity from Turks who come over from mainland Turkey in present day. Turkish Cypriots have five hundred years of common history with Greek Cypriots, and common rituals and words in their respective dialects. Greek Cypriots have far less in common with the growing number of recently uprooted settlers from eastern Turkey, and the shift in the identity of Turkish-speakers in Cyprus has further complicated the thorny Cyprus problem.

Christine and I separated and I explored the castle alone, my confusion and the sound of Turkish pricking my eardrums like the soundtrack of a banned film. I looked around the ruin a while, then out at the view. My eyes strained toward the Turkish mainland that had sent over the settlers who kept Cyprus divided. A haze rose from the sea, though, and the Turkish mountains were concealed.

I met Christine in the cafeteria and we bought lemonade. There was no problem using our Greek money, even though Cyprus wouldn't adopt the euro for another year. Good thing, because what would we have done with leftover Turkish lira? I felt odd handing the cashier my Greek Cypriot pound—apologetic but also proud: "I'm sorry I've been deriding your people all my life, but you did oppress us first."

I didn't try out my *tesekkür*, the Turkish thank you I had

practiced from Christine's handbook. I said thank you in English, and I tried to find something else to say but faltered and sat down on an old plastic chair in the shade. A soft, sweet breeze blew.

We headed down the mountain again, this time for the beach. Our picnic was long overdue. If I'd asked someone, maybe we would have found a tourist beach, but instead I drove around and we both looked for a road that looked like it led to the shore. When we found one, I parked and spread our blanket close to the sea among lots of other bathers, none of whom looked like tourists. There was a run-down-looking restaurant open. The pointy Turkish ü sounds poked at my ears again; I felt invisible, and again like a spy. None of the Turks that surrounded me could hear the angry words yelling in my memory. I longed for my phone, angering myself with this pettiness, this dependence on the cell. But I needed to talk to my Greek friends about the crushing, infinite complexity of our country.

Christine agreed that we would leave Kyrenia district without ever seeing the city or its marina. We just headed for our next landmark, Bellapais. I had always thought it was an Italian name meaning pretty country, but it turns out the name was originally *Abbaye de la Paix*. The Abbey of Peace was built by Augustinian monks who fled Jerusalem when the Crusaders lost the city to Saladin's troops in 1187. Like a lot of Cyprus's medieval architecture, the building looks strikingly Western with its pointed Gothic-style arches, and contrasts sharply with the older, characteristically Greek column, pillar, and statue bits that litter the excavations of earlier periods. By that point I was awfully tired of exploring history, so I stayed outside while Christine went in. I climbed a carob tree to get good shade and relief from the boiling heat of the parking lot. I felt kind of at home up there.

A group of Greek Cypriots sat down under the tree without noticing me, and I listened to their plans to travel all the way along the northern shore to Apostolos Andréas without leaving behind a penny, in protest against the illegal and unjust occupation. When Christine came back, I climbed down, and before we left they offered us some of the water and cake they had brought with them. "Don't be tempted to buy anything!" they warned. I didn't mention the lemonade.

By the time we headed back to the car, it was late afternoon and I was even more ready to go home. Driving back, my anger dried up. The trip was done and over. My heart beat only a little faster while we passed the police officers who sometimes check cars for drugs and cheap cigarettes being smuggled from the North. Christine and I laughed at the "Happy Turk" sign with less heart this time around.

I was too tired for scorn. Too worn out from driving and wondering what hope there is for Cyprus after all. I smuggled back jaded hopes, impatience, and the ashes of an anger that used to make so much sense. They oppressed us first. They conquered this bit of land and that, and then we fought back and then they fought back.

Perhaps what makes me angriest now is that I cannot do a thing about it. I can question why I felt no reason to talk to a Turk during my time in the *katehómena*. I can question the defeatist attitudes into which my polemical ones have degenerated. But I can't fight anymore.

I guess I can understand now, after going, why it would have felt so wrong and impossible for my father to go. I'd never bothered to talk about it when I went, since my feelings were drained, emptied, and not worth discussing. I just told him it was as beautiful and as sad as he had described. But one year, my aunts came to Cyprus to stay with us for two weeks. My dad's youngest sister asked him to take her up to

Apostolos Andréas, as she had made a *táma* to Saint Andrew asking him to help her daughter, who wasn't responding to doctors' treatments. She's always been my father's closest family. They've helped each other out since they were kids stealing sweets from their father's store, and I was taken aback when I heard that not even she could get him to go. She had to take a taxi with their oldest sister instead.

"I went there when it was ours," my dad explained when I asked. "And it's no longer ours. They put their flags everywhere, and so on." My father hated going to Nicosia because of the enormous flag built with white stones on the Pentadáktylos. His youth had been consumed with the dream of freedom for his island home. Not in his wildest nightmares did he see that island cracking in two, one side crushed under a foreign army and the other left as a tiny so-called sovereign state, flung onto the international scene with missing limbs.

"You see the hostility everywhere," my dad said. Though I had told him the facts of my journey but never mentioned how I felt, he put his finger on what had made me so uncomfortable that day: the Greek's wariness of Turkish hostility, our centuries-old collective memory. Love Cyprus as he did, he preferred that I live somewhere else. To remind me, he reiterated, "and I don't see the situation getting any better. Talks, talks, and nothing changes. After all, *aftá eíne zóa.*" These are animals.

You can see how all efforts of rapprochement between the Greek and Turkish sides have led to impasse upon impasse. The "I Don't Forget" campaign has succeeded in preserving the collective memory of our own suffering. With not forgetting as our goal, though, we haven't learned to act, to forgive, or to compromise. We have been fighting over small but strategic bits of earth for one thousand years. In school, we learn details of the massacres and oppressions our respective sides have suffered. Having suffered an invasion seems to make it the Greeks' right to retrieve the island on our own terms, Turkless. I wonder if we want to go back to 1571.

A resistance song calls the Pentadáktylos to "rise up and shrug off the conquerors who have subjugated you." I sing the song and imagine the mountain tearing off that mile-long stone flag that flaunts the victory of guns. If we hope to unite this country, we cannot be shoving ethnic triumphs in each other's face.

Digenís's Pentadáktylos receded in the rearview mirror as I drove south and home, and I felt relieved at the fading of that enormous stone flag. The flag may represent a state that does not exist, but it represents people who exist and suffer as much as we do, and more in the abjection of their illegal regime—I learned that much in my trip over to the other side. And I need to learn more. For when we gain the understanding that a new, two-blooded flag might represent, and that our only borders are our shores, then we will have a country that's as strong as Digenís Akrítas.

—

Wild Honey,
Locust Beans

—

If you live, as I do, in a world where an overabundance of food is more a plague than hunger, you might be given to scrutinizing ingredient lists, and so have seen the words *carob bean gum* before tearing the plastic wrapper from, say, an ice cream sandwich, or the foil from a tub of cream cheese. Small quantities of carob bean gum do the trick, and so this natural stabilizer appears at the ingredient list's end, the part that even serious health food nuts expect to find uninterpretable (for me, it's a list of plants I can't quite place, and words I remember from high school chemistry). *Carob bean gum* sounds harmless, natural, salubrious, even—beans healthier than meat, carobs healthier than sweets—and, indeed, harmless the carob bean is. Such harmlessness is all most of us want to ascertain when we venture into the ingredient list's largely chemical tail. I have never made the effort to learn what lecithin is, though I often see the word—ditto for guar gum, potassium sorbate, xanthan, and xylitol. There is a limit to how much thought we can devote to the origin of our foods, to their ingredients' history.

I do happen to know, though, about the carob bean, about

the little seed and its sweet-fleshed case. Alternately called locust bean and St. John's Bread, the carob is a hand-length, inch-wide, woody pod that hangs from the branches of the carob tree. In late August, pale-green carobs ripen to a dark, chocolate shade, ready to be plucked from the trees and consumed. Carobs are grown in California, but the species's origins lie in the Middle East. Today, the largest producer is Spain, followed by Italy, Portugal, Greece, Morocco, Turkey, and finally Cyprus. Evergreen, drought resistant, and squat (botanists call it a shrub), only slightly taller than the olive tree, smooth of bark, wide and deep green of leaf, the carob has held a key place in Mediterranean ecosystems since biblical times.

Its ecological importance notwithstanding, if my family had stayed in carob tree-less New York, I would never have learned anything about the carob beyond its failure to be like chocolate. But when I moved to Cyprus, where carobs abound, I became invested in the carob quite literally. My father had inherited acres of land, all of which was farmable if irrigated, but which was otherwise a wilderness of thorns, scraggly pines, terebinth, and carob trees. Among this independently thriving vegetation, the carob alone produces something to sell. For pocket money, each August I shook the pods from my father's trees, piled them up in burlap sacks in our front yard, and sold them to a man who passed by our house with his little blue dump truck en route to the market in town. It was my first summer job, and the fulfillment of a dream— as a New York kindergartener, I had played not house, but farmer. I had believed that this was a job I could have, and I kept believing it as I read *Little House in the Big Woods*, kept reading books about self-sufficient families on the American frontier. I ended up a teacher, but still felt driven to the fields.

I wanted to work with my hands. I wanted to shake carobs

off their trees. I loved climbing them, loved being alone inside their foliage. And I loved the way the carob tree depended so little on rain—I was attracted to the tree's indifference to weather, to its freedom from need. I longed to need nothing but my own body, nothing but my muscles and the earth. Over the years in which typing and teaching have become all I know of work, memory has lent to the physicality of carob picking a certain Wordsworthian romance. I have learned all I can about the carob, for the tree has become, to me, a kind of symbol, a promise of something that I want.

In 1988, when we moved to Cyprus, I was a Greek American ten-year-old, aware of Greekness as an abstract marker of my identity, like my age, my gender, and a fondness for pizza, purple, and playing outside. At five, my brother knew fewer Greek words than I did, and as a result I could employ Greek to tell my mother things I didn't want him to know. The purpose of our move, my father claimed after the fact, was "so that the children will know who they are." The move away from suburban Queens, while hard for us all, turned out to be hardest for my father. As native a Greek Cypriot as he may once have been, he left his birthplace at nineteen, and didn't start learning to be a Cypriot adult until he returned, a forty-nine-year-old history teacher who'd quit his job for a dream.

Life was hard because we kids spent the first year reeling from culture shock, our tears putting a strain on our parents' own efforts to adjust. We got used to our new lives, Dino and I—we learned standard Greek in school and Cypriot on the playground. We made friends, gained our new teachers' favor, joined clubs, aligned ourselves with identity-supplying groups: Apollon soccer fans (Dino), and youth who rallied around our island's national wounds (me). Asgáta's grassless soccer pitch, along with the empty hills where I ran, replaced for us the jungle gyms of Queens. We learned that while in America we had to wait patiently in line, in Cyprus we'd need to shove our way to a crowd's front if we wanted lunch. We became, in sum, little Cypriots.

In August, when the carobs turn brown, they may be ripe; but unprocessed, the carob is no treat. Nothing I know is similar to the ripe carob's texture or taste. Woody fibers go down scratchy and dry. The carob's syrup, tastier once extracted and poured over unsalted whey cheese, is aptly called carob honey (*haroupómelo*) because, like honey, it is sweet but has an added, incomparable twist.

In both Cyprus and America, I run a little recklessly, with neither cell phone nor ID, neither money nor keys. Such untethered movement exhilarates me. Once, though, running from Asgáta to Kalavasós too early in the day, before the sun had sunk behind the hills, I reached a nearby village and, parched, could find no public water fountain. With no money, I had to request a drink from a woman I could see through the back door of a tavern, who was standing at a stove stirring Greek coffee in an *ibrik*. This was the humiliation of need—abnegation's failure, reliance on others, the inability to reimburse. She gave me water, and in return, I gave nothing but thanks. Before I reached home I was thirsty again, and I plucked a carob from its tree, dusted it off on my shirt, bit in, and tasted the disappointment that the carob's sweet woodiness brings.

Great hunger is really the only state in which humans eat carobs raw. Muhammed's armies ate them when supplies ran low. A second-century rabbi named Shimeon bar Yohai survived on carobs for the dozen years he spent hiding from the Romans, against whom he had led a failed rebellion. Some Arab Muslims drink a sort of carob juice during the month of the Ramadan fast. Many Jews commemorate Tu B'Shevat by eating carobs—something to do with the patience needed to wait the long years that a planter must wait before a carob seedling starts bearing fruit. And St. John the Baptist, in his famed wilderness, lived on the fruit of the locust tree. Yes, the word in the Greek gospels is *akrídes* (ἀκρίδες), which can be read as locust the insect, but I side with scholars who read the word to mean *tips of the carob tree*, i.e. carobs. St. John ate not honey and bugs, but wild honey and locust beans.

When Nazi forces took control of Athens, they confiscated the Greeks' supply of food. They seized fishing boats and livestock. In 1942, *Time* magazine called Greece "the hungriest country in the world." A loaf of bread cost fifteen dollars, and those who survived did so by eating what the Nazis didn't recognize as food: the conquerors' potato peels, rat meat, shoe leather, carob pods. I read somewhere once that a survivor said that during the occupation, "Lemon rind was our lobster and carobs our caviar!" When I have mentioned my carob-picking to Athenians old enough to remember World War II, they have remembered: "Carobs, oh yes, that's what we ate in the occupation." Or they remember the stories—what our fathers ate in order to stay alive through the War.

>>·<<

After the war, during my father's childhood, carobs made up a significant part of the Cypriot gross domestic product—after copper pyrites, carobs were the British colony's largest export. They brought in more income than all other agricultural products, such as wine and citrus fruits, combined. Back then, carobs weren't just an additive or health food product, but an important animal feed, a significant supplement to hay. As twentieth-century science progressed, the world's demand for carobs fell. New, carob-free foods were invented to better facilitate milk supply in cows, sheep, and goats. The new use for carob as a kind of emulsifier required small quantities of carob; it was not enough to keep prices high.

By the 1980s, once-agrarian Cyprus had become a tourist economy. The local carob mill had become a carob museum, and the carob warehouses had been turned into restaurants. Now, before dining, tourists gazed at the rusting W and T Avery scales imported from Birmingham, and at the great cylindrical separators, conveyor belts, crushers, and sieves.

The waiters, managers, and restaurateurs were grateful to have work, and were unafflicted by nostalgia for a time when those conveyor belts moved. My father, though, re-membered fondly the era of bull-drawn ploughs and irriga-tion through long ditches from stream to field. Children dug them out with shovels once a year, before the rains came. I imagine him as if in an old black and white movie in 1940s shorts and leather shoes and a sweater knitted by my grand-mother. He described to me, once, the stone cisterns built in streams so that when the winter rains came, water could be saved for irrigation when the streams dried up.

Carob picking was work I did with my father, labor being my favorite way to spend time with a parent. We were no farmers. Both of us made a living teaching English in the afternoons, as foreign languages are big business in a tour-ism-based economy. The carob harvest supplemented our teachers' salaries modestly—one year's labor bought the family's groceries for a week. In a photo of me up among a carob's branches, I'm wearing a flimsy purple tank top that has caught a branch and torn at the shoulder. I am posing with a four-foot cane of bamboo clutched in both my hands, torso stretched along the trunk. I remember what it felt like to push my weight against the wood, reaching up, my feet seeking higher holds; I remember knowing, as I stretched my bamboo cane into the branches, trying to knock the carobs from the tree, that I could at any moment fall onto the clods of dried-up mud below, or onto a stone. It was the only time I'd tried to feed my body by putting my body at risk.

During Great Lent, I used to read from *The Lives of the Saints* about martyrs, men, and women aflame with yearning for truth, for Christ. The highest honor is the crown of martyrdom: choosing Christ over life. As a foretaste of this crown, Orthodox Christian Lent has strict rules of fasting—not total abstinence from food, but close to it, with meat and dairy forbidden throughout (like contemporary veganism) and oil permitted on weekends only (weekdays, we mostly eat boiled beans with only lemon and salt). An exercise, our theologians call it, a lesson in how much a body can do without—a way to learn from hunger. My mother had me fast from meat as a child, and when I was a teenager I volunteered to give up dairy, too. I never stopped missing milk, never understood how ascetics and anchorites shed the human taste for comfort, the drive to self-protect, to self-preserve. How, I wanted to know, did ascetics free themselves from need? What made a martyr yearn to die? Who could promise to leave a world as sweet as ours?

I saw a martyr leave the world. I was seventeen, and picking carobs, and when I went inside for a break, I saw a man be killed on television. His name was Tássos Isaác, and he was protesting the military occupation of Northern Cyprus by riding his motorcycle into the forbidden zone, past the Green Line. It was a risk the Cypriot President had warned was too great, but the thousand bikers didn't listen; they rode across Europe and into Europe's last divided city. Isaác was stopped by the nationalist group the Grey Wolves. I had gone inside for a glass of water and the biker protest ride was on TV. I stayed and watched until I was watching the body of a man be pounded with clubs and stones, his skull crushed, his bones all broken, in a cloud of August dust among the sage brush, low thorns, dry grass, fence wire. Since that day I think about carob together with risk, with freedom—from occupying troops, and from the need to stay alive.

Unaware of my metaphysical associations with the tree, or of my longing after courage and self-reliance and working with my hands, our fellow villagers thought it odd that my dad and I, the returned Americans, bothered with so outdated an enterprise as carob-picking. Aside from my old uncle Yórko, and one or two very poor families, my father and I were the only ones who picked. Theío Yórko's fields lay a few hundred yards from our house, and when I woke up around dawn, his long cane would already be clacking against the branches. For seventy years he'd gathered carobs. We were competitors in a way. I envied the old man's piling of carobs outside his house, sack by sack, day by day. I would peek at his progress each afternoon as I pulled out of the village on the way to teach my couple of hours of English.

Most land-owning Cypriots pick olives, not carobs, from the village land they've inherited, as olive oil is both useful and expensive. Olive trees are almost as drought resilient as carobs are, and a few trees had survived on our land. By turning the earth and watering the trees, my father nursed them back to olive-producing health. A few days in the olive grove can yield the hundreds of dollars' worth of olive oil consumed in a Greek household each year. But the work of olive picking failed to satisfy: the gentle, attentive combing required by laden olive branches gave none of the release which the carob tree affords. I loved to lift a long bamboo stick into the air and thwack the branches, knowing the crop would land on the ground unharmed. I let my father pick olives alone.

An Asgáta woman, a distant relative, once told me that when her family went out to pick carobs, she cooked in the fields. As a boy, my father used to carry lunch to my grandfather and the hired men, but this woman saw no need. Her people carried with them the cured meats they kept in a barrel. At noon, she would pick vegetables that grew next to the carobs: zucchini, tomatoes, green peppers, eggplant. Then, with dead, dry carob branches snapped into sticks, they'd make a fire and fry it all up as fresh as could be. Later they would sleep in the carobs' thick shade and, rested, climb back up with their canes and get to work.

Back then, they had none of the plastic sheeting that we used to spread over the prickly weeds below so that when the carobs fell down in a heap, they could be slid into empty paint buckets and poured into the burlap sacks we loaded into our battered pickup truck to bring back. No, they didn't have plastic, and when I insisted to my father that surely they could have used old sheets, he looked at me, puzzled. In an economy of preciousness, where for every thread an hour picking cotton or feeding silkworms could be traced, clothes were handed down from generation to generation, and there was no such thing as a sheet too old for a bed; there was no such thing as trash. The carobs fell onto the ground, and with their hands the laborers bent down and gathered handfuls from among the dusty thorns. Even the burlap sacks sometimes cost so much the poorer landowners had to lease them from wealthier men.

I like to imagine the entire village out picking carobs. During British rule throughout the first half of the twentieth century, no one was allowed to pick carobs until a specific date—August 20, my father thinks—to ensure that everyone was present in his own field, preventing early birds from harvesting other people's crops.

After Cornell, when I'd returned to Cyprus and commenced the same low-paying ESL job to which my once-a-principal father had descended, the other teachers laughed when they heard how I spent my mornings.

"Do you know what Joanna does in the morning before work?" one asked a similarly amused colleague. "She runs. And now that the carobs are ripe, she climbs into trees and collects carobs." In Greek, it all sounded silly. The odd American, trying to revive the old ways of Cyprus. Charming. "Did you read about it in a book? Will you write the first carob novel?"

The Prodigal Son yearned, in his hunger, to take the food from under his herd's snouts, and I learned only in adulthood that this food was a mess of carobs. Many translations give Luke's word *keration* (κερατίων) as *pod*, which could mean any kind of peas or seeds. Gospel Greek is legible to me, so I return to Luke's original words as if reading them myself could unlock a secret the translators withheld: "καὶ ἐπεθύμει γεμίσαι τὴν κοιλίαν αὐτοῦ ἀπὸ τῶν κερατίων ὧν ἤσθιον οἱ χοῖροι, καὶ οὐδεὶς ἐδίδου αὐτῷ." "And he wanted to fill his belly with the carobs that the pigs were eating." The words for belly, *kilía*, and pigs, *chíri*, haven't changed over the millennia, and I picture the youth in his mud, sporting a once-stylish, now-tattered robe and no shoes, holding his rumbling tummy and drooling as the chubby swine gobbled their sweet, sweet carob feed. He became the butt of the other swineherds' jokes. I imagine him with his bindle of gold setting off for a new country. We had the same reason for leaving our parents' houses: we wanted to leave behind the bodies from whence our own bodies came—for they are the bodies that remind us of our dependence, of the self-reliance that can never be.

When the Prodigal "came unto himself," gave up drooling after carobs, and went home, he intended to become a servant. By folly he'd forfeited his birthright. He had taken his fortune into his hands and lost it.

I suspect that my affinity for carobs belies the secret hope that I can still go it alone, that I could strike out on some frontier and turn my body's labor into food without help. I talk a lot about community, about helping others and accepting their help, but a part of me—proud—resists.

I know, even, this: that carob trees do depend on rain, and what is more, they depend on the absence of too much. Plentiful rains would kill them. And martyrs? They are free of the need to go on living, yes, yet they are in fact the antithesis of self-reliance. Tássos needed the unity of Cyprus more than he needed life. St. John, all need, stepped into the desert naked, looking for his God. Without humiliation, St. John took God's handouts, and ate that wild honey, ate those locust beans.

My father moved to Cyprus so that his children would "know who they are." I have a knowledge now that I would not have had if we had stayed. But it isn't what my father had in mind. I know that I'm a Greek, yes, a Greek Cypriot in fact; but my fantasies of peasantry are waning, as are my prodigal hopes of independence. I'm a Greek Cypriot, but I'm not a farmer of the early 1900s. I'm an educated New Yorker, an American whose food is earned by sitting at a teacher's desk. I can't take care of my body's needs with just my body. I won't ever be a martyr for an independent Cyprus or for Christ—I won't even be much of an Orthodox Christian if I keep on resisting humility, resisting the humiliating truth that every breath I take is a gift.

After college, I decided to live in Cyprus forever. I wanted to give up the privilege of an American life. But I was no less privileged in Cyprus. And though it might be an excuse for what I still suspect is giving in—relinquishing something I thought I needed, letting my patriotism slide—I have come to suspect that my ideal of the carob's independence has nothing more to it than the Prodigal's belief that he could make it on his own.

I am subject still to nostalgia's sweet deceptions, to the ease with which I remember as perfect my father's hardscrabble past. How powerful it is, this play of desire and memory—how persistent and how physical a draw—for when I return to Cyprus each summer, now, it is not the view of mountains, sea, and sky that brings me tears of joy, but the scent of carob—sweet and rich and warm—mixed with wildflowers, thyme, and drying hay.

—

Unsent Letter
to My Father

—

My father, I did everything you asked. I left New York with you, and while my mother (you said) didn't even try, I learned to love your land. I learned its history by heart. Each school year since kindergarten, I brought home grades to make you proud; and every year I won so many prizes that a shelf filled up, and we had to clear another one for all the plaques, best in math and best in chemistry, in physics and in literature. And I ran, trained six days a week, around and around the red rubber track in the Cypriot sun, so that you could tell even people you didn't know, "My daughter is an athlete." My high school basketball team never won any games, but I made sure your daughter was its captain and the best. At school parades, I held the flag and gave the speeches. After that, I brought home a good degree, with more honors on it than any of my cousins had.

Now that I have completed these, the things you asked of me, I want to find a way to ask if any of those efforts and achievements matter, or if, after all, all that matters is this one last thing you asked of me yesterday. Because although I learned to honor you with prizes, I'm not sure that I can find a man and marry quick enough to give you peace.

I want to know two things. First, I want to know if you will love me even if I fail to give you a grandchild, and second, I want to know how hard I should try to turn what I am into what you want me to be. You never seemed the kind of parent who raises children to be themselves and turns around later to ask, "Why aren't you more like my dreams?"

So I am writing this letter to you to ask the things I cannot when we sit and face one another from opposite ends of a small kitchen table. I want to know if my duty to the family is done, if it is enough that I became a human being who works and learns. I want to know exactly what I owe you. I want to know if bringing home first a man you didn't like, and then no man at all—if that will make the medals and the plaques and honors mean nothing at all.

For years, the idea of my family asking personal questions seemed like a joke, the sort of thing that happened to other girls. I felt immune because I did everything else right. You and my mother have always been discreet, although sometimes I'm not sure where to draw the line between discreet and evasive; we think we are tactful, sometimes, when we are only boneless. When silence is easiest, that is the time we are most obligated to break it.

I have no more courage than you, so instead of talking I am writing a letter.

Each time I leave your house, you wave goodbye before I can ever say, "Farewell, be well, my father." You hate the way most people toss words like *love, want, worry, hate, death, fear.* They don't understand how words, like blood, must not be spilled in sport. To honor our revulsion against the too-much-said, I am writing these, my measured words, to you.

I will preserve the silence and break it at the same time.

There were my aunts, early on, your three sisters who worried about me and yelled in a dialect about dangers I couldn't understand. You assisted me in avoiding them. After all, you still blamed your oldest sister Galátia for making you marry too soon.

I learned to protect myself from your sisters and to despise them. In fact, you and I conspired in despising your sisters. They pushed me around and you said, "Ignore them, they have no education." We had education, you and I. We had read history and novels. We felt sorry for the women that had only the kitchen, the ridiculously intricate stitches to make doilies that collect dust; women who had only the gossip gleaned from neighbors, soap operas, and coffee hour at church.

But yesterday you said the time has come. You asked me if I would please consider the son of this man named Gabriel. George Gabriel stood by you long ago, before my birth, when your first wife was dying. And although you and he haven't really spoken much since then, you still trust and love the man so much that yesterday you asked me: "Please, would you marry Gabriel's son?"

You started to talk to me, of course, with a truism: a neutral, bearable way into the subject that we hadn't ever talked about head on, though it has hovered for a while now. "There is a right time for everything," you started. Your molten eyes magnified by glasses, your skin sunburned like a day laborer's, you waited. I thought, "My God, wouldn't the time to say it was okay, now, to associate with boys have been ten years ago when I graduated high school—at the latest?" I admit that yesterday I was glad to see you hesitate, falter, nervous and weak, feeling just the way your own aversion to direct talk has so often caused me to feel. You should have admitted years ago that your daughter's perfection in school might not translate into an entire life of things just falling into place for her. Remember that on weekends I had to leave my friends behind at eleven, hours before anything interesting ever happened. It was the latest you would pick me up. Your bedtime was nine. Eleven was a generous compromise. There still isn't a bus between the village and the city.

Remember that for nothing other than good grades did you ever promise your approval, which was all I wanted. If I'd known it then, and if I'd had sufficient spine, I would have pointed out that there isn't any chance of gain in anything related to the heart unless some kind of security is put on the line. I think you should have let me stay out as late as everybody else.

Truth is, even if I had had the freedom I so wanted, I would have probably turned out just the way I have, solitary and aloof. And yet, I think you would admit that in those years, when I had to find out the next day who kissed whom, where they spent the night, whose feelings were hurt, etc., I had to fall in love with loneliness in order to survive. And now, who will make me sever my old, necessary tie to solitude and silence? Is it not a little late to remember that I am a girl?

Of course I can write these things, but I can't say them. When we sat at the small kitchen table yesterday, and you told me about this man named Gabriel whom you'd never really mentioned before, I cried. For my sake, you broke your tight, necessary silence, and in the hope that I might enter the arms of another man, you spoke about your most personal pain, the most painful, difficult thing you have ever had to say.

I am not sure that I can make a return on such a sacrifice. After twenty-eight years of obedience and success, today I have to say: I don't know, Dad; I don't quite know that I can. And so to put my heart, at least, at ease, so that I can stand next to you in peace when you are lying on one hospital table after another, I have written this letter that I will never send.

Dad, I would love to have loved young. But my love is for the stars, for the ocean, and words, my work. And if I have learned anything at all about love, it's that love requires melting, a smallness, and a wonder at the magnificence of all the world. If I learn to love nobody else, I want to learn to love my father, and if I've learned anything yet about love, it's that a grudge can poison all goodness. I am writing to learn to forgive, to be forgiven.

We have done everything in silence and hand in hand. Your end has begun to become ugly. I am so afraid of the enormity of your liquid-filled belly, I am afraid of the purple spots on your face and afraid that you will suffer the knowledge of all of these fears of mine because never, ever were we spared the knowledge of one another's feelings. You would have loved to die valiant and beautiful; I would have loved to ride on your arm, a bride.

When I sat next to your stretched-out belly as the doctor explained that the navel could burst because there was so much fluid, while I waited for the nurse to draw blood, it seemed so apt that I was there. This year we have grown smaller together, weaker and more human. I often wonder if you know how proud of you I am. Do you remember in the first years of your illness, when you said every other day that you were a sick man and we couldn't make noise in the house? How you refused to take a shower and I was ashamed and wondered who had stolen my father away and left me with a wreck of self-pitying flesh that spent all day in a chair? You have learned to live, and so I too will learn to live— in spite of the family's pity and in spite of their suspecting, hungry eyes. I only hope that it will be enough.

Do you remember how you used to say you didn't need to

go to the doctor because you ate a lot of fruit? You taught me to eat oranges without peeling the rind off all the way, leaving the spongy white bitterness, which purges illness. The man who never visited a doctor has now become the dependent of doctors. And I, who was proud and smart and much admired, have become the butt of my family's pity because it doesn't look like I can do the one thing that actually matters, it doesn't look like I can make any use of my charms: I will not catch myself a husband in time.

Dad, I'm glad you can't imagine what it's like to live this way, the women relatives always waiting, always sizing you up. I wonder what makes your sisters so vicious when they talk about my body. "Did you eat?" "She hasn't eaten." "It's one thing to be careful but another to eat nothing at all." "Why aren't you eating?" "Why are you so skinny?" "Why aren't you as skinny as you were last year?"

I read theoretical articles about female bonds but none help. Your sisters are powerful and their love is strange. Why do they tell me they love me and then rip me apart, Dad?

I am glad that you have had to shoulder their questions too. They ask, "What were you thinking when you moved away from New York?" They ask why you sold this, didn't sell that, bought this, not that. They note that it is a shame you never managed to make any money. They ask about your daughter and about your health and then nod as if they'd known already: no improvement. We must live through their questions, their weighty affections, their most difficult brand of love. And we must bear it all, my father, not hand in hand—for when did you ever reach out to touch my skin?— but heart in heart.

Sometimes I hope that I will never have to send this letter, Dad. For I hope, sometimes, that you have already forgiven me. Sometimes, as you ask about my plans and say, "It's all right, it's your life," with resignation, sadness, and that dogged hope of fatherly love, I feel that you have already forgiven my failure, already absolved me of this guilt, and I can let go of that feeling that I cheated you of the wonderful, intelligent, talk-to-able son-in-law, the wonderful, bright, boast-of-able grandsons that my illustrious report card once promised you.

I want to earn that forgiveness, which I know you've already given me as a gift. To really earn it, though, I promise: I am going to work to become human and to become honest and to become true, husband or no husband. In some things I will try to match you, and in some, I will avoid your mistakes.

I observe your sense of failure, and I observe your life of fear; I have seen how fear of others has wrecked a good man's life. I weighed the risk and wagered my loneliness—and in losing that, I won. I cast the die; I cast myself out into the eyes of strangers as merely myself, and I have found myself loved; I have found good friends, the kind that wrestle fear alongside me, the kind that wrestle with me and tell me when I am wrong in a way that lets me listen, bear it, grow. They are the friends who know me for the littleness that I am—and love that.

Neither of us have led a life to prepare us to confront these, our small and silly selves. But here we are, my father. I ask you now: is it not enough? In our smallness, have we not started to fall away from all that contempt with which, once, we poisoned our own minds? We are learning to respect the uneducated, for we know life is deeper than education, even though we gave our lives to it. It has been a long time since you had to tell me to ignore Galátia. You say now, "Let us remember that she means well."

I'm not going to argue that the work I hope to do, though

I intend to do the work all day every day for all my days, is as good as having children. How can we compare the two? I'm going to do the work that it's been given me to do. The other work, of homemaking, matchmaking, I will teach myself to respect, if I can.

I think, Dad, that if we want to respect anything honestly, we must suffer some humiliation. How else could we make space in our hearts for real appreciation of what is foreign to us, and strange? After all the years that I was the family star, the good one, the dependable one who brought home a B only once every other year, who said yes to everything and went to church—after all my years as the little wonder who'd come first in physics in spite of being a girl, I am exposed: I have a flaw. "There is something wrong with her," your sisters say. They didn't know it before, they say. "Poor thing—what is wrong? Where is the husband?"

I know that you would forgive me for having once blamed you for my marriage-lack. Now, I am going to live the life I've got, and I am going to believe that it will be enough. After all, we are human, my father, only human; we give gifts of love, we offer one another thanksgiving and forgiving and nothing more is needed—as you and I grow ever smaller and ever more terribly ourselves, I believe we're learning how it's possible that one human might have love for another.

If we are ever to become ourselves, we must first learn to be ugly, and stupid, and disobedient, and sad. My father, how will we part? Will you promise to forgive me this last disobedience, and if it is a disobedience of shame, and if all the family and other families laugh at us and say, "What is wrong with his daughter?," will you love me anyway, honestly, all the way? I am waiting to know.

How to take this humiliation and make out of it the stuff

of love—that is the question, the daughter's work, our work. And though we have been rich inside, and though we have been strong, today we are only ourselves, by the family's pity humiliated, and by our own failures made small. Small enough, I wonder, to slip through a needle's eye? Grow smaller and smaller with me, whatever the price—whatever the reward. Nothing comes without a fight, not even love.

—

Shopping for Story

—

In the days following my father's funeral, I bought wheat, pomegranate, and almonds to make *kólyva* for his nine-day memorial, made phone calls, and fielded condolences. After those duties were done, it became time to find a present for my friend Vasilikí, who would be married in Greece exactly forty days after my father's death. I had called Vasilikí while Andréas was in the hospital in Cyprus, where the Cypriot doctors ignored my mother's requests for information. Vasilikí, then a physician and research fellow at Harvard Medical School, called my father's doctor from Boston. The man was forthcoming to a colleague, and she relayed to us the doctor's plan to perform surgery on my father to repair a hernia that had occurred in childhood and become dangerous only now. From my friend, I learned what it would mean to perform what is typically a simple routine surgery on a man with a failing heart. Because Vasilikí cared so much, and because she helped us, I felt grateful that her wedding would be the first event I would attend after he left us—after the surgery was canceled because his organs had begun to fail.

The last time I spoke to my father, it was late March, and Andréas still believed he'd be well enough to travel to the western Peloponnese in June. He expected to purchase our family's gift himself and had very specific opinions about what the gift should be. He dismissed my mother's suggestion that we should buy crystal. It must be something aristocratic, he insisted, though not exactly in those words. He said he wanted our gift to be the very best of what our island had to give. Lace or needlework from the village of Léfkara, he said. Vasilikí, companion of my undergraduate years, was marrying a fellow Greek doctor whom she had met in her endocrinology program at Harvard. Because ours is a family of farmers, teachers, tailors, and cooks, the prestige of Vasilikí's profession, along with her Athenian accent and generally refined ways, made my parents look up to her. Even when we were college freshmen, not yet out of our teens, I noticed that my parents got out the nicest dishes when she visited, and spoke with a delicacy not exactly affected, but also not their own.

One morning, about a week before we flew to Greece for Vasilikí's wedding, my mother and I began the forty-minute drive through the Cypriot hills toward Léfkara to look for the perfect tablecloth for a gift. I braked in front of the second shop I saw—a split-second decision. What prompted me to choose so quickly was either the large parking spot or the sign: "STOP AND LOOK AT THE WOMEN MAKING THE LACE."

Stop I did, not only to look at the women, but also because such a sign would make an excellent opening for an account I hoped to write up about my shopping. The sign made explicit all manner of themes in my nascent book: labor, tradition turned spectacle by tourism, and the touristic gaze. You see, my father's death hadn't dampened my desire to document life in Cyprus. If anything, grieving him only sharpened my drive. And I found that my heightened focus on writing down what I lived made me anxious about the authenticity

of my experience. Walking toward the shop, I suddenly felt
as though I was undercover and disingenuous. For I posed
as a woman focused on shopping while I was actually more
drawn to the stilted, awkward English of the sign than the
delicate lace and embroidery the women produced. Even
though the money I carried was real, the excitement I evinced
was not. Or rather, I would pretend to care about shopping
when really I wanted to acquire the lace-sellers' story.

Handicrafts are not something I personally admire—my
grandmother's doilies always seemed like pointless impedi-
ments to my furniture-polishing assignments as a child, and
maturity has not brought with it any new appreciation. No,
when it comes to objects, there's a strain of philistinism in
me—utilitarianism if one wants to be kind—and I still only
appreciate decorations if I am expected neither to construct
nor dust them, and if individual ornaments have already been
integrated into a harmonious, unified design. I am passionate, however, about the *lefkarítika* as an abstraction—about
the tradition the folk art signifies rather than for the beauty
of the signifier. I understood that my father, who moved us all
to Cyprus so that his children "would know who they are,"
believed a gift of lefkarítika needlework would reflect a high-
society refinement and an authentic Cypriot identity. Just as I
appreciate flowers mostly for their names, and the way names
like *jasmine* and *rose bay* anchor narrative in a place, so the
traditional objects turn abstract things like history, identity,
and culture into a concrete thing that we can touch.

The UNESCO page for Léfkara lace and embroidery
confirms what the shopkeepers would soon explain: Venetian
courtiers brought the tradition to Cyprus in 1489, and locals
learned the trade, adding Byzantine Greek designs to the
existing repertoire of Venetian motifs. Nestled (as the bro-
chures put it) in the Troodos mountains, Léfkara offered cool

summer weather to Venetian nobility, who used the town as a resort. It was for this reason that it was the women of Léfkara who developed this critical source of income as the centuries progressed.

It is easy to see through the discourses that constitute the lefkarítika as a symbol not only of Venetian (western European) superiority, but also of a pure Cypriot identity. In a British video from the 1970s, the documentarian cites the Léfkara women's "innate artistic nature," which allowed them to create handicrafts that reflected the character of the Cypriot: "dynamism, sensitivity, and power of observation" since it is inspired by details in nature. Seeing through the discourse doesn't make me any less eager to carry out my father's directions, and live whatever story those directions might prompt.

After we parked outside the "LOOK AT THE WOMEN" sign, we were greeted warmly and ushered in by a shop owner, Yórgo, who sported a bushy blond mustache, a yellow shirt and black jeans, and pointy-toed boots, which led my mother to compare him to a cowboy.

"Are you Cypriots?" Yórgo asked in Greek. I expected my Greek American mother to begin, as she often does, with a litany of her own origin cities—Constantinople, Epirus, and Sparta, places where people speak proper Greek, not the Cypriot dialect, which in comparison sounds hokey, back-water, low.

Before she could begin the long story, I answered, "My father," in a distinct Cypriot accent that itself answered the question. Once we were inside Yórgo's lace shop, he let his wife take charge. She asked us if she wanted a *gnísio* (authentic, pure) or *paremferí* (comparable) piece. We didn't understand why she was asking if we wanted something pure or something not quite until she unwrapped the dull olive and beige authentic cloth and told us that the price would be €900. We were prepared to spend more money than we ever had before on a gift, but even with the half price for Cypriots deal, €450 could not be justified. The shopkeepers explained that the label of *gnísio* could (as per UNESCO rules) be applied only to tablecloths made with French thread embroidered on Irish linen, just like it was in the days before industrialization and the diversification of trade routes.

Registering our discomfort with the authentic tablecloth's price, the shop owner unwrapped for us a beautiful ivory comparable tablecloth with white stitching. It was a cotton-linen blend, she told us, not pure linen like the authentic, but cost only €400—and €200 for Cypriots. In fact, the traditional, authentic piece of Cypriot folk art struck us as a little too folksy looking, and we went for the cotton comparable piece, cheaper and classier.

Before walking back to the car after what felt like both an accomplishment and a bit of a defeat, since we'd settled for something that wasn't an authentic lefkarítiko, I asked my mother if she would be willing to spend a little time exploring the streets of Léfkara with me. We soon saw the little old ladies embroidering on their pillows on tiny chairs outside their shops, and the encounter I had envisioned really happened. An old woman looked at me, introduced herself as Mrs. Eleni, and asked if I was interested in buying some embroidery. I lied and said I was, and followed her in. Inside, I met Mrs. Eleni's garrulous husband and former Léfkara mayor, drank most of the proffered orangeade to show that I accepted their hospitality, and listened carefully, torn between the impulse to take notes and the need to keep my notebook (and my identity as a writer only in it for the scoop) hidden.

Mrs. Eleni told my mother and me that the needlework costs so much because it takes so very, very long to make. I asked her if she ever felt bored, sitting in one place stitching for days on end. She said that embroidering all day doesn't bore her unless she catches herself making something predictable for the sake of speed, something that doesn't make her excited about needling on. If she's not going to be doing something different than she's ever done before, not combining the set patterns in ways that challenge her imagination and her skill, she might as well do something lucrative, easy on the eyes and hands, and leave tablecloth-making to the machines. She waved toward some of the tablecloths hanging outside a nearby shop, on sale for five or ten euros because they were mass-manufactured by machines in China. I said, "That's exactly how I feel about writing. If I know what I'm going to say before I start, I feel bored, or like I'm faking it."

I sat with Mrs. Eleni and the former mayor for half an hour, gleaning stories about Leonardo da Vinci, who brought a cloth back for the altar of Milan's Duomo cathedral; about the men who traveled, in the last century, to cosmopolitan Alexandria where demand was highest. When I had enough material in my head, I was ashamed to leave the second store without buying anything, so I bought a small placemat-sized decoration for an end table. It was tiny but authentic, and cost forty euros (Cypriot price). I gave Mrs. Eleni the money and slipped it into the package that contained the tablecloth. Placed thus, it implied that the tablecloth, too, was a €900 authentic piece. I felt a little ashamed of my duplicity, but also thought it could have happened by chance. And anyway, would it make a difference whether Vasilikí thought I'd bought her a real lefkarítiko or knew the truth? Would she even want me to spend a whole month's salary on a UNESCO stamp? As I removed my hand from the package, I thought about the writing, and whether I would be able to find in my action symbolic weight.

In the end, my mother and I made the trip to Vasilikí's wedding in the Peloponnese without my father. We flew to Athens together, then took a public bus to Sparta, three miles from the village where my mother's own grandmother grew up in the late nineteenth century. We spent one night in Sparta. Then we took another bus north to Kyparissía, where Vasilikí would be married. The wedding was glorious. I danced endless circles of *kalamatianó*, the dance from nearby Kalamata, and *tsámiko*, which I'd thought was more of a northern dance but is apparently popular in the Peloponnese, too. We stayed in town four nights, long enough for my mother to attend several church services, and my mother raved about the way she could actually communicate with the parishioners there. Even after fifteen years in Cyprus, she still struggled to understand the Cypriot dialect. The speech in this place was clear to her—it was the Greek her grandmother had taught her.

Next, we took a bus up to the capital of Epirus, which is the state in which my mother's family on her father's side had lived for generations before they emigrated to the city then called Constantinople. *Pappoú* Spyros's actual ancestral village is currently part of Albania, so we stuck to parts of Epirus south of the border. While there, my mother looked at the people and kept pointing to them and saying, "Look! Look at their foreheads! Look at their faces! Look at the back of that head! Don't they look exactly like me?" Long after she went back to Cyprus (alone, because I stayed in Northern Greece for a summer job), my mother would recount how she felt that week in Kyparissía and Epirus—how she felt she had belonged, and how these places where her grandparents had lived were, at last, pieces of land that matched her own authentic sense of who she was. She had seen the earth from whence she'd come.

While we are making choices that forge our identity, we are driven by the hope of being legible to others—and accepted as who we say we are. I ask others to accept the claim I make with my clothes, my gait, my haircut, my glasses, my makeup, my car, my jokes, my bumper stickers, my water bottle, and my shoes. People often tell me that I shouldn't care how others read me, that I should "just be myself." That advice hasn't worked out for me. Without seeing myself in the mirror of other minds, I feel like a ghost. I don't exist. And I know that I crave to be read as the person I feel myself to be—even as that person is influenced by the way others see me. I also know that I can benefit from letting go of that demand, at least a little.

Letting go of notions of authentic selves—embracing needlework that's close enough—means admitting that when I decorate my house in a Spartan manner, I am expressing who I am not just for me, but also because I want my visitors to acknowledge that my nondecorating matches who they think Joanna is. And when I resist someone's suggestion of frillier dress or decorations in my house, because that's not really me, I am acting for the sake of the story—the story of self—we all compose.

After all, even the authentic lace is woven the hard way, with months of labor, only because shoppers (Cypriots and foreigners alike) believe that this handicraft, made in the age-old way, represents who the Cypriots really are. To accommodate them, the women of Léfkara produce the commodity the shoppers expect. The people of Léfkara put out the signs—"STOP AND LOOK AT THE WOMEN MAKING THE LACE"—and they perform their authentic Cypriotness, and I . . . I stopped to look.

—

Dancing Greek

—

I am going, again, to Greece. *Going back* is a phrase that applies, if not because my mother's roots on the Greek mainland make it a kind of homeland for me, then because this June 2014 trip marks the fourth consecutive summer for which I'll be flying to Greece to teach. I'll spend one week in the northern city of Thessaloníki and three on the island of Thássos, a Balkan place with gray stone rooftops and steep, pine-covered hills that reach down to a rocky, windswept coast. Thássos lies in the sea, the poet Archilochus wrote, "like the backbone of an ass." Its quarries supplied marble for the sculptures that populate museums from the Louvre to the Met. Flatbed trucks still carry enormous marble slabs on ferries to the mainland, and walking along the island's marble-strewn footpaths feels a little bit like walking through a fancy courthouse or a church.

Leaving for the Writing Workshops in Greece is a summer ritual for me now. Each June I leave behind Joanna, my Cypriot American self, and become *Ioánna*, the Greek teacher. Swinging between badly paid jobs in Cyprus, Greece, and the United States, as it has so far, my life has had little room for travel to countries other than these three. After college, I joined an English friend of mine for a month-long

Eurail adventure from Calais to Bari, but that's about it. By limiting my last thirteen years of travel to the three countries in whose languages I'm fluent, I always feel at least partly that I belong. And I forget what it feels like to hear a buzz of foreignness around me. To get small, low-cost doses of feeling entirely foreign, I choose flights with long layovers in cities where I've never lived—Paris, Munich, Amsterdam, Istanbul—and I steal out of the airport for a few hours so that I can listen to a language I do not understand. For this is how our American students feel during their four weeks in Greece. Sure, I will teach them all the Greek I can, and they will study hard, and learn enough to order food and ask for directions from patient waiters and eager salespeople. But the rapid everyday conversations around them will remain an unintelligible buzz. That buzz will tell them: "You are not at home."

My flight into Thessaloníki lands at ten o'clock at night, and though in the past I've made a show of my thrift by taking the city bus, this time I hop into one of the taxis waiting for all three workshop participants who came in on my flight. I serve as interpreter as the driver asks people where they are from, and I field further questions about what our group of Americans is doing in Thessaloníki. Soon, the tall man driving the taxi looks into the rearview mirror and asks, "You are a Cypriot, eh?" This near-instant recognition is my favorite thing about being in Greece. "Yes," I say, with enthusiasm at being correctly assessed, and smile eagerly at the back of the driver's long, gray ponytail.

In Greece, whether I ask a gas station attendant to fill up the tank or a kiosk owner how much a pack of gum costs, I am almost always recognized as a Cypriot. In Cyprus, frequently I'll get a few sentences into a conversation and then my accent will provoke the assessment, "Englezokypréa!"

British Cypriot! I say, "No, American." Often, the other
Cypriot shrugs, as if to say, "Same difference." It's British
Cypriots who are familiar to them, not Americans, so that's
what they decide I am. In Greece, on the other hand, the
Cypriotness of my Greek tends to mask any inflections that
come from being a native speaker of English, and I am read
as native; I pass.

After the taxis have dropped us off at the El Greco hotel,
Christopher, the director of the workshop this year, meets
me in the lobby and suggests I dump my suitcase in my room
and come out for an ouzo right away. I equivocate—I need
a few more hours to gradually transform. Once I become
my Greek-teacher self, I will feel like I'm under obligation to
have fun—to drink and dance, regardless of my mood. Once,
at the hotel-tavern at which the Workshop is anchored, I
had been dancing for a few hours, and I went to sit down.
Tássos (the owner, who is the same age as me) yelled at me,
"Don't sit! If you sit down then everyone will stop dancing!"
I believed him and have since then always felt an obligation
to have fun for the sake of those who've paid for an experience in Greece.

When I get to my room, Erika is there waiting for me.
Now that I've moved to the US and she lives in Cyprus, we
can't spend time together like we did in high school and the
years between college and grad school, so I have invited her
to come to Greece and share my room. I feel like I have only
one night to catch up, just the two of us, before our social
circle widens to include the other faculty and workshop
participants. Two decades into our friendship, Erika and I
maintain a common, secluded space bound tightly by our
common high school experience in Cyprus, our bilingual-
ism, our common interests in science and literature and liberation, common friends and common histories of trouble and

joy. I envy the way she lived in Cyprus her whole life except for college, and so can grasp nuances in Greek that I miss. She can also code-switch between Greek and Cypriot pronunciation, so that bizarrely, people's first guess is that *I'm* the Cypriot one and she's from Greece, even though I'm the one with family roots on the Greek mainland.

Once we get to Thássos, though, we'll both just be the Cypriot girls. We don't have to introduce ourselves—people talk about us, compare notes, remember us from last year. The ice cream truck owner says, "The Cypriot girls are back!" and promises to put in an order for my favorite popsicle. Neither Erika nor I have a Greek cell phone, but we find that the neighbor network serves just as well. I walk into the mini-market and ask, "Did the other Cypriot woman buy yogurt today? Eggs?"

The room here in Thessaloníki smells like long-extinguished cigarettes, as Greek hotel rooms often do, and I ask Erika to put up with the air conditioner for the first night so that the cool air will lessen the intensity of the heat and also the smell. I'm unaccustomed to heat and smoke now that I live in Missouri, whereas living in Cyprus makes Erika too unaccustomed to air conditioning to sleep when it's turned on. Our decision to live in different countries makes compromises necessary—we'll use it on alternating nights until we leave for the sweet-smelling, dry island of Thássos, where both of us can sleep with just the breeze.

The next morning, I begin my teaching duties by greeting students and other faculty in the hotel's mezzanine. My teaching persona is activated as soon as I encounter the students, and spontaneously I teach them the word *xenodoheío*, a *doheío* (vessel) for *xénous*, a word that I'll be able, in time, to define as foreigner, stranger, and guest, all at once.

Christopher is handing out maps of important historical

sites and explaining the self-guided tour they'll be taking, asking them to divide into groups called "Team *Kolokythákia*" (small zucchini) and "Team *Melinzána*" (eggplant). The ritual of using Greek words as tokens makes me cringe a little, although I don't know why—maybe it's the same discomfort I'll have all month when the Americans use the wrong word, get the customs wrong, make faux pas that I imagine reflect on me because I imagine myself responsible, as the Greek teacher, for every Greek word they say.

On the first night of each workshop, we take all the students to a local tavern for one of many dinners that will leave them in awe. In Greece, going out to eat typically means getting a number of *mezéthes* (singular, *mezés*). Everyone at the table will get a taste of any dish they want. The usual twenty or so workshop members will sit around a long table in a Thessaloníki tavern called *Myrovólos* (myrrh-flowing) *Smírni*. True to its name, Myrovólos Smírni specializes in dishes from Smyrna, now İzmir, and other cities in Asia Minor. Like so many restaurants in Northern Greece, it was opened by Greeks expelled from their homes in Smyrna during the 1922 population exchange.

We gather for dinner around half past seven in the lobby of the El Greco, and as we walk together, members of the group (half are college students, half graduate students and professionals) ask me if the restaurants are empty because of the economic crisis. I explain that we are going out for dinner at an hour when most Greeks aren't even making dinner plans. At seven in the evening, folks are just wrapping up the afternoon coffee they drink after waking up from the still-prevalent afternoon siesta. I feel defensive about napping, even though I can't practice it myself, but since no one has asked, I keep to myself my argument that the siesta *increases* productivity. After all, sleeping during the hottest hours means that more work can be done during the cool evening. When we return from dinner around midnight, we'll see the waiters just bringing Greek people their meals.

Instead of holding forth in defense of napping, I explain that the austerity measures imposed by the International Monetary Fund and European Central Bank have indeed left many Greeks penniless, without money for electricity or food. But those who do have jobs continue to spend money on eating out, because they so deeply value the sense of community that arises from a shared meal eaten in a public, communal place. When I told my relatives that my American students had asked why they Greeks didn't try harder to reduce their spending, their response translated roughly to: "The Germans have already taken away so much—we won't let them take this too." Really, they said, *"Ke ton kafe tha mas kopsoun?"* ("Are they going to even deprive us of coffee?" "ε, και τον καφέ θα μας κόψουν?").

Once we've passed through the arcades of the open market, we reach the Myrovólos Smírni. The appetizers arrive quickly, among them the best *melinzanosaláta* (smoked eggplant dip) I've ever had. Erika helps me explain its origins and the way recipes that developed among the various Armenian, Jewish, Turkish, and Greek communities of what is now Turkey came over in 1922 and radically changed the Greek cuisine. The restaurant owner, Thanássis, was born in Thessaloníki, to parents expelled from Smírni. What I've read about world history tells me that the only comparable event in history was the partition of British India. Over the coming weeks, I find that this year's workshop is especially interested in history, and thanks to their questions, and the knowledge they bring to

our class discussions, I discover all sorts of things I knew but
didn't really understand about Greece. When Thessaloníki,
for instance, became part of the Greek republic in 1913 after
the Second Balkan War, Greek speakers were in the minority.
It's hard to imagine Greece prior to 1913 as a country without
its second-largest city, yet it existed for almost a century that
way. I suppose it's as hard as trying to imagine the United
States before the Louisiana Purchase. During the nineteenth
century, Thessaloníki became a city with a majority Ladino-
speaking Jewish population, with a large Turkish-speaking
minority and an even smaller minority that spoke Greek.
Today, if you listen to the buzz around you, you hear few
traces of that history, since almost everyone speaks Greek, but
history's complexity retains a presence in the food.

One of the next *mezéthes* to arrive are snails. Thanássis
beams widely under his bushy gray mustache. "*Karaólous!*"
he bellows, and I laugh, asking him where he learned the
Cypriot word for snails. The Greek is *salingária*. He tells
us he was visiting relatives in Cyprus the year an old man
left his house on the free side to gather snails after it rained
and accidentally found himself in the buffer zone. I was in
high school in Cyprus at the time, and I remember—it was
around the same time the motorcycle club tried to cross the
Green Line. This man who had been gathering snails was
shot dead by Turkish soldiers. Thanássis read the headlines
that morning and had to figure out from the context what
the man had been doing. I knew the Cypriot word for snail
by then and hearing the news story caused me to picture
myself wandering among the dry grass, carob trees, and
sagebrush, losing my way as I so often did, and then being
shot. In Greek conversation, even eating snails prompts a discussion of regional dialects, and of belligerent Greco-Turkish
relations.

As the dishes continue to arrive at our table in Myrovólos Smírni, most of them more familiar than snails, those of us accustomed to *meze*-sharing nudge the newbies to keep circulating the food. Christopher tells the group how much I like to dance, that I can't stay in my seat, and what a good time we'll have soon when the musicians pass by. This is true. I have a hard time sitting down when music I like is playing. In my effort to make sense of just how much pleasure I take in my mediocre performances of dance, I've been reading about mirror neurons and kinesthetic empathy. Brain scientists are figuring out the mechanisms behind the special relief I receive from communally expressing a song's beauty through dance.

Because I take not only pleasure, but also a sense of spiritual relief and psychological catharsis from dancing, I have felt uncomfortable about getting paid to do it. It's not so much the ethics of gleaning both joy and money from the act, but a problem of performance. My experience of pleasure functions as a spectacle of authentic Greekness for foreigners. I feel like I am performing Greekness for money and selling someone out. I have anxieties about minstrelsy, but I do it anyway.

Thanássis's son Thomas asks if we want him to call the guys who play live music. "Of course," I tell him. It's been months since my hips got to swivel in the way of a *tsif te téli* (a bit like a belly dance), and my anticipation heightens as Thanássis talks to the unknown musician on his cell. I don't really believe he can just call up a man with a drum to come play for us, but this is Greece, and within minutes a boy of thirteen or fourteen arrives and starts to play. I get up— the boy has, after all, come for us to dance, and I call to the students not to leave me alone. Shyly they rise, and soon I have several students up and imitating my movement. We fill up the end of the arcade between our long table and the wall. It feels forced to dance to just a drum, and so early in the evening—I don't think I would if it weren't my job. A young Michigander named Josh also rises, takes the tambourine someone offers, and I take pleasure in the communication with everyone. Photographs from that dinner show me with my arms in the air and my hips out, but my brows are furrowed like I am concentrating a little too hard.

After the boy leaves—it seems he has exhausted his drumming repertoire after half an hour—Erika realizes we haven't tipped him. Someone runs out to the street and calls the boy back as we explain to the students that the boy survives on tips from people like us. He passes his drum around and we drop euros into it. Erika and I explain everything we know about tipping in Greece—less money needs to be left at restaurants, but because of austerity measures, almost everyone the students meet is barely hanging on, and it's only right that we share the good fortune of our American jobs. Those of us on graduate student stipends, I explain, feel like money is always tight, but still we earn much more for six hours per week in the classroom than many equally qualified Greeks working full time, while everything except medicine and vegetables is more expensive in Greece.

On Tuesday, we make our way to the island of Thássos. At a rest stop on our bus trip eastward from Thessaloníki, the soups and sweets are labeled in Turkish as well as Greek. There's a ferry boat and more road, and then we reach the Archóndissa Tavern and Hotel, which will host us for three weeks.

Christopher has known our hosts for decades, while the other teachers, Natalie Bakopoulos the fiction writer and Carolyn Forché the poet, are returning for a third year just as I am. Three summers—three month-long stays—have been enough time to develop in us a strong affection for our host family, and we greet them with the hearty emotions of distant but enthusiastic relatives. Stamátis Kouzís, deeply beloved to us all, is a fisherman who told me he built the Archóndissa cinderblock by cinderblock with his own hands. He supplies the tavern with fish now, and has told me that he built and worked the tavern for decades for the purpose of supporting his family until he could have the life he wanted, which is the life he has now, as a fisherman whose sale of fish barely pays for the fishing boat's gasoline. His wife Eva runs the small hotel attached to the tavern, and also governs the kitchen. Tássos, who will inherit the restaurant from his parents Stamatis and Eva, is my age. He is in charge of the wood oven that is advertised on a billboard on the road, shoveling in loaves of bread and ceramic pots of food his mother and her workers have prepared. These people will shock the American students with their warmth, and with hospitality that to the Greeks feels like basic decency and to the Americans an overflowing generosity.

As I begin our first class on the island, I ask if they have any urgent questions. They do. "How can we hang out with Tássos without getting shit-faced every night?"

I explain my trick for dealing with the hospitality requirement that the hosts keep filling up the guest's glass. I try to illuminate the way individual wishes in Greece are subordinate to the demands of the *paréa*, or group, such that their personal desire to drink more, or to stop drinking, doesn't matter—each member of a *paréa* must at least appear to be drinking for as long as everyone else is. "Accept that your glass will always be full," I suggest, "no matter how much or how little you drink."

Also, I remind them that when their glasses are filled on

the house because of the owners' cultural urge toward hospitality, they have already paid, in a sense, because the cost of the meals is substantial. In fact, after Tássos spends a night giving the students wine for free, he would be frustrated if they didn't order meals from him in return. I avoid these awkward misunderstandings by cooking meals in my apartment, and celebrate my decision to live the rest of my life in individualistic America, where I rarely get into such scrapes. So far, no one has done me unsolicited favors and then asked for payback.

Teaching others how to navigate the emotionally charged and complicated Greek social structure brings me relief. I don't expect that to happen, but it does. I am just aware, at first, of being *so happy* to be doing this work, and just marveling at my good luck, being paid to do something so therapeutic. Later, with reflection, I consider the way that teaching Americans to decode Greek interactions and unspoken systems of reciprocity, and navigate a minefield which it's impossible to navigate without insulting someone, normalizes my own difficulty and eases the stress of being so often unsure of how to act—the stress of not knowing what exactly is expected of me, because my eleven years in Cyprus aren't the same as a whole lifetime, and my Greek-speaking parents aren't the same as parents who never left.

The same problem of not-quite-belonging follows me into American contexts: Greek music is the only music I know, and when my American friends sing or discuss music, I can't participate. English literature in all its high and low forms is beloved to me, but when it comes to music I only listen to Greek music. Erika, whose family-level closeness entitles her to say this, attributes my Greek-only attitude with music to stubbornness. Other people just think I'm strange.

But it makes sense to me. The only music that sounds to me like *belonging* is Greek; I take a special and enormous pleasure at the opportunities to dance to Greek music that my island job affords. This year, Christopher has told me on our bus ride to Thássos, I will have a special opportunity. The German dancers we've heard about will have lessons concurrent with our workshops. Our first night on Thássos, we meet the Greek dance teachers Níkos and Bámbis, who is happy to joke about the implications of his name when said in English. It's a typical mainland-Greece shortening of Harálambos, but it's unfamiliar to us. Bámbis thinks Pámbos, which is the Cypriot abbreviation of the name, sounds silly, and will continue during the coming weeks to poke friendly fun at what he picks up of the Cypriot dialect Erika and I use with one another.

Bámbis knows a little English, but he and Níkos are fluent in German and Greek, so only members of our group who know one of those languages can communicate with them well. But when we sit around watching their practices, it doesn't take much language to understand how their dancing course works. The basic setup is a lot like our writing workshops. Student tuition pays for the instructors to travel to Greece and live on Thássos. The programs offer an active learning vacation that couples an escape from everyday life with the development of a skill. The German Greek-dancers are mostly novices, looking to pick up the skills from scratch. Some are more like our creative writers, who have been practicing back home and have come to Greece to hone those skills with uninterrupted focus on the craft. The German dancing students are mostly retired folk or teachers, who can afford the many summer days off that attending the class requires. I admire but can't entirely feel kinship with these amateurs, since the money, time, and attention they put into learning Greek folk dances doesn't compare with any pursuit of mine. When I ask myself why I don't have anything that would qualify as a hobby, I decide it's because I chose to make writing, which I love, into my job, so that my work takes all my effort and attention.

Bámbis and Níkos have day jobs selling cars, but by moonlighting as Greek-dance-teachers, they have made work out of what they love. Over the course of the next ten days, they spend a lot of time with Erika and me. They teach dance to their fifteen or so students during the day, and then at dinnertime hired musicians arrive, and the Germans practice their newly learned dances. By the first night, the Germans have learned the two most common dances, the *kalamatianó* and *soústa*. The musicians play a song about the woman who falls into a well and bangs her bracelets to call for help. *Droung*, it goes. I remember the song from childhood and jump up to join the *kalamatianó*. The Germans whose hands I've clasped on either side of me beam. I am embarrassed when I realize that, instead of recognizing that they were just happy to embrace another fellow reveler, I have quickly made up a whole story to explain their beaming. I have imagined that they received me as a token real Greek, who could enhance their experience by providing authenticity.

My defensiveness about my identity, about how I am perceived, often rears its head when I'm not expecting it. And my misinterpretations force me to face my own prejudices, paranoias, and preoccupations. Mishearings seem to me the flip side of Freudian slips, and happen often when I'm operating in my second language. Although I lived in Greek-speaking Cyprus for a long time, I've never spent more than two months at a time in mainland Greece, and never more than three weeks on Thássos, and so there are both regionalisms and current turns of phrase that I miss.

For example, I used to see a road sign in Limassol, Cyprus that said on it "← *poreía epanastrofís*" ("Πορεία Επαναστροφής"), and beneath the Greek, the English translation: "← WAY BACK." It was positioned on the meridian of cement and rose laurel that divided the lanes of my city's shore road. In the direction the arrow pointed, there was only a tiny side street and some small shops, a souvenir shop or an ice cream parlor, and perhaps an optician. But the arrow pointed north, so I deduced that it must be a political message about the occupation of the island's north by Turkish military forces. Later, I'd realize that while *epistrofí* means return, *anastrofí* is a U-turn, and *epanastrofí* indicates the retracing of one's steps.

Another example. Tonight in Thássos, the musicians begin to play a popular *hasápiko* (the butcher's dance, a sort of synchronized improvisation danced in rows with shoulders clasped, the combination of moves agreed on beforehand or sensed by someone who gives cues). When we hear the introduction, we all get up to dance. I have my right hand on Bámbis's left shoulder, and his left hand is on my right shoulder. I wait for him to start so I can follow—I don't have the skill to lead—when he taps my shoulder and says, "*íseh eléftheri*" ("είσαι ελεύθερη"), literally, "you're free."

I freeze. *Free* also means *unmarried*, and I stand gaping at Bámbis, terrified that he has asked me an uncomfortable question. As in many languages, in Greek, "You are free" and "Are you free?" are identical sentences but for intonation. Is Bámbis asking me out, I wonder, or admonishing me for not being married to a man? My panic is irrational, but paranoia by its very definition makes no sense. After a few awkward seconds, Bámbis gestures for me to begin dancing, and I realizes he means I am free to start the dance. I explain what I thought was obvious: that I need him to lead. We switch places and step into an exhilarating, beautiful dance.

The German dance students, who learn old folk dances but not the more contemporary *zeimbékiko* or *hasápiko* dance in their classes, stand around us watching as we figure out a combination of the various moves we know (hop-and-twirl-around, bend each knee to the ground, cross one foot over the other in one of several standard ways). They stand out from the Greek tavern customers, who wear high heels and fashionable, slinky dresses. One German man with tiny round glasses and thin-soled black sneakers wears striped, pajama-like pants, and wears them again for three nights in a row, until he switches to similar pants with different colored stripes. There is a sweet, mountain-tall woman with whom I dance a *tsif te téli* when the music changes. Her red-brown hair falls past the elastic waistband of her colorful skirt, and her sequined moccasins sparkle in the dim light. Some of the Germans dress up in flats and pretty shirts; others wear yoga pants, T-shirts, and sneakers. One woman with short hair is always dressed for the gym. Another wears clothes you might find at a mid-range thrift store, her dyed hair held up by a pin.

The night ends with a final *tsif te téli*, and the students approach and dance with me and seem excited when I tell them they are doing great. These moments will, experience tells me, become part of why they will eventually love their experience of being in Greece. Participating in a dance generates a strong union between individuals, and those for whom Greek dancing is not fraught with anxieties about Greekness and belonging take even more pleasure than I do. Erika tells me that it's very annoying when I yell out invitations to the students to join me, and I feel ashamed. When she mimics my overly cheery call, I experience all my anxiety about appropriation, exploitation, and the gaze. Thus, it's rare that I get lost in the moment, or in the pleasure, because I feel alone in an anxiety that isn't shared by my students, who are happy to be tasting Greek culture and just having fun.

I would like to know what it means to parade in a costume that belongs to another culture—and whether I'm doing something ethical by teaching the Americans to dance like Greeks. I return to my room eager to go on dancing with these strange people who don't share a language with me, but share a passion for Greek dancing in spite of our not-quite-belonging to the Greek nation.

The next night, the German dancers have proceeded to dances of northeastern Greece and have already surpassed my range. I can't join, but I clap when I can and chat with the students as we eat and drink. As I make my way toward my room, a sweet older-looking man whom we had dubbed last night "the German Santa Claus" stops me as I am leaving the tavern. He speaks to me in German, flapping his arms and widening his eyes behind the wire frames of his glasses. His cheeks are flushed, and his white hair blows in the breeze, and I have no idea what he wants.

A girl seated at a table next to us looks my age, and northern European, and my helpless glance prompts her to translate the German Santa Claus's concern into very American-sounding English. He is upset, concerned that I am not dancing because I am sad. I guess he wants me not to be sad. I ask her to explain to him that I can't participate because I just don't know the Thracian dances. I want to tell them the whole story of my dancing life: being sidelined in kindergarten, then participating in after-school Greek dance lessons in second grade, only to find following the teachers' instructions so difficult that I got terrible headaches after practice, so that my parents let me drop out, and the headaches stopped. Then I took a decade off until undergrad at Cornell, where all my friends were Greek. We danced together on weekends, and I learned a few dances. Then came a handful of lessons in Asgáta village in my early twenties, along with a bunch of little kids. While a master's student, I joined some friends in learning the regional dance from the island of Icaria. There are nine steps in this dance, and it took me four hours to learn them. My friends took me around and around and around until I finally managed to match my feet to the song. Everyone else in the group took about ten minutes to master it.

Over the course of the coming ten days, I repeatedly fail to impress upon this sweet, enthusiastic German Santa Claus the limits of my Greek dance ability. The confusion seems generalized. Most of the German dancers seem to assume that since I speak Greek, I will know all the Greek dances. By the end of the Germans' stay, when they have mastered an astounding number of complicated dances from many distinct regions of Greece, I realize that these capable, agile folks just can't fathom how difficult learning a dance is (and always has been) for me. I'm just a weak dancer. When I eventually perform, years later in Beaumont, Texas, in costume for the first time in my life, my fellow dancers will lend me the costume with the longest skirt because in spite of many, many hours of practice, they know I will botch at least a couple of steps.

After the German Santa Claus is appeased and accepts (I think) that I'm not terribly sad, the young woman who has translated my English into German introduces herself as Denise. She asks about our program, and I explain the writing workshop. In turn, Denise explains that she is not one of the dancers but likes to visit Thássos along with them so that she and her husband can have German-speaking company. We talk about how hard the dances are, and how amazing it is that the students learn so many. We wonder together what motivates the participants to invest so much time, attention, and money into learning the folk dances of another country. Then Denise asks if my sandals—tan with a brown plastic sole and straps of woven plastic made to look like leather, which buckle around the ankle—are from Target. Standing on a Greek terrace in the Aegean, listening to the music of clarinets and sheepskin bagpipes from Thrace, I wonder how this German woman knows the origin of my American (made in China) shoes.

I tell her they are indeed, and I remember how I worried, when I bought them ahead of this trip, that the braided imitation leather would resemble the tacky faux-ancient sandals sold at most Greek souvenir shops. Tourists buy them along with unflattering dresses decorated in ancient Greek symbols of meanders and laurel, to imagine, I suppose, that they are wearing sandals just like the ancient Greeks and therefore getting an authentic Greek experience during their vacation. My German shoe-sharer explains that she has family in Houston. She visited a few months ago and tried on the very same shoes, but they didn't quite fit. I am at this moment still a permanent resident of Missouri, a college instructor, and a graduate student who can't imagine life beyond graduate school. Within eight months, I receive a call inviting *me* to Houston, and I go, and I teach there for four winters, and myself shop for a new pair of plastic sandals in the very same Target as this girl from Germany. In a few short years, I'm fully employed, and there in Houston, I join a Greek dance troupe of my own—my first and only hobby.

For now, we possess knowledge only of our past and of our wonderful Thássian present. In that present, Denise asks if I would like some *halloumi*. I balk because I think I'm

being essentialized. The name of our national cheese is frequently the only distinctly Cypriot thing any non-Cypriot
has heard of. This isn't the case—rather, it just so happens
Denise and Stefan have already ordered some. She lived in
Cyprus for a while and wrote her master's thesis on the political integration of Cyprus into the European Union. And
I have done it again, had my feathers ruffled because I feel
the victim of tokenism. Being seen as a symbol of a place
prevents me, I suppose, from feeling seen. Seen, that is, as
just myself—but as which self? Joanna, or Ioánna the Greek
teacher? I'm not sure what it is I'm after, or what will make
me feel confident and calm.

At night, with the musicians paid for by the Germans, I
experience a different sense of who I am. I become a person
full of delight. The musicians who play for the German
dance students are Níkos, on guitar, and Páris, who plays
bouzouki and also waits tables at the Archóndissa when he
isn't playing music. They play my favorite songs—songs I
know well but have only sung along with the radio in my
bedroom, always alone. Erika elbows me at times to remind
me not to sing along loudly, because I'm off-key no matter
how hard I try to hit the notes, and excitement only makes
me sound worse. But I can't contain my singing, because
singing the music I've loved for decades together with other
people makes me feel like I belong.

It will be short-lived, I know, this feeling of belonging, but
it's a better feeling than I have had reason to hope for. Over
the course of the Germans' stay, musicians even more accomplished than the locals Níkos and Páris are hired, and they
are given rooms at the Archóndissa, and Erika and I stay up

until sunrise listening. We struggle to fall asleep as the world turns from black to gentle blue.

I have never been able to sleep during the day, and after these two full nights of song, I am red-eyed and dazed, but happy—happy especially that my one responsibility, the teaching of Greek, comes even more naturally to me than sleep does at the normal nighttime hour. And I do fine. The students progress, making their way through the alphabet and learning new idioms like *póso kánei* (πόσο κάνει), for *how much does it cost*?

The one thing that troubles me is the way a few members of our group laugh at the Germans when they dance. The dance lessons last from midmorning to early afternoon, the last hour of dance class overlapping with our American students' lunch hour. My students stare as they eat. When I look back on these days, I don't recall names, but remember only the insistent snickering at the Germans for looking like marionettes. "It's as if they are made of wood!" I don't know what to say—I feel dissonance; I am the only one who notices that the Americans had no reason to be laughing at the Germans for pretending to be Greek. By this time, the Americans have themselves danced with Greeks many times and attempted to join in the less complicated dances, like the belly dancing that requires no steps, just imitations of hip swiveling and shoulder shimmying. They make no connection between their own performance of Greek dancing— true, they make none of the attempts at accurate imitation they are laughing at—and the ridicule they are heaping on the Germans.

I want my students to like me, and I want them to give the Writing Workshops in Greece good reviews, and also I'm not accustomed to calling people out on their problematic statements. It's self-righteous. So I refrain from pointing out just how quickly the Germans are learning to dance. Since they learn in one day what would take me (the authentic Greek) a month to master, it is only natural that they are a little stiff. They focus on the specific, complicated way in which a different culture's rhythms are expressed in steps of a particular order and duration. It is entirely understandable that the Germans, on their first iterations of a new dance, look like they are overly intellectualizing the art. Practice alone brings mastery, and with it comes the appearance of effortlessness. Only great artifice produces an appearance of artlessness. But my fellow Americans are attributing it to the scientific meticulousness that is the German stereotype.

Over the course of our stay, after the dance group has gone home to Germany, they continue to be remembered in patronizing terms by the Americans, and I fail to make sense of this scorn. Maybe they are laughing at German failure to have fun. When the Americans imitate Greek dances with little attention and even less accuracy, they have no qualms about authenticity because they are enjoying themselves. When the Germans dance with meticulous attention and the resultant accuracy, they do not seem to be *having fun*, regardless of how likely it is that succeeding at a difficult task probably brings them great, if hidden, pleasure. They look inauthentic to the Americans, because they are concentrating, and therefore worthy of ridicule. This teaches me something about perception, and about how assumptions about belonging pass through several layers of prejudice before judgments are made. And how much harder I have to work on catching my own hasty reactions, because we're worst at noticing prejudice of our own.

Instead of addressing the problem directly with the students, I try to sidestep into the charged problem of culturally determined ideas of *fun*. I encourage my class to explore their experience in Greece, and think about things that are surprising to them as Americans, hoping to let them see, through the existence of a whole word that's not available in English, that their culture determines their perceptions of what is fun and what is work. I send them two recent articles in the *Journal of Modern Greek Studies* which attempt to articulate in English what *kéfi* is. Simply put, *kefi* is that spiritual momentum that a gathering takes on, the communal sense of excitement, transcendence, and being outside time. One of them, about dancing in a Greek Australian community in Adelaide, links kéfi to another word I teach my more advanced students: *meráki*.

Passion in Greek music-making and dancing is constituted as a cathartic experience of the individual symbolically (through music and dance) asserting a strong sense of the self within the collectivity of the community. The externalized expressions kéfi (communal excitement during a party) and meráki are read as celebratory signals by participants, and function to generate an event with kéfi and much social interaction.

Meráki is also crucial. It's one of my favorite words in any language. I try to explain that to do something with meráki means that pleasure is derived from attentive, caring, passionate labor. It sort of undermines words like *overthink*, *overwork*, *obsess*—because within the definition of the word is the notion that a sort of transcendent, spiritual pleasure comes from spending a great deal of time and focused attention on a task.

The work I do here, I do with meráki. My job as Greek teacher produces not just joy but also healing. Articulating the untranslatable words and having students see their meanings at play in everyday Greek interactions confirms for me that I'm not crazy, that it really is impossible to translate them, and so a whole part of my life and thought feels hidden while I operate in English-only contexts. Empowering Americans to speak Greek with confidence makes me feel like I matter. And when I empower them to dance—I think this is the best job in the world. One student tells me that dancing along with strangers makes her feel connected to them in ways she hasn't ever felt connected before, even when she *could* speak the same language as her new acquaintances.

And so I love being here, and dancing here, in this country where I speak the language but don't have citizenship. I like having an outlet for the perpetual translation that goes on in my head. I also like being suspended between the countries in which I have citizenship. Once, a young Frenchman who attended Russian Orthodox churches and had one Armenian grandparent explained to me that there are people who can *only* live in diaspora. He meant there are people who can't live in their countries of origin and feel comfortable only in countries where they are outsiders. They need their outside-ness to be seen. The Armenian and Russian ex-pats of the Frenchman's parish would never have been able to go home. They were comfortable in exile in France. In a similar way, I figure out that I feel comfortable in Greece because here, unlike in America and Cyprus, I'm *supposed* to feel like I'm not at home.

Both in American and Greek cultural contexts, there's something not-quite-native about my sensibility. My knowledge is stretched across two cultures so that I feel recognized as native in neither. I often need cultural references or phrases explained to me, and that has made me feel like an outsider when I lived in America, and when I lived in Cyprus. Here, in this in-between space, my failure to be entirely Greek or entirely American permits me to function as a bridge. Being a part-time Greek, and one who translates for Americans, makes my in-between-ness and my not-quite-ness into an asset rather than a liability. My anxious perception that Greeks are always suspicious of me stems from aggressive questioning about my failure to be married. Because of consistent aggressive questions about the absence of men in my life, I haven't been able to relate to Greek strangers calmly or believe that they accept me as one of them. Still, I feel myself inching toward reconciliation with the way I'm always treated as peculiar, because in *this* place my difference is useful. In Greek circles, I still expect to be ridiculed or attacked for being a lesbian. In 2011, I was about to come out to a college friend when her husband started asking me if the poet Cavafy was from the island of Sérifos, because I had just visited that island. "No," I said, "he's from Alexandria," and then I let the friend's husband go on joking about gay people, thereby deepening my sense of shame and not-belonging. In 2019, after the music ended at the Archóndissa, the keyboard player asked me out and I told him I was gay. He insisted that I have sex with a man to find out what I was missing. Over and over, I said that I only have sex with women. I didn't want to leave the conversation and let him think I had conceded. At five in the morning, when the sun rose, the keyboard player still insisted that it was impossible I could desire anyone but men. We parted ways; I felt defeated. Later that morning, the keyboard player was seen strutting around the tavern with his shirt off asking where I was.

I finally understood my predicament better when I reread James Baldwin's essay "Equal in Paris." In racist mid-twentieth-century America, Baldwin endures violence because he is a black man. In France, Baldwin is sneered at by the policemen because he's an American. He's held in disdain, a disdain that is identical to the disdain they bear the white Americans. Being seen as just an American releases Baldwin from his rage at being always targeted because of the color of his skin. It's not the same at all—I have suffered none of the violence or the oppression or the lack of opportunities that people of color do in America. But "Equal in Paris" is the only piece of literature I read in college that helps me reckon with my own rage at feeling like no matter what I do, no matter how hard I try, I cannot get other people to look at me the way I want to be seen.

Realizing that Bámbis wasn't trying to find me a husband, and wasn't preparing to indict me for not having one, but was just saying that I was free to begin the dance, prompted a little epiphany of my own. I see now that a very real history of oppression has conditioned me to perceive the whole world as oppressive. I recognize that if we can see our prejudice, our paranoia, and our conditioning clearly, we might give voice to our rage, and break free.

—

Out

—

1

—

By my mid-twenties, I knew that one thing wouldn't change: I felt attraction powerfully and exclusively toward women. Facing this scared me, not just because of the social stigma and the rejection I expected from my family, but because it demanded a more personal reckoning. For before I really *realized* this human love for what it was, I had loved God, and with passion. And that simple temporal fact would underpin my decision to spend the next several years denying all of my sexual and romantic yearning.

Terror and shame were there too, but to my mind this was a decision about love. It was a decision about preventing the loss of my earliest partner in love. Simplistic, yes. And yet. For me, prayer was an outpouring of love, an expression of love; God was the being that received my love when all my many other loves, all my many crushes, heterosexual woman, married women, closeted gay women perhaps (how could one know?), were all forbidden. My love went unmirrored, left outside language and outside thought.

There is a scene in D. H. Lawrence's *The Rainbow* where a girl character looks at a woman's body with desire, and I read this scene repeatedly, just because it alone made my own experience real. I had no other mirroring beyond those five paperback pages; nowhere else did what was inside me match what I saw in reality outside me. The title of the chapter is "Shame."

Because books offered a rare portal to worlds in which bodies were described, God was contemplated, and yearning both physical and spiritual was articulated, for me the sensual and the religious got all tangled up. Orthodox worship is physical, with incense, prostrations, and real wine animating the senses in church. I was eight when I was introduced to the Jesus Prayer. It's practiced all over the Orthodox world with a rosary made not of beads but of knotted wool. I was then instructed to inhale on the first half of the prayer, "Lord Jesus Christ, Son of God," and exhale on the second half, "have mercy upon me a sinner." I didn't do it too much as a child, only when told, or in church on Sundays and holidays. Still, a blueprint was laid. I don't think I was more or less interested in religion than other curious kids. But I was wild to understand the universe, its spirit and its physicality, and as a teenager, I grew more interested in both theology and science. Orthodoxy requires scary, face-to-face confession, without the screen that protects Roman Catholic penitents from view. (In New York there was group confession for children. We kneeled in front of the priest, who spread his stole on top of the children closest to him, and confessed silently in our own heads.) After we moved, there were no group confessions. Starting in autumn 1988, my confessions took place in my Cypriot confessor's cluttered office. There, across from his swiveling desk chair, among towering stacks of religious books, I had to state what I'd done wrong. The point is to be freed. I did often feel lighter afterwards, although I was terrified of encounters with a priest—of this existential discussion that cast me as bad. Yet the truth-telling demanded by this part of my religion had great allure. I read whatever theology I was given.

I was fifteen when my confessor gave me a book called *His Life is Mine*, and I began to pray in the manner described there, directly and insistently and with absolute concentration: no words but the repeated Jesus Prayer, and an expectation that God would visit. I don't remember how soon after this prayer began to bring with it states of ecstasy, elation, and transcendence, but it did, pretty dependably, and it felt like I held in my grasp the most important secret of the universe. Soon, I could sense in other people whether they'd had contact with whatever divine thing this was. When I waited in line for confession, sometimes I would experience the inner lifting just before the person ahead of me emerged, as if the priest could communicate with me telepathically. I felt it in a few monks and nuns, like a handshake of the heart. I had absolute reverence for the sanctity of this gift—I didn't consider it a feeling, but God himself. This is not something one can experience and then easily give up. It is a sense of absolute connection to the universe, of tranquility, of joy, and even of knowledge—in this state, I felt that the Trinity made sense, along with many other paradoxes of the world.

One way I made sense of my indifference to boys was by casting girls who dated as conformist or superficial (or both), whereas all of my passions (for girls) were *spiritual*. To prove how devoted I was to the life of the mind, I read my parents' books. When I opened Plato to a random page, *Lysis, or Friendship* appeared, and I can still feel the scratchy cloth of the old book against my palms as bewilderment hit. The men spoke of loving men as if it were natural. I slunk back into the house and slipped the volume back into its place as if my purpose, rather than confirming the superiority of my mind, had been to perpetrate some kind of perversity or crime.

Later, in college, a professor asked the class to turn to an Adrienne Rich poem: "My Mouth Hovers across Your Breasts." He read the lines out loud, or a student did, and I felt the whole room receding from me, or myself receding from my body, something like that. That poem simply could not be read as straight. Well. It could be. But not in that college classroom. There, the delicate and wild fingers, the hovering mouth, the exact tongue, and the breasts all came together to mean nothing but two women making love in one shared bed. I don't recall whether there was snow outside or only in the poem. In the poem, there is a daytime candle and its light is peculiar, but I recall that in the classroom the light was typical. Natural. No one else worried that two women, together, relished the pleasures of winter. I recall terror and longing and sitting frozen silent at a wooden seminar table feeling dangerously exposed.

I spent my undergraduate years reeling from the openness of a liberal school, which put my repression and denial under threat. Beauty became a threat. My body, too. I clung to religion. After college, I lived with my parents in our small village in Cyprus. I taught, got a car, and developed a bit of a social life, as well as powerful crushes that I kept as silent and as hidden as I could. One of my epiphanic moments involved a woman I was very much attracted to, who artic-ulated the physical experience of arousal when she assumed I felt it for a boy I was dating. (I dated a boy once because I believed I had to, but then my father got mad because he wasn't Greek and I abandoned my effort to fulfill this obli-gation after that.) I freaked out because what the woman de-scribed was precisely what I felt when I saw her, and up until then I hadn't yet forced myself to face that fact. Nothing had before compelled me to reckon with the implication of my physiological reaction to girls.

Once I had realized at last, consciously, that I experienced intense and exclusive attraction to women, I reasoned that since I'd fallen in love with God first, I must ignore this second love. I would stick to loving God and keep on ignoring my want and my lust. Given the solace, safety, and ecstatic joy I got through prayer, one can imagine what a crisis my epiphany provoked. I bore it alone. I spoke to a couple of friends, and their kindness was not enough. I believed I had to choose between one love and another. When I was thirty-two, I heard a voice in my head saying, "Never." I envisioned dying having never touched a woman, never expressed longing, never tasted mutual desire, and that vision of myself unloved and dying changed me forever. I decided I would try to date.

When, on one of my dates, I kissed a woman for the first time, it felt normal. When I had sex with a woman for the first time, it felt natural. None of this could fix my fear. Here is the paradox: I still feel my faith holds the keys to spiritual liberation, total connection, and absolute peace, but by rejecting homosexuality, it becomes, for me, also a cage.

One day, shortly after I returned from my first year of graduate school in the US to spend the summer with my parents in Cyprus, I went to Costa Café with Erika around noon. She was smoking back then and lit a cigarette before taking a sip of coffee. I had my back to Makaríou Avenue, while she faced it. I remember that I posed it as a question. Something like "You don't think I might?" or "It's not possible that I'm?" I definitely didn't use dangerous words like queer or lesbian. It may have been only the silence at the end of these half-questions that made it clear: I was asking Erika if she thought I was gay.

The coffee shop was new to me then. I remember its newness only and how much light there was—too much light. One of us was squinting, even though an umbrella provided shade.

"Well, yeah. Nick and I used to say it. 'If Joanna wasn't religious she would be a lesbian.' "

It's embarrassing that my immediate response was something to the effect of, "How could you keep this from me?," but you can imagine the shock of learning that the words I couldn't even say had long been discussed among my friends. I knew it was never my friends' job to inform me of the desire they could see. And yet that's what I said. "How could you keep this from me?"

I had an appointment for confession right after our coffee, and when I said that I should probably confess my lesbianism now, Erika said that there was no way the priest didn't already know. I felt, of course, exposed. Also (and it's difficult to be sure about emotions I didn't write down), I might have felt a little glad—that I had been seen. That my loves had been seen by my friends, and now perhaps even by my priest.

There was always a tiny part of me that loved the power I had to see the beauty of women, and to desire and love them.

2
——

I wonder at my students, who speak with ease about their desire. I have benefited from other people's willingness to be frank. Frankness is highly valued in America. I am not entirely American. On matters of desire, I speak sideways. Words are bigger than I am. I am small. Words are dangerous. To secrets, there is a sweetness. The beauty of women. Beauty begets reverence. Why speak? A sweet center, silence—outside it, terror.

When I told my oldest friend that I loved women, she told me that she already knew, and I said, "How could you hide this from me?" She didn't run away. I told someone else, and she also did not run away. I did not run away. Again and again. Twelve times.

Then, a priest. God has pity on those who are ill. I still go to church. It is hard to walk in there every week and be thought of as incurable or unwilling to be cured. But if I disappear from the church, what good is done? I lose my God, and my church loses its one gay woman: more emptiness than before, loss upon loss.

Two friends tell me: "You don't have to choose." God or love? I have not chosen.

I write about coercion, now, and confession. I read Michel Foucault. I understand that human churches, human societies, make truths into secrets. I know that power wrenches words from us, turns lovers to sinners. Outside church, I am shamed for my shame, and love is withheld from me when I do not conform.

I think the definite article in *the coming out process* is dangerous. I think it is dangerous to believe that the receipt of three words has told you much about my inside world, about the fears and the loves and the rages and the wants that make up my person. Saying, "I am gay" asks a dangerous lot of three words.

It is more dangerous not to say them.

Cyprus Pride

My island has been awake for hours by the time I, in my Midwestern suburb, rise and hunch over a screen to wait for news. It is May 31, 2014, and on the other side of the Atlantic Ocean, Cyprus is having its very first gay pride parade. Victorian sodomy laws remained on the former British colony's books until I was in college, when the island's lawmakers gave in at last to the European court, which had ruled in favor of the change. In Modinós v. Cyprus, the European Court of Human Rights ruled that Cyprus could no longer keep a law that made sodomy punishable by five years in prison. I was fourteen when the court ruled in favor of Alécos Modinós, but Cypriot religious and political institutions formed a Committee for the Fight Against the Decriminalization of Homosexuality and through its influence managed to resist pressure from Europe until 1998. This is the Cyprus in which I spent my adolescence and half my twenties. This is the island on which I tried not to believe that I, too, was gay.

Between Nicosia's long rows of towering palms, a sea of people moves, rainbows on their chests and on their backs, love in three languages: αγάπη, love, and aşk. It is impossible to tell which of the people are the Greek Cypriots, which are the Turkish Cypriots, which are gay, and which are the thousands of straight allies who have driven from all over the island for this parade. The island has been partitioned for forty years, and the Pride organizers' invitation of Turkish Cypriots to the southern Greek side is a radically progressive political act.

My friend Erika has ridden a bus from our town of Limassol into the capital, and when she calls to tell me she's arrived, I thank her for marching for me.

"I'm not just here for you," she answers. "I'm here for everyone." She tells me she can't reach the parade's starting point yet because members of a group called the Pan-Cypriot Christian Orthodox Movement (ΠΑΧΟΚ) are trying to block access to the parade. The police have formed a line to keep the marchers safe.

ΠΑΧΟΚ is one of many right-wing Greek Cypriot organizations that pay lip service to the rights of Greek Cypriots and Turkish Cypriots, Armenians, Maronites, and Roman Catholics, but are really saying that their own communities' rights haven't been protected enough. Their rhetoric is an "all lives matter" of sorts, with *all* meaning *our*. Until I went to graduate school and started reading on my own, I bought into the perspective of my conservative Greek schoolbooks, which presented Greek Cypriots as the only victims of intercommunal violence, and the only ones who needed their rights restored. And when teachers and priests and politicians said that the Greeks had suffered and deserved to have their human rights better protected, I understood that they meant only certain Greeks—the Greeks who dated the opposite sex. When Greek Cypriots demanded their human rights, they were fighting for heterosexuals like themselves. Gay Greeks weren't really Greeks. The archbishop of Cyprus has made a statement in anticipation of the pride parade, and in it he insists, as the church has for decades and will for many years to come, that homosexuality is and has always been an imported foreign disease. The disease of homosexuality can be treated, but it must not be confused with good health.

Greek Cypriots don't seem to know or care to remember that in the nineteenth century, British colonizers thought the contagion traveled in the opposite direction. A British scientist named Richard Burton theorized that gay was an inclination particular to geographic place, congenital but possibly contagious. Burton gave to southern Europe, northern Africa, most of the Americas, and Asia the name Sotadic Zone, and warned that in this region, people were by nature prone to sodomy. After colonization, the people indigenous to the so-called Sotadic Zone worked extra hard to prove they were not so prone at all. A kind of "It's not us, it's you."

Burton, of course, wasn't much of a scientist, and it's possible that his research condemned homosexual practices of people southeast of Britain just in order to get a publication about homosexuality past the censors. In any case, widespread beliefs that the darker-skinned colonial subjects of the world naturally tended toward sodomy produced a wide-reaching psychosocial response. Understandably on the defensive, colonized people reimagined the precise deviant inclination attributed to them as inherent, instead, to the former colonizer. Greek-Cypriot American immigrant communities, for example, tend to be especially vigilant against the deviance-producing force of the formerly-colonial now-host Anglo culture. Discovered in New York to have been loving men, one of my first cousins was sent to Cyprus to be changed. His parents' unspoken logic must have gone something like this: "No gays in the homeland; send him there, to a land very blessed and very Greek, and he will be cured." Nothing about sexuality or exile was spoken to me.

My cousin Elias just turned up in Cyprus one winter day, not yet thirty years old, neither working nor on vacation, and ate some meals with us before disappearing again. When he died at thirty-eight, the family said it was cancer. Decades passed before I learned that he had been gay like me, that AIDS had killed him, and that for all those years my family could not speak of his suffering and of his love.

Today, all this is different. Today, the rainbow flags make gay Cypriots real.

Suddenly, I exist.

Children are raised up on their parents' shoulders toward the sun at the same level as the flags and the signs: "SAME LOVE—EQUAL RIGHTS." Above a first story of adult bodies, the bodies of children, the rainbow flags, and the signs form a second story of hope: "HOMOPHOBIA HARMS YOU AND THOSE AROUND YOU."

In place of a picket sign, one demonstrator has made an effigy of an ostrich, and it stands with its head buried in a heap of fake sand in the shape of Cyprus. It hangs in a real cage.

Anna Víssi, the Madonna of Greece and Cyprus, greets those who have gathered to begin the parade. She pulls a folded page from her pocket, smiles almost bashfully, and tells the crowd she wrote down a few of her own thoughts, if we'll listen.

"It's already been stated many times by painters and by poets: whatever our skin color, whatever country gave us birth, we all have the same right to love, the same right to life, and the same right to a peaceful daily life."

Whoever these painters and poets are, they haven't ever taken a public stand in favor of gay rights in Cyprus. I, at least, never heard any of them address sexuality directly. For as long as I lived in Cyprus, through all my teenage years and my early twenties, all I heard on the radio about human rights was talk of the violations suffered by Greek Cypriots forced from their homes in the Turkish military intervention of 1974. The continued occupation of Northern Cyprus by Turkish troops underpins, oddly, one of the most popular conservative rationales for maintaining a ban on gays. In May 1997, when I was receiving my high school diploma and the repeal of the Victorian anti-sodomy law was being debated in Parliament, clerics led a protest of some thousand people to keep sex between two men a crime. Greek Cypriots were arguing, as they continue to well into the twenty-first century, that if homosexuality was legalized it would spread, and gays couldn't fight, so the rest of the island would be therefore conquered "by the Turks."

Behind Víssi, as she leaves the stage, I see signs: "Kuir Kıbrıs Derneği," which a Turkish-English dictionary tells me is "Queer Cyprus Association." Another sign says, in Greek, "FOR THOSE WHO CANNOT YET BE HERE." I'm sure it does not only refer to people like me, who live far away in places where it's easy to hide out, easy to wear T-shirts from gay events and say that I'm gay because no one will hurt me. Rather, the sign also refers to those who are living in Cyprus, but would risk being beaten or put out of their houses if they were seen at the pride parade.

I never thought it would happen, not, at least, so soon, not before my hair turned white and my sadness grew so heavy I could not find a way back. During my eleven years on the island, I heard the word gay every day and always as the slur *poúshtis*, like *fag* is used in America. Like many teenagers all over the world, I heard of homosexuality only in the context of sin or insult. Much later, when I moved to my progressive Missouri college town for graduate school, I became able to talk about my love of women, and to use words I'd once heard only as insults to describe myself. In academic circles of twenty-first century America, I was called brave. It was sweet to earn praise for speaking so uncomplicated a truth. I felt, however, that if I'd had real courage, I would not have left Cyprus, where being gay was hard, and where pride parades were not safe.

I've been going to protests I believed were safe for many years—anti-occupation demonstrations in Cyprus, progressive parades in progressive New York, Take Back the Night marches in Missouri, and anti-racism marches in Greece. Last July, a Greek nationalist–fascist parliamentarian from the Golden Dawn Party slapped another parliamentarian—Liána Kanélli—on live national television. The Golden Dawn MP hit Kanélli with three left-right blows, almost knocking her down. I was in Thessaloníki at the time of the televised assault, and the very next day I joined a rally against all discrimination. We protested misogyny as well as all of the Golden Dawn's insidious nationalist agenda. We called on our fellow Greeks to stop harassing immigrants and stop making them the scapegoats of the country's financial ruin. Somewhere near the middle of the large parading protest, a small group held a rainbow flag, and I walked closer and closer to them, then stopped a few feet off and hung back a little. I could get no closer because I still feared being outed in a Greek space. I was safe, yet still it felt like a risk because I felt exposed. Also, my fellow protesters were chanting a slogan that equated policemen and right-wing people with fascists, and this terrified me because it felt like a provocation. In the sixties, the police conspired with the military junta, who arrested suspected progressives and had them tortured, imprisoned, or sent into exile.

As the pride parade proceeds, though, on this morning in May, some counterprotesters from ΠΑΧΟΚ gather at "NO"

Plaza, named for the famous rejection of an ultimatum from Mussolini. The Christians carry no guns, no knives, and no clubs, and it is possible to believe for an instant that they will make their procession in peace. On their banners I spot the word *kólasi* (hell, κόλαση), and in English, *disaster*, along with quotes from American demagogues and from quacks: "cannot be strictly genetic."

Some men peer over the policemen, bouncing in place, yelling, "Hey! Are there gays back there? Eh? Are there gays?"

They strive for a glimpse of the gays as if there is a show for which they have bought tickets, as if they are entitled to gaze upon the circus of freaks. The ΠΑΧΟΚ people carry banners with Bible verses and slogans. They are men in polo shirts and faded jeans, with sunglasses masking their faces. They begin to shove the police, who are in their riot gear. The police are bearing the blows, whatever their history of collusion with right-wing totalitarians, and they are being hit by the men carrying banners of Bible verses, nationalist tropes about the blood of Cypriot martyrs, and translated propaganda from right-wing America.

The helmeted police officers lock their arms. I have seen arms locked before, on television and in my dreams. In my world, police are still the ones who deliver blows, like the tall British policeman who brought his bayonet down to kill my father, a tiny teenage freedom fighter with orders from the guerrilla leader to break through the line. My father scampered under the policeman's legs and lived. I have seen sticks raised this way before, sticks beating down onto flesh. Wood used as a form of torture, a big stick with a man nailed to it, for instance.

Priests in their long black cassocks and their cylindrical priests' hats try to stop the banner-bearing men from beating the police. These clerics must not have realized when they recommended printing gay-bashing banners that they were arming their congregation not only with words, but also with sticks. In several videos, I watch the banner-bearers use the heavy wooden rods from the banners to beat the police. The clergy runs into the fray but cannot stop the barrage of sticks, so they flee. The police stand firm, raising their clubs to shield their bodies. The Christians bludgeon the police.

"*Ya sena Kypros*!" "For you, Cyprus!" a deep-voiced counterprotester shouts as he heaves his body against the officers in riot gear and breaks the police line. He sprints toward the parade, but a policeman catches him eventually, and he is not permitted to hurt anyone.

When a television reporter asks one counterprotester why he is there, the interviewee seems puzzled by the question, as if the reporter has asked why he is defending the country against an invading army. He answers with a question. "What are they trying to do? Proclaim their . . . their . . . perversions?" He doesn't understand why they (we) aren't hiding.

During my first year of graduate school in Missouri, when I was thirty-two, a Greek Orthodox priest told me that being gay was not a sin, but more like being deformed.

"It doesn't damn you," he said. "It merely keeps you from some of the pleasures of being alive."

Later, after I had left that incense-filled church and that cushioned pew, where at my side the Orthodox priest repeated the words *club foot* while pumping his shiny black shoe, I recalled Sparta, and the mountain where the Greeks discarded infants that had been born deformed.

When I was thirteen, my family toured Greece. Using a relative's house in Athens as our base, we visited historical sites in the Peloponnesian and Attic peninsulas, among them Sparta's tallest mountain, Taygetus. We drove together up the slopes of Mount Taygetus and stood on the spot where, I'd learned in school, the ancients had left their infants out to die if they were born sickly or imperfectly formed. From that mountain, every Greek-school student learns, children whose bodies did not match the Spartans' ideals of strength and health were tossed. This was not taught as a legend, like Odysseus's journey or the stories of the gods, but as history. None of my history books questioned this story.

I remember standing on the mountain top, firs and pines all around, looking at the gray stone on which my body would have been broken had I been born earlier, and imperfect. I felt lucky to have a body that was properly formed. I was safe.

My maternal grandmother was Spartan. Recalling the mountain after visiting the priest, I imagined that if I had been born two thousand years earlier, and my *deformity* had been visible at birth, I too would have been taken to the mountain by the parents that had given me life and left on its glistening limestone for my flesh to feed jackals and hovering birds of prey. Many accounts suggest that parents felt pain when they exposed their infants, but not remorse. The death was difficult, but necessary: a brutal sacrifice made in the name of the nation—for the strength and the purity of the Spartan tribe.

And the priest's message was not a new one, either. It was the first time I made my sexual desire explicit during confession, yes. Still, since I'd first apprehended a whisper of the erotic pull, I had received notice of myself as unacceptable, impermissible—exactly what the church hymns and prayers referred to in phrases like "dark pleasures of the night," "impulses of passion," and "turbulence of our flesh." I had felt the impact, and incurred imperceptible, persistent, devastating damage. What was new was that it was said out loud, directly to me. For years I had been told implicitly that my very self, as it was constituted, was a problem, a perversion, and that my bodily integrity was at the mercy of a culture that required its members to conform. The message often arrived without words. Those naked Greek sculptures, once brightly painted, had not simply faded over time. Restoration projects chose to ignore the sculptures' original color, so the whiteness of once-concealed marble could proclaim the clean restraint of virtue, the containment of our animal nature, and the reining in of all things abject and repulsive, including homosexual sex.

When my priest stated this old, unspoken message out loud, something in me cracked open. The sensation was not unlike the feeling of falling uncushioned into a rocky crevasse.

The appearance of videos and online reports on my Missouri computer screen slows, eventually, as the parade in Cyprus comes to an end. No one has been hurt. I search obsessively for more videos of the religious banner-bearing men. I want to watch even though it hurts. I later ask myself what drove this compulsive watching, over and over, and why it felt good. I realize that it felt good to have proof that all these years I've feared a hatred that was real. That this is what they do. This is what they would have done if I had shown them who I am.

Behind the closed police line, another man who wants to get past it to the pride parade holds a stick ripped from his banner, the tatters of the word-bearing cloth fluttering in the wind. He raises it high in the air so that the blow will crash with great force onto the helmet of a policeman. Instead, his blow hits the cassocked shoulder of a running monk raising his arms up to prevent more violence. The monk walks with his hands outstretched and begs the Christians to stop hitting the police, but men with sticks keep charging past him. It is too late. Their official decrees and their sermons about the threat posed by gays and their supporters have already been taken to heart.

While I wait for more videos and images to come from Cyprus, I tune into an American tribute to James Baldwin, honoring the writer's ninetieth birthday. During a discussion of Baldwin's queerness, someone challenges the panelists: "Would you die for the word *queer*?"

Are you willing to die—or would you lie?

When I was a kid, my mother read me the lives of the saints as examples of how to live. Martyrdom was a calling for which I should have been, as a Christian child, diligently preparing. The only stories I remember are one of a nun, Anastasia Logacheva, who sat naked on an anthill for Christ, and another of St. Christina, whose breasts spouted milk when her anti-Christian father had soldiers raise their swords and slice off her nipples. My mother told me I'd have to risk everything for God. To be safe in eternity, you have to be ready to die.

Soon, Cyprus has gone to sleep, there is nothing more to watch on my computer, and I go for a run in the humid Missouri heat. I think of my friend the poet Carolyn Forché, who told me about the talks for James Baldwin's ninetieth birthday, and who has always insisted that one person, one person's art, can change the world a little bit. She went to El Salvador when war was brewing to bring back the truth in her poems. The year we met, I explained that I was trying to decide whether to give up my Orthodox faith or renounce my love of women and remain celibate, because there aren't any people who are both Orthodox and gay.

"Then you'll have to be the first," she said.

I'm still running in Missouri, but I'm thinking of my village in Cyprus, where I ran on lonely roads cut into the mountain forests as protection against wildfires. I felt like that lonely running kept me alive. One evening all those years ago, a pop song called to me from the radio. It went something like, "Why don't you believe that I love you? Why won't you come back?" And I, a teenager, believed it was God speaking through the pop song, because he had noticed a hesitation after a year or more of passionate, deep, and ecstatic prayer. I apologized to the pop singer (or Christ) and said I would come back. I wasn't yet aware, then, of my homosexual desire, but I had been feeling the resentment the church's rejection of that desire had produced.

Twenty years later, running on a Missouri trail, I feel it again, someone asking: "Why won't you come back?" I respond to God with a condition: you'll have to take me as I am. The girl I used to be, the girl willing to pretend she doesn't fall in love with other girls, she's gone. This is who I have become: a woman who sees the beauty of women as the brightest of all beauties. I can't love a God who doesn't love me this way.

I head back to the house, feeling like maybe that conversation changed something. It's getting so dark I can hardly see, but it is still hot, so hot I feel different in my body, different about my body. The endorphin ecstasy that takes me over while I stretch brings with it a new way of seeing. I see that there isn't love without body, that there isn't person without body, that this soul I used to associate with love isn't real without the reality of bodies, of desire. I wasn't just scared of being gay—I was scared of the body that responded to women's beauty in ways my mind could not control.

When my sweaty self turns on my computer, I find that Erika has posted an image of the demonstration to Facebook, writing, "For Joanna Eleftheríou and all others who could not be here." For a minute, two minutes, I want to take down my name. I imagine my Cypriot neighbors shouting that I, a shameful, deviant, perverted lesbian, don't deserve to be called Greek anymore—I have brought shame upon my parents, and must not be allowed into Cyprus, not even to visit my father's grave.

I leave my name up. I turn off the computer, and go to sleep, changed.

Two months after the parade, I am in Cyprus. No one has blocked my entry into my village as I'd feared. No one even mentions the parade. Yet Cyprus feels different to me. Erika and I go to a new bar named Sousámi, where men hold hands with their boyfriends and women refer to their exes as "she." I meet graduate students, academics, and writers, many my own age and gay. I speak Greek to gay people for the first time and for the first time discuss queerness in Greek. We introduce ourselves, stating our names and occupations or fields of interest. They ask me where I am from. This question has always been a difficult one for me to answer, as all simple answers skew the truth. So I say, "Pou Néan Yórki ch' Asgátan." "From New York and Asgáta." Everyone laughs at the wide gap between the places of origin that I claim, New York City being New York City, and Asgáta being a tiny backward town of four hundred folk.

The next morning, I ask Erika if it sounded pretentious, attention-seeking, or too flip, to claim two places.

"No," she explains, "you answered exactly where you are from." She is right. Those are the birthplaces of my two parents, as well as the only places in the world where I have lived for longer than five years.

And so, it seems, just like that, the gay bar revealed to me a way to answer the question that has plagued me: "Where are you from?" I was born in New York and I own property in Cyprus. I have two driver's licenses and two passports. I'm *from* both.

Several days in advance of my return from Cyprus to Missouri, I dedicate an entire morning to seeking gifts. With my American friends in mind, I choose handicrafts and shop for religious icons in a shop owned by the church. As I walk around the store, I remember the Cyprus Pride pin on my backpack. When Erika fixed it there last month, we were travelling together in Greece, where I know no one, and I didn't care. No one there could hurt me. Now, I turn my bag around and clutch it in a way that keeps the Pride pin hidden. The entire island of Cyprus has fewer people than greater St. Louis does, and it feels like everyone is my relative. The clerks at this religious store wear the rosaries, black garb, and long beards of the men in the Pan-Cypriot Christian Orthodox Movement. I continue to clutch my backpack to hide the pin while I get my money for two icons. Only once I am almost out the door do I risk being mocked—and I swing my backpack onto my back for all to see.

I confess this failure of courage to a friend months later because I am still ashamed of my faint-heartedness. My just-when-it's-convenient activism seems as hypocritical as my enjoyment of the freedoms I did not help attain. The friend asks if I absolutely have to be a martyr all the time. We recently spent a morning at the LGBTQ+ table during Parents' Weekend at our university, passing out supportive pamphlets for students whose families had renounced them when their queerness was revealed. My friend warns me against fantasies of martyrdom and heroism and asks why I can't be satisfied with what is actually within my power to do. My cousin's death of AIDS at thirty-eight makes me feel survivor's guilt. But by the time I turn thirty-eight myself, I have marched in two Cyprus Prides and one in Thessaloníki, with students of mine in tow. In 2017, a major Cypriot news source reports on that year's Pride and posts to its home page a photograph that includes me, and I am not afraid. These are little risks—risks I can take without being paralyzed by fear and without damaging myself irrevocably—and I realize that perhaps it is enough.

Though I meet others after I start to come out, I am, indeed, the first gay Orthodox woman I know. But that doesn't mean becoming some lone hero, some desert-dwelling martyr, fighting alone. Maybe this is what marches are for. For courting risk together. For overcoming danger together. For not being alone.

—

Inheritance Law

—

Yet the question of fidelity and responsibility remains.
 —Pascale-Anne Brault and Michael Naas
 on Jacques Derrida's *A Work of Mourning*

Έπρεπεν, κανονικά, όταν πέθανε ο Αντρέας, η διαθήκη να εκτελεσθεί.
According to the rules, when Andréas died, the will should have been executed.

 —Antónis Salahóris, Esquire

Hearing my father's death referred to by his lawyer not only in the past tense, but also in a subordinate clause, brought the finality of his death into a new focus. Once itself the chief matter at hand, and the main clause of all our sentences, the death had now become a donnée, something to take for granted and move on. It was a significant event among many other significant events. Death had become a marker of time. When my father died; before my father died; after my father died. After my father *had* died. More than anything else, the grammatical shifts signaled to me that the period for mourning my father had come to a final close.

New problems now eclipsed the immediate problem of

death. Namely, the problems of inheritance, of property. Antónis Salahóris is a specialist in property law, and his job is to help us make sure land is properly transferred to the next generation. For the first few years we lived in Cyprus, my father mentioned him constantly, always by his surname, so that I didn't find out his first name until years later, when my turn came to seek Antónis Salahóris's help. One of the first new Greek words I learned after moving to Cyprus was *htimatológio* (κτηματολόγιο), Land Registry, because when my father arrived on the island of his birth, he began to regularly pay it a visit. Also, I learned the word for *property*, which, when it's used in the sense of an estate or inheritance, is *periousía*. The word's root is *ousía*, which means *essence*. *Real* estate. Upon his return from Pittsburgh, my grandfather Cóstas married the only daughter of an Asgáta landowner, Agáthi, and quickly began to build on her substantial dowry. He bought plot upon plot of village land. Although Cóstas Eleftheríou liked his nickname, "The American," his land investments tied him to the small Cypriot village where from a rooftop he could look upon the broad expanse of what he owned. There's a word for property in the sense of *what I own* in Greek; it is *idioktisía*, and it does indeed share a root with the English word idiot because it connotes *private* property. But like the word *estate*, periousía is used more often to connote ownership that is in a way communal, since land is used by families together; periousía is something that produces status and a connection amongst kin.

I called Salahóris's office in late July 2014, some two years after my father's death, because my family wanted to ensure that all the work my father had started—all the property gathering—would be completed by those of us who were still alive. My father had not bought much land in Cyprus, not after the first purchase, in his youth, of a piece in the

Troodos mountains. Instead, he had salvaged it. He safe-guarded family inheritances from being repossessed by the government, since that's what would have happened after the land had remained the property of dead ancestors for too many long, non-tax-paying (because dead) generations.

>>·<<

Shortly before my father entered Limassol General Hospital for what would prove to be the last time, I scrawled three of his words—*grandson of Cashanós*—in an upward slant across the whiteboard in my Missouri kitchen. During the years I lived in that apartment, that whiteboard often bore the questions that arose during my writing week. It was easy to locate them there when my parents made their weekly phone call, and to scribble onto it their answers. As a result of this practice, during the five weeks of my father's last hospital stay, my whiteboard became a kind of prayer list, remembering the ailing to God, along with my departed great-grandfather, in the hasty grayish streaks of a black dry-erase marker nearing its end.

I had been writing, that March of 2012, about my father's childhood, and in early March I had asked him how it was that a small boy found the *kouráyo* (κουράγιο; will, resolve, peace of mind, stamina) to dig the long ditches used to irrigate a vegetable patch. "*Ímoun o ángonas tou Kashanoú!*" ("Ήμουν ο άγγονας του Κασιανού!") he answered me in a voice bewildered by the question. "I was the grandson of Cashanós!" He told me that the *periousía* of this grandfather had to be protected, *na min hatheí* (να μην χαθεί), that it not be lost or go to ruin.

The words *grandson of Cashanós* remained on the whiteboard for many weeks, and remained there still during the first hours he was gone. It was St. George's day—Monday, April 23—at least in Cyprus. In Missouri, it was still the evening of Sunday, April 22. When midnight passed, when Sunday turned into Monday, I wiped the words away. In their place I wrote notes to my subletter: the landlord's phone number, trash and recycling days, the internet password, and my neighbors' names.

Back in Asgáta, a year after my father's death, I sit down at the Lemoniá restaurant, and men who knew my father speak to me. The men, fellow villagers, each of whom I saw almost daily during my Asgáta years, have never spoken to me before. I was, to them, something of a ghost, running by their fields as they stood watering the potato plants, standing behind them in church, buying my candle and nodding to them as they stood where parish council members stood, waving to them when we crossed paths in our respective pickup trucks. I spent a total of eight winters in the village, and more summers, between the ages of fourteen and twenty-six. These men have watched me grow. When I sit among them now, and remind them who I am, they make a motion with both arms, elbows at right angles, back and forth, to confirm that they remember me. To them, I am the girl who would take to the hills and run.

I am the daughter of the *Tsoliás*. At this table, the men don't know and don't ask for my name. My father acquired this nickname when, as an elementary school student in the 1940s, he played the role of a soldier in the Greek Revolution. He wore the gold and velvet vest, the flaring white ruffle skirt, the woolen tights and pointed pom-pom shoes of the *tsoliá*. (In spite of this nickname's congruity with his eventual vocation as a history teacher, he didn't like it.) The village men say they are glad I made it back from America to Asgáta and I say, "Yes, yes, it's good to be back." I like the way it feels when these men tell me I belong to a place where my forefathers lived for centuries. In order to enjoy this taste of connection to the land and to my father, I push to the back of my mind the classist problem of my emotion as well as the fact of my own gender. I ignore the oppression women endured in this village as my grandfather built his estate and permit myself to savor, for a bit, the prestige and privilege that it's now possible for me to access by identifying with my father and his father before him.

The men talk to me about my father's grandfather. The structure where we sit once belonged to him. While my father was a boy growing up during the Second World War, the building served as a grocery store and coffee shop with my great-grandparents' house behind it. My youngest aunt and namesake of Cashanós's wife, Myriánthe, used to spend most nights here, away from the crowd of older siblings she shared her own house with. My father, before he died, had entered the Lemoniá while renovation was still underway. The new owners include a friend of mine from our high school days who had become a civil engineer, and she'd asked my father to look around and assess the faithfulness of the renewal. Andréas haltingly made it up the two steps into the dusty, empty shop and showed me where the counters once were, and where his grandparents' bedrooms had been, behind the store itself. He confirmed that the place looked just like it had in the forties, and I conveyed this fact to the new owners. The renovation was sponsored in part by a European Union program for renovations that made new buildings match old ones. I told my friend that Andréas had pointed out only one window that, as he recalled, had been much higher up and harder for him (when he was a boy) to reach.

As the men and I continue to talk about my great-grand-father Cashanós, seated at the Lemoniá which once belonged to him, nibbling on appetizers, a man named Agathocles waves his arms toward the mountains in the south. All that land belonged to Cashanós, too, he tells me. Agathocles is a little older than my father and tells me that he plowed that land himself for my family with a *zefkári*, a pair of mules, when he was young. Sometimes, they used oxen.

Somehow, the discussion moves on from ploughing with mules and oxen to the digging of the *avláki*, or irrigation ditch. I tell them the story of my father, the last words of his that I transcribed. Phítos (short for Neóphytos, think *neophyte*), who looks about ten years older than me, says that he too worked to clear the system of ditches each year when he was a child. Children and teenagers, Phítos explains, were responsible only for the work of maintaining the ditches, which wasn't as arduous as the first opening of the ditch. That job had to be done by a grown man.

As night falls, the blue neon cross on top of Saint Peter and Paul lights up. We engage in dinner-table philosophiz-ing, agree on the importance of savoring the here and now, living simply, being thankful for what we have. By this time another man has joined the *paréa*, so that when I say, "My goal is to recognize, right now, how good it is to make *paréa* with Christákis, and Dína and Phítos," they supply his name—he, too, is another Neóphytos, probably a cousin.

"That is what I always wanted," I tell the part-time farmers, hiding as best I can the awkwardness I feel about baring my soul to almost-strangers. Because this is a pro-foundly personal desire I'm revealing to these men I barely know: I want to learn to rejoice in the place where I am, the company I *have*, rather than long for some future happiness or, like my father, for a place I've left behind. Staking a claim to this difference between my father and myself feels like an infidelity, like apostasy, as if there were some law that obliges us to continue in the suffering of our departed fathers.

Happiness, for the mourner, feels like a betrayal.

The next day, I'm seated at a table with a woman named Erasmía. I used to see her often when I lived in Asgáta because she farmed the land near my house. "Land," Erasmía tells me, "is all you need to survive." I often bought bags of cucumbers and tomatoes from her. Their quality was high and the cost low. "If you have land, you won't starve," she says. Still, she tells me eagerly that her oldest son is learning a trade. He is apprenticed to a man who makes signs.

The landowner Cashanós died in 1929, ten years before my father's birth. It is not, therefore, a sense of reverence or affection for the man that underlies my father's statement that he dug ditches in the sun because he was the grandson of Cashanós. It must have something to do with legacy. It's the family name. An estate built over time is an inheritance for everyone, access to security and status for generations. Is it not the financial security of land so much as a sense of importance, of belonging, I wonder—the same longing for a connection to a piece of land that makes me listen so eagerly to the old men reminiscing about my great-grandfather and his mule-tilled fields? And do my emotions prove that I subscribe to this classist source of joy, this access to power that is either capitalist or feudal?

My father's two older sisters, Galátia and Faní, received the bulk of their parents' land, as well as linen, furniture, and cash as their dowries. In addition, a lot of land had been in my great-grandmother Myriánthe's name when we arrived. Most of that she left explicitly to her namesake, my father's youngest sister, in an oral promise if not on paper. After they had been in America for decades, all three sisters sold off what they owned, with my father facilitating the deals. For property that the aunts had in their name, my father just had to facilitate the sale. For property that was left to them in a will, or worse, in an oral promise, my father had to first work on getting a title deed in the sister's name. Then he could make a sale. And then there was the property for which there was neither a will nor a promise. For that, he gathered signatures to ensure that all the potential heirs of his dead progenitors' land gave him, Andréas, the authority to sell the land and distribute the money. Almost none of my relatives in Australia or America wanted to keep any Cypriot land in their name. I heard the Cypriot word for title deed, *kochâni*, very often in those days.

When a decent amount of time had passed after my father's death, one of his friends (someone who had assisted my father in his *kochâni*-getting efforts) told me that there was an open case regarding a large piece of land worth half a million euros. I knew better than to believe this number. I was, after all, at the time failing to find a buyer for my parents' house, which was listed for less than half that, and situated on property far closer to the city, with a paved sidewalk, an asphalt road, and water and electricity. And was, well, a house, not a tract of wilderness. I repeated the claim nonetheless, foolishly, to my siblings, who in their turn urged me to pursue the case and procure our half a million. Because I was the one who kept on going back to Cyprus, this became my responsibility.

And so, a year after my father died and a year before I

eventually called the property lawyer Salahóris, I went to the Land Registry and found that there was indeed a piece of land that still belonged to my father's paternal grandfather, Elefthérios Panayí. This great-grandfather is also my cousin Dina's grandfather. Together, we counted forty-one potential heirs to this Elefthérios. Nevertheless, she too urged me to pursue the case.

In the summer of 2014, I finally get our property lawyer Salahóris on the phone. He speaks to me more frankly than I expect—as if he knows me, as if we are family. Salahóris explains to me about the land that doesn't yet have a *kocháni* and pauses to say *title deed* in proper Greek (*títlos idioktisías*) and in English too. I assure him that like the word for *land registry*, *xtimatológion*, the Cypriot word for title deed, is very familiar to me.

Salahóris says he will look into the case. My siblings and I hesitated to call him because we worried the lawyer might claim our father owed him money, but he mentions no debt. Instead, Salahóris just seems interested, earnestly, in getting all property still registered to dead people into the hands of the living. When I ask him how much the property is really worth, Salahóris says it's about fifteen thousand euros probably. I ask, then, if *worth* translates into *will actually be sold for.*

He replies, "Just between *us*, no." He admits that he hasn't heard of any piece of land like that (large, in the middle of nowhere, with no decent roads, no water, and no electricity) being sold in the last three years. At all.

Salahóris goes on, "*I axía tou eínai mithén.*" ("Just between *us*, to be honest, its real worth is zero." "Η αξία

του είναι μηδέν.") Salahóris tells me about the day he, my
father, and the village mayor at the time tried to visit that
very property, the one still owned by my great-grandfather
Elefthérios. Their jeep got stuck in a ditch, the dirt road was
so bad, and they had to call someone with a truck and winch
to come pull them out.

Salahóris is in the mood to talk, it seems, even though
he's never met me. "What," he asked rhetorically, "could you
possibly grow on such property?" No water, no crops. He
speculated that one could plant olive trees, which can survive
with only rain after the second or third year. But even people
with mature olive trees already growing on their property
aren't harvesting their olives, because selling olive oil returns
less than what they spend on watering the young trees and
transporting the olives to the olive press.

Salahóris is forthcoming about my father's adventures
with the family's land. All I know comes from overhearing
my father's accounts of court battles, signatures, and petitions. Salahóris explains that to sell the land, my father
couldn't simply have become the owner of it, even if it was
nearly worthless, because in spite of the land's near-worth-
lessness, his brother in Australia had refused to sign papers
ceding it to my father. Instead, he had become owner of
much of his parents' and grandparents' land through the law
of adverse possession. The law of adverse possession required
my father to prove that he had been taking care of the land—
tilling it, paying taxes on it—for a substantial number of
years. After proving he'd done that, my father had obtained
rights to the land without his brother's consent. Salahóris
doesn't think we can make a case for me to inherit any of the
remaining land, however. I agree that I can't make a claim to
have been caring for the land when I don't even know where
it is. Even though the bar is pretty low for adverse possession

of arid land—claiming to have been using land that is essentially useless—I simply can't imagine it. I can't even pretend that I farm.

After he's explained why the property left in Eleorthérios's name is worthless, Salahóris starts, unprompted, to tell me how much my father suffered as he worked to gather signatures so that the property belonging to long-dead grandparents could be transferred to the living. The oldest brother had died young; the three sisters were content to sign over their property rights to my father with no certainty of compensation. But the middle brother Christóphoros didn't trust his little brother, even if Andreas promised to pay him his share.

"Christóphoros attacked him viciously," Salahóris laments, "as if your father were a criminal rather than a man just trying to do the right thing." Salahóris emphasizes that saving the family estate wasn't merely an effort to get some money to make us a little more secure. Rather, making sure that the land was titled and sold was the right thing to do because, first, it honored the sacrifices made by those who worked to acquire the property. And second, selling off family land is good for the community, since it means it can be transferred to someone who will use it. If my father hadn't done anything about the land owned by his dead parents and grandparents, it would have remained there, unusable, for years and years. Because so many Greeks and Cypriots emigrated, and their heirs live in different countries all over the world, abandoned properties riddle the landscape.

"You know what else?" Salahóris asks me. "When Andréas did get his brother's signature for certain properties, instead of giving him one-fifth of the money for which the land was sold, i.e. his share, your father gave him *four*-fifths. Andréas wanted to do the right thing. He wanted to appease his siblings, not hear them cursing him."

What is eerie about this portrait of my father as being so good, working at thankless tasks on principle, rather than for the money, is that this is the picture he painted of himself but no one really believed. And by no one, I suppose I mean myself, and maybe my siblings. Andréas was given to exaggeration, and what was worse, he was of the penny-wise sort, maddeningly careful with small sums of money but not so good with big decisions. For example, he would go to three different supermarkets on the same day to save a few nickels on groceries, but he sold our house in Queens at bottom market because of the urge to *go home* to Cyprus and one year's worth of frustrations renting it out. And so it was easy to feel uncertain about how he managed the finances of the family land. Now, Salahóris has faced me with a portrait that exactly matches my father's *own* self-portrait, the one I have not fully believed. It is the kind of thing that should gratify but doesn't because it comes too late.

Before he hangs up, Salahóris asks me to call him a second time before I leave Cyprus, to see if he's made any headway on the cases. I procrastinate, though. I return to America, still saying to myself that I'll call. I don't get the memorial ordered or make any headway on finding a buyer for the Parekklishá house this year, either. None of the things I'm supposed to do in the wake of my father's death seem to get done.

>>·<<

While the supposedly half-a-million-euro piece of land in the middle of nowhere can wait, as can the stone memorial to replace the wooden cross at my father's gravesite, what is urgent is the house. It must be rented out or sold.

My mother left Cyprus (forever, she says) six months after her husband was gone. By October 2012, she signed a rental agreement with a Russian welder, sold the family car, said final goodbyes to the few friends she'd made, and boarded a plane to New York. It unsettles people when she says, responding to their "When will you go back to Cyprus?" questions, that "Fifteen years was enough—I did my duty." It is customary to pay lip service, at least, to a longing for the homeland.

In March 2013, the Cypriot banking system collapses. It's a very complicated story, but Cyprus is essentially deemed too small to save. The largest bank in the nation ceases to exist; our welder disappears overnight. Once the house is empty, I begin to worry about squatters, about the place falling into disrepair while I get on with my American job hunt, my American life. Neglect of the house wouldn't just cause my family to lose our only asset or be bad karma. It would be an affront to my father, a failure to care for what mattered to him. The house remains empty until I return, alone, to Cyprus.

The Parekklishá house management falls to me. My brother works a nine-to-five job in New York all year. My sister never lived in Cyprus, whereas I lived there for most of my youth. I have no teaching responsibilities in the US during the summer, and my job with Writing Workshops in Greece pays for me to get to Greece, which is a short, cheap flight from Cyprus.

Because he works in Manhattan, my brother has taken full responsibility for the inheritance on my mother's side. She has come into half of a Manhattan co-op, on the Upper East Side, bought for our grandmother by her Wharton-educated second husband half a century ago. When our grandmother Joanna dies at home in 2014, my brother quickly begins cleaning the apartment. He puts it on the market. Our lives are so different, so separate, normally, that this work on our inheritance puts me into better touch with my brother and sister. The law of inheritance reminds us of our connection and further binds us together. Our mother reminds us to communicate and cooperate, so that what happened between our father and his brother doesn't happen to us.

It is a thankless task, preparing a house for the market, and there's an embarrassment to it—the reason the house can't be inhabited by its owners, my father's unwillingness (or inability) to accept the proximity of his impending death along with my mother's inability (or unwillingness) to live in Cyprus alone. I wax apologetic when I show prospective real estate agents this house that I told my father not to buy. I feel that our house ought to be in better shape. But I am powerless to address its problems. The garden, for instance, is overgrown with weeds.

Furthermore, there is the general humiliation of house-selling, one's ability to clean and maintain a house on display along with the walls behind which one has conducted the most private of one's affairs. These, after all, are the walls behind which my father confronted the inexorable deepening of his frail body's condition and the first drops of blood that signaled the end. I should feel thankful that my father died without enormous suffering and humiliation, and without giving up his only asset. I know that if the complication with his hernia had occurred in New York, and he had spent five weeks in the hospital there, he may have joined so many lower-middle-class Americans whose deathbeds cost them their very last asset. I should be grateful that I have the house, and that I have the time to take care of it, but instead

I just feel stress, and I resent this house that I told him not to buy, and this task of caring for a building that I never loved.

On top of all that, I cut the most bizarre figure as a home-owner. I'm old enough, certainly, in my mid-thirties. But I am a graduate student, in the humanities no less, and I dress like one. The concept feels farcical, almost: penniless me, taking the bus in my faded skirt, Walmart tank top, and Old Navy flip-flops to sign a contract entitling my family to a year's rent. The rent, five hundred euros a month, is money I will count on to help me scrape by, pay for groceries and car insurance and dentist's visits.

In July 2014, I meet our new tenants Tanya and Yorgos for the first time. I take the bus to Tanya's work, and she drives me up out of the city to the house in Parekklishá. It's a ten-minute drive. I'm a bit taken aback by Tanya's easy good looks, the way her graying white T-shirt and the impossibly blonde hair escaping her ponytail seem only to add to the effect of her features. She has the glow of one whose skin has seen much more sunlight than their ancestors' did. Yorgos, when I meet him up at the house, has the same skin as me. To call it olive is a cliché, but an accurate one. We are actually the color of olives, the light brown ones, the ones with the faintest hint of green.

The house looks beautiful. The kitsch decorations that decorated the walls when my parents bought the house have been replaced with tasteful ones, so that even the furniture, which hasn't changed, looks better. The many patios are all spotless, and the bright new paint job impresses me. It's the paint, I think, though it might be the overall aesthetic success of the house, that makes it look much better than when it was inhabited by its owners.

This is the law of inheritance: after you, someone else does what they like with what you built, and sometimes what they do is better. I ask them how they managed with the garden, if they brought a professional gardener.

"How you do this?" I ask in my pidgin English. "I fill seven bags, and still I do nothing, I make it even worse than before," I explain, remembering how I didn't know what to do with the clippings, how I threw some weeds into nearby fields and dragged branches down the street to the dumpster, unclear about what was the most ecological way to get rid of green wood. Someone told me much later I should have hired a skip.

They say no. It took them a whole week, though, the two of them getting scratched up as in battle, working all day.

"We fill seventeen," Tanya laughs. When English is the speaker's third or fourth language, everything happens in present tense.

When Yorgos leaves, I mention to Tanya that he seems to be a very good man. I am making conversation and also fishing—the tyranny of business—for clues about their marriage. They will be our tenants only as long—I am sure— as they are one another's spouse. As Tanya talks, I wonder if I've ever met anyone this good-natured. I feel opened up by her, and I understand where her success as a salesperson comes from—this goodwill, this happiness in her presence, this trust.

After more than an hour, I am thanking Tanya (and she is thanking me), and I get ready to return to my friend Erika's, where I am staying.

"How will you go?" Tanya asks.

I point toward the bus stop, then flip open my wallet to

show my bus pass. "By bus," I say. "I bought a pass and I am going up and down, to shops, to library—my friend she lives on the sea." Tanya insists on driving me down to Erika's.

Even though I stay with friends rather than up at the house, I do have to concede that it feels good to tell people that I own (part of) a house. It gives me a stake in Cyprus, and others seem to respect me more, as someone who has a claim to the place. I don't have property of my own, since I have never earned a salary that exceeded my expenses. I have never been able to save money for the acquisition of a *periousía* (property). All the same, periousía has come to me, because although I have not had the luck or the diligence required for such acquisitions, others did, then died and left it to me. For my siblings and me, our periousía—our estate—depends wholly on the luck—the gift—the fate—*the law*—of inheritance. Not only the house we asked my father not to buy, but also land, land still owned, officially, by Eleuthérios Panayi.

When I deplaned at Odysseus Elytis airport in the capital of Lésbos one year, I told the young man waiting for the city bus with me that as a writer, I wanted to visit the places where favorite writers were born and which they had described. I told him that Stratis Myrivílis's *The Mermaid Madonna* was my favorite novel, and that in its honor I was making a pilgrimage to the chapel of Prophet Elias in Skala Sykamia, on the northern coast. I did not share that I'd had five days between a conference in Iceland and my job in Greece, and that when I wondered what to do during that time, I decided that the best way to spend it was on a journey to the Sapphic mecca, and birthplace of Sappho herself. *The Mermaid Madonna* pilgrimage had come as an afterthought.

On the night before my flight to Lésbos, I went for a jog along the White Tower promenade, en route to a particular Thessaloníki bakery from which I was to purchase a white-chocolate-covered sweet bread (*tsoureki* tastes a lot like challah) for the grandmother of a cousin of mine. Well, a cousin-in-law of sorts. When this relative heard of my plans to visit Eressós, the birthplace of the poet Sappho, she told me that her grandmother lived there, and I should stay in one of the rooms she rented, and could I please bring her one of these breads as a surprise?

On the hot, bumpy bus ride from Mytilene to Eressós, I told everyone who asked (and people asked) that I'd chosen the town because I had relatives there, and I hoped for a discount on a room. Although I'd been out to my friends and colleagues in America for years, I was still nervous in Greece and didn't want to mention Sappho. But what I was really after was a peep into a different kind of inheritance than land. I felt that all my reading of Greece had been of writers who were men, and I had aligned my longing with theirs, and in them I could no longer see myself. Sappho had been written out of my education, and reading her fragments as an adult, alone in my midwestern apartment, hadn't much helped. I imagined that by standing where she stood, Sappho might become real to me, and I might feel that I belonged to a lineage of Greek women who saw the beauty of women, and who named their desire.

In more practical terms, I also hoped that if the number of lesbians in a small place reached a critical mass, I might receive the attention of a woman. I had been hit on by men all my life and felt attraction to not a single one. After a very slow struggle against a crushingly homophobic world, at thirty-eight I still hadn't figured out how to signal to women that I was interested. What I'd read about Sappho's birthplace (that gay women from all over Europe vacationed there) made me hope that the environment would work sort of like training wheels for my baby gay self. It did not—I'll get that out of the way—and my romantic résumé remained painfully short.

All my life I followed the rules of my religion and culture, and for many years did not speak about love. Now, I have words for my desire. I call myself gay because I've been undone over and over by the beauty of a woman, years of successive, secret crushes, girl after girl, since the first erotic thrill. But my lesbianism remains an abstraction when I talk and write about it. I still don't feel comfortable enough to vocalize desire, let alone get very far past a first date.

And so in late May, 2017, I was eager to change that and I spent my days in Sappho's birthplace walking around. I found an abstract piece of art that looked a little like a woman, and I guessed that was probably the island's tribute to its famous poet. There was the Sappho Hotel, owned by my cousin-in-law's aunt, and a Sappho Travel Agency. I walked the streets all day because it was early June and not yet very hot, and once a man asked me about the kinesio tape on my knees. I explained how it kept my patella from sliding out of place and inflaming my knee, and somehow we got to talking about Sappho. "They have turned her into a dishrag!" he complained, which if I understand correctly was a complaint about the commercial use of the poetic inheritance. Instead of explaining that I'd seen worse, I asked to buy a bag of fruit from his pickup truck and said goodbye.

Later, I sat down with a notebook and ordered a drink at a bar where a few couples (all women) were already seated.

A woman about my height, but very well-dressed, with tall heels and big curly hair, came over and struck up a conversation. Her name was Ioánna, same as mine, and before I knew it she was urging me to travel back to the island in September for the International Women's Festival, which she directs, and which had sparked my hopes about finding a lesbian oasis—I hoped the effects of a September lesbian festival might spill over into June. I explained that, unless I got a sabbatical, I couldn't leave my teaching job for a week, and this seemed to be a silly excuse to her. I enjoyed the argument, because I enjoyed the attention, and I enjoyed thinking, "Here I am, here I am, in Lésbos, among the lesbians."

On my last day, I passed for the dozenth time a small lot near the seaside, a rectangular heap of rubble with a small blue sign in the middle that said, "Property of the heirs of K. Kazazi." I raised my smartphone to snap a photo, and as I was doing so, an attractive woman some years older than me appeared in the road and asked why I was taking a photo. I got embarrassed and flustered. I felt like a voyeur, someone looking at pain porn. I had guessed that the sign represented a situation like some of the problems my father had run into while settling the estates of his grandparents. I told her so and apologized for turning her problem into a spectacle. The woman brushed off my apology and invited me to her house. She unlocked a door that opened into a garden, then disappeared into the kitchen while I waited for her in the old-style courtyard and looked around at her gardenias and jasmine. When she came out with two Greek coffees and glasses of water, she confirmed that there was indeed a dispute about the ownership, and she'd been arguing with her cousins for decades. She told me her name was Andromache, just like the Trojan wife, and we talked for several hours about family and love.

I told Andromache that I was a lesbian, out to everyone but my mother, and she was accepting and warm, and told me details of a legal dispute that I had heard about on the news. In 2008, a few male Lesbians (in the sense that they were residents of Lésbos) had brought a lawsuit to try to ban the use of the word *lesbian* to mean homosexual woman, and as a means of comedic catharsis I had watched with my friends a video which showed a deep-voiced, mustached old Greek man waving his cane in the air and yelling, "I am a Lesbian! I am the real Lesbian! They have sullied my name!" The NPR report had given the name of the man as Dimitris Lámbrou and used the headline "Lésbos Resident Wants Name Back from Lesbians." I knew nothing more.

Andromache told me what the news had left out: the shop owners of Lésbos had rallied together to shut Lámbrou up. The businessmen cared more about the lesbians' willingness and ability to pay—for hotel rooms, taxis, souvenirs, rental cars, fancy meals, and alcohol—than about their sex lives. I didn't want to leave Andromache's house, and secretly I wished that I could stay there with her.

Andromache held me for a long time when I got up to leave and slipped a notebook page with her email address into my hand, asking me to send her my writing (in Greek or French! No English!). I didn't find a connection with Greek women writers on that trip to Greece; I found no sapphic foremother. But I found Andromache. And that was something.

Six years after my father's death, the house in Parekklishá was sold at last. The land that still belongs to Elefthérios Panayi is all but forgotten. I have a better job than I did before, my brother is married, and we're both thinking about acquiring

property in America. If we manage, it will be because generations ago, our people were landowners, and enjoyed the sur-
plus value of their mule-driving, field-ploughing farmhands.

This, then, is the meaning of inheritance law: that a person
has a right to what their parents did, and to the place where
their parents lived. As an American, I buy into the fantasy of
the self-made man, but when I look at my life, I know that
everything I have, I have because of the law of inheritance.
And it is because people have to die that people like me enjoy
what was theirs; it is because the land they made theirs can't
follow them into the afterlife that it goes, by law, to us. Even
and especially as a gay woman, my inheritance as a lesbian
is there (in noncanonical books, in out-of-print books, and
in the archives) for the unearthing. Queer writers and activists have for decades—centuries—now written against the
silence. Thanks to an inheritance—a gift—from them, I tell
my story.

For beyond family inheritance, there is the gift. During
my meetings with property lawyers for the sale of the house,
I learned that Cypriot law caps the amount of property
that can be left to nonrelatives in a will. A person who has
children can leave no more than 50 percent of her property
to nonrelatives upon her death, but before that, she can give
it all away as gifts. Legally bound to me, my blood relatives
make me their heir. There is space beyond inheritance law
for my queer kin, with whom I take stock of my desire and
what it means. As Derrida suggested, "the question of fidelity
and responsibility remains." Both those who leave the earth
and those who remain have a responsibility to the past and
to the future. But what exactly that responsibility is remains
an open question, and we keep on asking.

—

Without Goodbyes

—

I sat on a faded loveseat opposite my mother in her small Brooklyn apartment and listened, in unseasonable May heat, as she announced that the week before, three decades after her father's death, she'd learned that he had not fled Turkey in 1920 after all, but five years earlier. He had spent half his childhood in a refugee camp in Greece.

"For seventy years," she said, "I thought they came straight from Constantinoúpoli to New York, when my father was thirteen."

His family had made it only as far as Greece after their first escape. They had stayed there—we will likely never know what city—through to the end of World War I. The memory we had each constructed of Spyros Papadopoulos's flight required revision. Now, the refugee boy who had spoken Greek at home and Turkish at school, who had attended an Orthodox Christian church and helped restock the shelves of his parents' store, had not been twelve, but seven years old when without warning and without goodbyes he had been put onto a ship and taken away from everything he'd ever known. At seven, he would have just begun to play the violin.

"Why," wondered my mother, "did my father never mention that he spent five years in Greece?" During the music

221

lessons or the Greek language instruction he'd given her at home, during long car rides from Brooklyn to their vacation spot in New England or the weeks they spent together on a steamship to Greece, the fact could easily have been disclosed. Instead, my grandfather had spun his narrative this way: he began with his childhood in a city that was at the time still called Constantinople, mentioned a stop in Greece as if it were a brief, steamship layover, moved on to his job as a thirteen-year-old shoeshine boy in Boston, and finished with his studies at the Boston Conservatory.

When I asked my mother what had prompted the overdue revelation, she said she'd seen a World War I film called *The Promise* and had called her cousin to talk about it. In that conversation, the cousin had mentioned that her own father, Thomas, my *Pappoú* Spyros's older brother, had been drafted into the Ottoman military and sent to the eastern Dardanelles to defend the empire. The Allies had invaded, and all Ottoman men had had to fight. Thomas turned eighteen sometime during the ten-month-long Battle of Gallipoli. My aunt had thought my mother knew this part of the family story.

"But," I said as we pondered together the astounding news, "I thought they left so that Uncle Thomas could *escape* the draft."

"Yes, that's what I've thought all my life," my mother said. "But no, he was drafted, fought at Gallipoli, and then when he was injured he ran away. Somehow he got himself onto a ship traveling west. He hid in the ship's toilet." A boy younger than his own seventeen years had found him, and my uncle had begged the boy not to tell. Somehow, Thomas had gotten to the Bosporus's western shore, where his house was, and returned to his family.

With muscular, piano-playing fingers, my mother turned

the pages of a dusty encyclopedia opened to its entry on World War I, and as she scanned it for an explanation of his silence, I said that my grandfather's omission did not strike me as so very strange.

I knew very little about refugees, mostly from novels like *The Mermaid Madonna* and from the film *Polítiki Kouzína* (*Political/Constantinople Cuisine*). In them, Greek children born in Turkey were taunted by the local kids, Greeks who called them *Tourkóspori*, or "of Turkish seed." The children took cues from the grown-ups, who resented the influx of people from the east. These eastern Greeks were different. Their Greek sounded strange and they cooked with exotic spices. Worst of all, they were hungry, and they were desperate for work. I knew that, wherever my grandfather's family had spent those five years, more and more refugees would have joined his family as Turkey's nationalist project proceeded.

This was the end of what I knew about the Greeks who fled the Ottoman Empire as it fell. But I did know something about silence. I had recently done a lot of reading on trauma, and it was because of that reading that, to me, my grandfather's omission made sense. The brain freezes as a kind of protection. A gap would thus be left in the memories of a child whose parents chose suddenly to uproot themselves because if they stayed at home, at least one of their children would die. For if the deserter-son Thomas had been found, he would have been sent to a forced labor camp. No one came out of those alive.

We figured out that my uncle Thomas, a skilled teenage musician and graduate of the same Robert College that the novelist Orhan Pamuk attended, had been one among many thousands of Christians drafted into the Ottoman army after a 1909 law ended centuries of a Muslim-only draft.

And that Uncle Thomas had not dodged that draft by emigrating to America as we'd once believed but had put on an Ottoman uniform and gotten onto an Ottoman ship and fought at the Battle of Gallipoli. And when he had reached his parents' house, a deserter, they had held him close and smuggled him out of the empire so that he wouldn't be sent back to die.

Although I couldn't tell my mother that the reason I'd been reading about trauma was that I'd obtained some new insight regarding my own psychological wounds, incurred in a homophobic world and a family that evinced no willingness to protect a gay daughter, I could tell her what those investigations had taught me: that if a boy had been overwhelmed by terror, and if his caregivers had been themselves too terrified to receive and comfort their child, his brain would have ceased to encode and store. The five years in Greece would have been forgotten.

I did tell my mother this: if the family fled Turkey in the middle of the night with only the shirts on their backs, as she described—if my grandfather left behind him a cosmopolitan, modern city that had been a jewel in the crown of two empires; if he left friends and safety and school for a refugee camp in a rural backwater of a small country bankrupt from the still-recent rebellion of shepherds-turned-militiamen fighting against a global superpower—then of course he told no stories.

"Memories of terror," I thought, "go up in smoke."

Because the revelation of my great-uncle Thomas's desertion gave my mother and me something to investigate together, in those days of May 2017 we managed a few conversations that were a little less strained. Tension had been building between us in recent years, as I'd grown tired of protecting her from knowing the adult that I'd become. Her churchgoing, anxious-to-please, rule-abiding-perfection-ist teenager had become a lesbian as skeptical of capital-ism as she was of her church's claim that one can't practice Orthodox Christianity and same-sex love at the same time.

I believed my mother to possess, by now, the almost-knowledge that so many parents of gay children recall as a lurking shadow. The same almost-knowledge had haunted my own long years of terrified denial, when my friends saw in me the desire I could not, myself, see.

But by my thirty-eighth year, I'd learned to say *I love women*, I'd served as president of queer student organiza-tions and had published poems in lesbian magazines, so that among those who knew anything about me, my mother alone remained ignorant of the slow, inner revolution that in my thirties had changed me. Family history was rare ground on which we could meet, where we could name abuse and persecution while remaining silent about the way we each felt ourselves to be oppressed.

Together, I on the internet and she in libraries and her enormous collection of books, we learned that just before our family's flight, a series of anti-Greek pogroms had occurred in the region around the Dardanelles—here six hundred, there a thousand. When she claimed that this proved the Ottomans had been trying to wipe out the Greeks since Byzantium fell to them in the fifteenth century, I countered with arguments about how when the Ottoman Empire was strong, it was happy to let Greeks and the other *millets* govern themselves. I tried to explain what I had recently learned about the rise of the European nation-state, starting with France and spreading later to Greece and eventually Turkey, with the young Turks imagining a Turkey-for-Turks rising from the Ottoman Empire's impending collapse. Empires, I argued, contained different ethnic groups, but nations only one—this was why they tried to exterminate the Armenians at around the same time, and why Nasser expelled so many Greeks from Egypt later, in the fifties. My mother said she remembered that. She had been in middle school when she had heard about Greeks who had been in Egypt for two thousand years being forced to leave their country as refugees.

"It's our own Greek-nationalist education that effaces long centuries of Greeks thriving in places like Egypt and the Ottoman Empire," I said. Effaces, also, all the bloodshed that permitted the Greek nation-state to arise. Neither the Greek nor the Turkish nation-state was founded without the deportation and slaughter of hundreds of thousands of people who, once an empire had re-imagined itself as a nation, no longer belonged. I promised myself I'd learn more about the complicated emergence of the Greek state, because trying to rehearse the details to my mother only exposed my failure to fully comprehend it.

Still, even without fully understanding what had happened and why, my mother and I were able to conclude from our reading that my great-uncle Thomas must have joined thousands of other Ottoman Greek soldiers who refused to die for a nation that no longer wanted them. He decided not to die fighting against the Allies. I remembered that the protagonist of the first novel I ever read in Greek had also deserted around the same time but had been caught and imprisoned. After years of forced labor and imprisonment, Manólis had escaped because the war had finally ended, and he had run toward the sea and swam toward an island. That was the fate that would have awaited Thomas if his family hadn't run. And so it was for Uncle Thomas that my mother's grandparents had joined the tens of thousands of Greeks who during the First World War left their friends, their shops, their animals, their money, their clothes, their homes, and the lives they knew, because if they did not leave, they would join the tally of the dead.

This tiny island of facts became ground on which my mother and I stood, fleetingly, together. A relative fleeing gunfire fit into the grammar of our frightened lives. A family fleeing a spate of recent nearby massacres satisfied our shared desire to prove that the world is fundamentally unsafe.

My mother's mother, Joanna, was born in New York City in 1916. Like her future husband the "Turkish seed," and like so many American children of immigrants, Joanna suffered a childhood full of blows dealt by nativist jingoism. I grew up believing my grandmother spoke only English, even though I'd heard the story of how she was beaten in first grade for speaking Greek. She had learned only Greek from her immigrant parents. Then they had sent her off to a New York City public school. When my grandmother spoke, the teacher beat her and told her that only when she spoke English would she be permitted back at school. I grew up believing my Yaya Joanna had forgotten all her Greek. She had, by the time I was born, married her second husband and taken his last name, Umbach, and their apartment on the Upper East Side bore traces of only his Anglo-Saxon heritage. It wasn't until my grandmother was well into her nineties that she surprised me by heaping upon me compliments in Greek, because her aging mind had at last released the language such an early trauma had suppressed.

My paternal grandfather, Cóstas Eleftheríou, abandoned his job as mayor—as a British colonial official—only to die in his American exile when I was six months old and he was seventy-eight. His Brooklyn house burned down as he collapsed inside it, and when his children entered the smoky ruins, they saw that their father had fallen just a few feet from the door. Without goodbyes, he too left his life behind.

I never endured a beating like my grandmother Joanna, and never fled a war like my grandfather Spyros. I didn't find the empire that employed me under attack by my compatriots like my grandfather Cóstas. I've never witnessed war. I have never even seen violence. But when my parents led me out of the nation where I'd barely finished growing up, when I invented for myself a way to keep on growing up in an alien culture and a language I couldn't entirely comprehend, then I too felt alien. I too felt unsafe (and more unsafe as adolescence proceeded). And because I lived that way—because that *leaving* marked my life—I suppose I feel a special kinship with my forebears who suffered *leaving* and wondered all their lives if they'd go back.

In a different way, I felt that learning about the wounds from which I came would help me to accept that I, too, bear wounds. Telling my family story could offer liberation from this ghost that lives inside me: a sense of exile, a sense of not-belonging, a sense of being trapped and unable to flee.

In a *New York Times* essay about the Modernist poet Cavafy, Orhan Pamuk expresses a kinship with the poet, who is descended from an old family from Istanbul and who lived in the City briefly during adolescence. Of his visit to Cavafy's house in Alexandria, a museum now, Pamuk writes, "The only people in the museum were tourists. The shuttered shops, the handful of old pine trees, the run-down buildings, the narrow streets, the squares, all helped me realize that versions of the Istanbul of my childhood still survive in cities all over the Mediterranean." Reading Pamuk describe his connection with a poet I read in middle school, I remember a fact that is intellectually obvious but difficult to remember: That

Turkey borders Greece, that the countries are so very close. That a man can jump off a Turkish pier and swim to a Greek island without drowning. "I love Cavafy's poetry not just as a reflection of his exemplary life," Pamuk goes on, "but also for the landscape it depicts, for its crumbling buildings, and because I immediately identify with the texture of Greek life." Today, decades after I read "The First Step" for school, this Turkish novelist teaches me what the name Cavafy means in old Greek: maker of cheap shoes.

I started reading Pamuk's memoir *Istanbul* when I flew to Greece via a layover in that city. My mother had recently expressed a fear that I would visit the City after she died and could no longer prevent me, so I kept my itinerary secret. Then, when a delayed flight precipitated a free overnight stay, I spoke to her, standing there in the city whence her father had fled, and fibbed that I had arrived safely in Greece. Months later, she found my Turkish Airlines boarding pass bookmarking my place in the copy of *After Antiquity: Greek Language, Myth, and Metaphor* that she had borrowed. I told her everything.

I told my mother that the Hagia Sophia was there, majestic as I remembered it from the pictures in my elementary school religion books. I said I'd roamed the streets and asked young people to tell me about the riots in Taksim Square. And that near the Blue Mosque, I'd observed a festival with little children dressed in traditional costumes that look exactly like our own. I told my mother that a song came on for the kids to dance to, and it was a song I recognized. The words were in Turkish, but I hummed the Greek words to myself until the language switched, and there in Istanbul/Constantinople I became a lone Greek among hundreds of Turks watching little kids dancing, and I sang the Greek words alone with the recording.

Constantine Cavafy holds a key, I believe, for undoing
some of the nationalisms that in his day had already begun
to brew storms of lasting war and conjure fantasies of racial
purity. Cavafy subverts all this and names a Hellenism that
is cosmopolitan and grand because it is Syrian—it is African:

> And from this exquisite pan-Hellenic mission,
> victorious, bright,
> world-famous and glorifious
> as none before it
> beyond compare, we came forth:
> the Greek new world, the great.
>
> We—Alexandrians, Antiochians,
> the Selefkians, and the myriad
> other Hellenes of Egypt and Syria,
> and those in Media, and Persia, and the rest:
> with our broad dominion,
> our varied practice of careful assimilation,
> and our Common Greek Tongue
> which we took all the way to Bactria, all the
>   way to the Indians.

Cavafy's work can model for us, today, what it means to
queer our notions of Greekness, of ethnicity itself, so that
when "Where are you from?" comes to us, there is something truthful we can say. It is an alternative to the perpetual addition of boxes upon boxes of identity. In the world's
youngest empire, the empire of my birth, more and more
Americans are seeking ways to queer the rigid categories of
the last century, such as those of Greek, Cypriot, or American.
Wherever I go, I feel myself labeled as a person from elsewhere. This label wounds me. It is a necessary wound, for it

is the price I pay daily for my own effort to abandon fantasies of being purely Greek or purely American.

All over the world, countries from France to Australia to South Africa to Cyprus are seeking a language for the way nations now include so very many differently skinned, differently tongued, and differently religioned people. The dream of modernity, that ethnically homogeneous nation-states would replace the multilingual empires—the old, nativist dream—is falling apart. It is not falling apart quietly; it will not go out gently. It is writhing; its death throes threaten everyone.

I spent the summer of 2017 traveling to Greece and to Cyprus as I do every summer, teaching for a spell and taking care of the property in Cyprus we've not yet managed to sell. Every week, I called to tell my mother where I was—Thessaloníki, Lésbos, Thássos, or Cyprus. I asked if anything more about Uncle Thomas had turned up, because it helped keep more personal questions at bay. Friends from both Cyprus and America said they understood the stress of keeping such a secret from my mother, especially when I recounted the way (without telling me what prompted her) she'd pleaded with me to confirm that I still believed in Jesus. "You have to come out to your mother," my American friends said. "Don't tell her," my Greek friends said, "it will devastate her." Or, "She will never give you peace once you tell her." I kept quiet.

I was restless all summer, inwardly unquiet, and the earth was restless too. In early June, I was in Lésbos, with the Turkish coast so close I could see buildings, when an earthquake shook the island where I was visiting the site of *The Mermaid Madonna*. After the earth shook, I went out and talked to shopkeepers and kebab sellers, and they told me their town was unaffected because it was built of stone. They kept on talking, as though one could talk away the threat of a powerful aftershock, and during all that talking, I learned that everyone on that island seemed to have at least one grandparent who had come from Turkey as a refugee in the 1920s. These descendants of the refugees spoke with suspicion about the NGOs that had descended upon the island since the war in Syria had broke out, and with infinite empathy for the tens of thousands of Syrian refugees who had spent the preceding year on their island.

In the American West, the mountains started burning. And my country—the country where I'd been born and where I had chosen, at least, to work for most of the year— seemed to be feeding fuel to its sociopolitical fires. In August, I arrived in Houston, where that winter I would teach, and I watched images of young men in white shirts march across the campus of the University of Virginia carrying fire. "You will not replace us!" they chanted, and the blood chilled in every person who remembered a time when a powerful, dominant group set out to destroy anyone who threatened their dominance.

My mother was, to my relief, appalled. I pushed her to say how dangerous this was, and how cruel, because I hoped to detect in that admission a tacit concession that everyone persecuted for their difference deserved to be kept safe. But she didn't do what I wanted. Instead, she said the white-shirted rioters had a point, actually, and that historical monuments, even Confederate ones, should not be removed. I was too hurt to argue or ask her which oppressor of Greek citizens should be honored with a monument. I didn't point out that Kemal Ataturk had been born in Thessaloníki, but there's no monument to him there because his side lost the city in a war. I also knew that it was unfair of me to keep trying to wheedle out of her empathy for other minorities, just in order to protect my own wounded fantasy that she might protect me.

I'd barely finished putting away the last contents of my suitcases and distributing souvenirs to my friends before worry began to stir about yet another danger from the restless earth. Hurricane Harvey was coming toward us from the Gulf of Mexico, and Houston would be sure to flood. I'd lost my car in the previous year's flood (the Tax Day Flood) and knew that the city, with its cemented-over wetlands and inadequate infrastructure, would be underwater for days. Grocery stores had only bottles of Gatorade and iced tea on their near-empty shelves by the time I went to purchase supplies, so I prepared to hunker down for a sugary week should the drinking supply be cut.

My one-time boss from a long-ago summer job at the Parks Service, though, called and urged me to get out—"You have no pets, no children, so forget supply-buying and get out," she said. When I said I was too anxious to drive, she found me a flight to Missouri that would get me out before the rains came. So I pulled all my notebooks off the floor, where they rested in my writer's spread, and put them on high shelves. I let my roommate know the Gatorade and iced tea was his if he wanted it and got onto a midnight bus to the airport. Two of my closest friends had recently left our former grad school home, though, and I realized I had to figure out a new place to stay, and fast. I texted a young woman named Néri, whom I'd met only a few times before, but who had invited me with the sincere, urgent hospitality of her native Turkey, and sure enough, she texted back immediately, with apologies for her uncomfortable futon.

And so I found myself, at the end of that summer, in the

small apartment of my new friend, watching with her footage of a not-quite-natural disaster ravaging the city I'd narrowly escaped and telling her about my grandfather, and how he'd fled Istanbul. She'd grown up in the city. She knew about the battle my uncle Thomas had fled.

"Gallipoli? Oh, yeah, we learn about it in school as a big victory for Turkey."

I asked Néri about the tales of oppression of minorities within the Ottoman Empire, which I'd heard about in Greek school but couldn't confirm. She told me that there were indeed extra taxes imposed on non-Muslims, and that there was a big incentive for them to convert. There's always been an incentive to change the mind of an infidel, Néri explained. Even her parents, upon hearing that a Christian would be sheltering from disaster at her house, had suggested she might earn sure entry into heaven by getting me to become a Muslim.

Néri set a plate of food on the low coffee table in front of me, and as I shifted my position on her floor—all my grad school friends seemed to eat this way—I thanked her, overwhelmed and shy at the generosity of a young graduate student who hardly knew me. Our conversation turned to the way we both felt pulled toward America and, at the same time, east toward cultures that madden us with their demand that we prioritize our families. I told her that when I gave my manuscript the title *This Way Back*, I couldn't even figure out if it meant my attempt to get to ancestral Greek lands, back to New York where I was born, or whether it just meant that I had been saddled with a restless sense that the home I have to get back to is always somewhere else.

"My parents won't even acknowledge that I told them I stopped praying two years ago, and I'm not sure I believe in God anymore," Néri said, "and they definitely don't know I

have a boyfriend." She explained that if the news of her relationship reached her community back in Istanbul, it would
bring shame upon her whole family. I realized that, for her,
this was just as big a secret as my sexuality was, with consequences just as grave, and that she could understand how
torn I felt better than a lot of my gay friends could, because
their allegiance to an authentic individual self makes coming
out more of an imperative for them. We talked about the
American right to privacy and how we both loved it and also
felt isolated by it. We felt safeguarded by American privacy
but oppressed, too, by the relentless prioritizing of communal
norms in our Greek and Turkish cultures. We shared exasper-
ation at midwestern over-politeness and the absence of yogurt
at meals. I asked Néri to listen to a Greek folk song that has a
Turkish line in it—many do, because of all the centuries of in-
habiting the same space—and she couldn't make sense of the
Greek singer's pronunciation until I found a Turkish translation of the whole song, and she explained it to me. At night, I
wriggled around looking for the futon's softest spot until I fell
asleep, my heart filled with thanks for Néri's kindness and my
sleep reddened by the taillights of cars I'd seen in Houston the
night before, in their interminable northward lines, inching
their way toward a brief, self-imposed exile.

The next morning, Néri FaceTimed her parents and
beckoned to me to greet them. "Mérhabar!" I said. They
spoke to me, and Néri whispered responses for me to repeat,
since the seven Turkish words I know weren't enough for
even this brief exchange. Néri spoke to her parents for a few
more minutes and then made brunch for us both.

"You know something, Joanna?"

I look up from the eggs Néri had served me.

"Your mom and the Ottomans, they were thinking the
same way."

"What do you mean?" I sipped the tea she'd made for us.

"The Ottomans encouraged Christians to convert because, from their point of view, it was better for the infidels themselves. From the point of view of Islam, it was in a Christian's interest to become a Muslim, because that way he'd go to heaven. Our parents, they're pushing us to do what they believe is best for us, to stay virgins and marry men of our own faith." The simplicity of this truth unlocked some of the anger I'd harbored against my mother. I saw that she cared about me, and that it wasn't her fault that her effort to protect me was causing me suffering.

I also saw my own suffering as connected to the many centuries of one group casting all its weight against the resistance of another to, from the first group's perspective, save the second. Rather than beg my mother to abandon for my sake the way she'd always seen the world so that she could utter to me the words of acceptance I so craved, maybe I could decide, myself, to see the world differently, in a less wounded way, in the light of something other than my trauma. Maybe I could see that my bruises were the bruises of a human existence that's been nothing if not a long series of attempts to make others conform to a rubric that seems safe.

Even this disaster, this hurricane and the flooding it caused with its week of ceaseless rain, was another example of some human being's attempt to stockpile safety for himself. In the name of progress or profit, Houston developers had cemented over wetlands and committed many other design errors that had made flooding inevitable, while the slew of hurricanes that rose up at the end of that summer resulted from climate change. And that, too, is yet another disaster caused by people who stockpile capital.

Stockpiling money permits the illusion that in times of

danger, the holders of wealth will be spared. Money safe-
guards against uncertainty. Money makes people feel
shielded from death. And so, many powerless creatures,
human and not human, will be exiled from an increasingly
large amount of land that, in a desperate attempt to feel safe,
we will render uninhabitable.

From exile to exile, I thought, disasters keep on casting
people out. None of us exiles ever really rest after deciding
that our one-time homes cannot feed us or keep us safe. We,
the generations whose fate it is to migrate, keep trying to
make new homes for ourselves, but we still don't fit. I, of
a merely tawny complexion, am much safer than the many
who continue to suffer the nativist's beatings, who continue
to die because people with power are afraid of letting power
slip. I enjoy plane rides and air conditioning and remain complicit in the climate disaster that has already produced so
many refugees. I have a responsibility to work toward justice
for those who do not know me, but I have to start, at the
very least, by accepting the flawed love of those who (albeit
incompletely) do.

I called my mother from the grassy hillsides of a sunlit
park near Néri's apartment. A breeze blew. The day was cool
and dry for an August day in Missouri. I described the cloud-
less sky of the town to which I had escaped. I didn't begrudge
my mother, this time, her surprise that someone from Turkey
could be so kind.

"I guess they're just people," she said, and again in Greek:
"*Ímaste óli aplá ánthropi.*" "We're all just people."

>>·<<

A year later, I sat on the same faded loveseat opposite my
mother again, reading journal submissions on my laptop. She

was reading the gospel out loud in the original Greek. I tried to maneuver myself into a position that kept out of my mother's view the rainbow sticker on my laptop. The sticker was a gift from the editor of *Sinister Wisdom: A Journal of Lesbian Art*, whom I'd met at a writer's conference after she published a poem of mine, so (to me) the sticker was a symbol of my accomplishments as a writer. My mother interrupted my article-reading and asked me about a family friend, the mother of my brother's best man, and I mentioned her recent divorce. My mother got a little worked up at the news (our friend had been married for over thirty years) and started talking about the importance of commitment, then said that she thought I would have been married by now. I had succeeded in getting her to stop asking about that in recent years, and so, on the cusp of forty, I listened.

I said something about not being attracted to boys and about how the one time I entered into a relationship with a man, a boy who wanted to be a priest, when I was still living in Cyprus and teaching at the language institute, my confessor had asked, "Don't you have feelings for him? God made a miracle for you, giving you a good boy that's interested in you, and you are so thankless as to not have feelings?" I told my mother the confessor's words, but not the fact that I had considered dating a boy (there was only one) to be a kind of fate that I wouldn't be able to avoid forever, and that when he asked me out I went along, disgusted by the kisses but grateful that at least, as a religious boy who wanted to be a priest, he would keep his penis in his shorts for as long as we were unmarried. Once my confessor admonished me to start praying for God to give me feelings, I gave up my heterosexual charade. I gave my mother an abridged version of this report.

And then, after twenty-five years, it came, the long-awaited question: "Have you been attracted to women?" And I said yes. And I said that I hadn't told her because I could not bear to hear her, my mother, say that the most tender feeling I've known was of demonic origin. She acceded that in years past, she might have said just that, but by this year, her seventy-third and my fortieth, she had resigned herself to the possibility that it was a hormonal orientation that had seen an uptick because of all the hormones in the meat (I didn't laugh). She said that she'd felt our relationship had been strained for a while and that she was happy to be able to talk openly and directly, and she said that she loved me. The question was over; I was finally out to everyone, and I called my friends to celebrate. I was, in a sense, newly free.

Three weeks later, I was grading papers in a Houston coffee shop after church, and the sky suddenly darkened. I gathered my belongings and walked quickly to my car without getting rained on, but a downpour started as I pulled out of my parking spot. When I had driven only two of the three miles home, the Houston streets had become so flooded that I was afraid to keep driving. All the sedans like mine had pulled off the road and into whatever raised parking space they could find. I chose one outside a Roman Catholic church and switched off the engine as torrential rain pounded the car's roof. Since there had been no forecast at all of rain, I figured the unexpected flooding couldn't last more than an hour, so I decided to wait it out. I had books and my phone, and lots to grade. I called my mother to spend some of my trapped-in-the-car time performing one of my important weekend tasks.

When she picked up, I explained to my mother that I was safe but anxious, given that the streets around me had become impassable and the rain hadn't stopped. She reassured me that this flooding was nothing to worry about, since it was only physical flooding and of the world, and what I really had to worry about was the "spiritual flood," she said, which was coming for me if I did not "renounce homosexuality." I expressed surprise that, given the circumstances, she had chosen this moment to thus warn me. She answered that she had already decided to make this the topic of our weekly phone call, and that maybe the downpour was some kind of divine intervention with helpful sensory imagery. I spoke calmly, but inside I was a mess. I remember that she used the word *exhort*. "I exhort you to renounce homosexuality."

And so, there in the middle of yet another physical flood, I had to face the fact that I could not please my parents and honor my own heart at the same time. I had to face the rope of my own conflicted desires and recognize that while my parents' hopes and longings made up some of its tangled strands, the rope was only mine; the rope was me. I politely ended the conversation with my mother, put on battered flip-flops and a wrinkled rain jacket, and locked my car, and by zigzagging my way through the neighborhood's higher ends of each street I made my way back home. I called my friends, who shouldered my pain and bore it with me, and by the time they'd gotten me to feel a little better the sun had broken through and the once-darkened sky shone bright.

A few hours later, Houston's streets had drained, and I slipped into my sneakers, ran to my abandoned car, and drove it safely back into my garage, alone.

>>·<<

During that first conversation with my mother about my hormonal orientation, the good one, I told her a funny story I'd been holding back for as long as I had been shielding her from the knowledge of my desire (and myself from the repercussions

of her acquiring the knowledge). During my first year in Houston, I attended a meeting of the Houston Cypriot Society,
which I hadn't been able to find (no website) until I received
a message from an older Cypriot Houstonian, who had just
been back to Limassol and bought some jewelry at the store
where my cousin Dina works. Dina had asked him where he
lived, and when he said Houston, she told him that her cousin
Ioánna had been looking for the Cypriots of Houston. And
that's how I ended up at the gathering, introducing myself to
several Cypriot women and men around my age. When I met
Maria K., the first question she asked me (in Cypriot dialect)
was: "Are you here in Houston alone?" I said I was.

"All right, we'll start searching for a husband for you,"
Maria said.

"Actually, it's a wife I'm looking for."

"Oh," Maria said, without missing a beat. "That's a little
more complex," she said ("λιγάκι πιο σύνθετο"), "but I'll start
working on it." When she asked me what district I was from
in Cyprus and I said Limassol, Maria said that she knew a
lesbian named Nicoletta who lived in Limassol. One of my
Cypriot cousins had just broken off a ten-year relationship
with a woman, so I assumed we were talking about her, but
some other facts didn't match. When I emailed the Nicoletta
I had in mind, she wrote back to say that Maria K. must
mean our *other* cousin Nicoletta. I'd had much less contact
with this second Nicoletta, since she's farther from me in
age.

My mother interrupted this part of the story to say, "Oh
yes. She is definitely a homosexual." I didn't ask why my
mother had never told me.

A year after my new friend Maria inadvertently introduced me to my second lesbian cousin named Nicoletta, I was
sitting in this long-lost cousin's living room. She introduced

me to her longtime partner, Sophia. They ordered kebabs and asked me to stay and eat with them. We had a beautiful evening. We lamented the way we had grown up so close and yet so far—a decade my senior, Nicoletta hadn't been interested in hanging out with her teenage cousins in her early twenties, back when my family had visited hers. I remember seeing her come busily in and out of her parents' house when we visited and saying little more than "hello." Nicoletta revealed that her mother had, around that very time, opened up her mail and discovered that Nicoletta was a lesbian. They'd had a hard time, even harder than I would have guessed, but we agreed that I might have been spared some of my pain's enormity if she and I had only been able to talk.

Now, though, late but not too late, we were here together in that same house I'd visited twenty years ago. Nicoletta showed me the renovation she'd done to her parents' place, and especially the bedroom they typically rented out but would keep free for me any and every time I returned to Cyprus. I told her about my father's journals, and the way he described living with her family while he was in high school. I told Nicoletta how, along with his motorcycle jaunts and souvlaki nights, he describes living with her parents and grandmother and taking her older brother out for walks in the pram. She said she was sorry for his death. Then Nicoletta, Sophia, and I cried together, and laughed, and hugged, and then I left, and they said, "Goodbye for now, for just a year, for your room here in our house will be waiting for you to come back and stay."

—

Epilogue:
Moonlight Elegy

—

In the village of Asgáta, I used to run up in his mountains for an hour before dark. On days when the law prohibits hunters from shooting at the thrush and rabbits, I go out into the hills and run alone. Around and around itself a mountain takes you, up to its spine, a ridge of dips and peaks. And you can see the other side, the city spreading out toward water. On moonlit nights you can see the footprints of God scintillating on the sea. When I would return each evening, he would ask me, "Did you see the moon?" As if anybody could miss the moon that showers light into a sky just turning navy.

Dusk settles, but rocks and thorns remain visible in the growing dark. White light falls on my shoulders, the moon pencils sharp, black shadows on the earth. Bats flap by, then vanish. I run at night because of the moon, and I stay in the hills late because of the moon. I stare a little at the moon before rounding that last bend before the house.

But I would always ask him where it was, and he would point, and I would crane my neck and look, because the raising of his weakened arm was his gift. As a father ages, a daughter learns how badly he wants to go on as before, though his children aren't children and nothing is as before.

>>·<<

When I lived in my parents' house here as a teenager, my mother and father used to tell me that my running made them worry—it's dark outside, the snakes don't sleep, hunting dogs stray, you could trip and fall and nobody would find you until morning. My father quoted lines from Seferis, our favorite poet—

> And now the new moon's come up wrapped
> In the arms of the old moon, with the beautiful
>   island bleeding
> The wounded, the calm, the strong island, the
>   innocent

>>·<<

In cities, I can hardly see the sky. I live in an American city now, and night is only night, black patches of sky, dark trees turned yellow in electric light. No one sees the stripe of the galaxy, no one sees stars. One night, though, I was walking through a parking lot with friends and saw the moon between a hospital building and a school. "Did you see the moon?" I asked. Then apologized: "I don't mean to condescend, sound patronizing, or say that you didn't see—my father always asks me just that way."

>>·<<

Seferis, a diplomat for Greece all through the Metaxas dictatorship, the Nazi occupation, and the devastating civil war that followed, was a poet, too. He wrote by night of old trag-edy and new horror. He stayed in the British resort at Plátres when my father was sixteen and guerrilla warfare against the crown was starting.

> "The nightingales won't let you sleep in Plátres."
> What is Plátres?
> Who knows this island?
> I lived my life hearing names for the first time;
> New lands, new madnesses of men
> Or of the gods.

My father carried letters, passed out pamphlets. Seferis knew that independence would not bring peace. Soon after Cyprus became a state, another war tore the island open. A new solution has been imminent ever since.

My father's home is wounded by politics and drought. Our village draws water from its own underground vein, which is shared among many farmers and therefore weak by day. My father waters the apple trees, jasmine, and bou-gainvillea every night after sunset and every morning before dawn. He holds the hose over little moats around every tree and waits for each to fill. He forms a small sea around the roses, careful not to expose any roots. A hedge of rose laurel divides our land from the neighbors', and bright pink flowers bloom across the way.

When I return all pumped and sweaty from the hills, my father points to the moon just cresting over the horizon. It is red like blood, and I sometimes feel that he is pointing to a place of violence and torment that lives beyond our hills. When I run, I listen, half expecting to hear a wail, some sort of lament.

>>·<<

The neighbors' rose bushes do not grow tall like ours. My father prunes the older leaves before they die, before they stunt the growth of the bush. "The dead understand only the language of flowers. On the trail of asphodels, hyacinths and violets we find our dead," the poet says.

I ask my father how he learned to train the roses to bloom all year. "From my mother," he says. I ask, "And she, from hers?" "No," he says, "Yaya Agáthi learned about the garden by watching it fail and grow, day by day and year by year, as a child learns to speak by listening."

After answering a question, my father walks around the house. He has worn the grass thin, one large circle, more like an earth-colored square scratched into the thirsty grass around the house. He stoops at odd moments to inspect the flowers, pluck some mint or lavender to rub between his fingers. My mother never gets his shirts quite clean on account of all the leaves left in his pockets.

The violent sun has burnt blisters onto the vulnerable skin of my father's head. He lost all his hair at twenty but rarely wears a hat. His cheeks are fallen, his face drawn back against the skull; sadness and strength-sapping medication have turned his eyes into upside-down crescents, softened and still. When he smiles, his mouth bends into the shape of a half moon.

When my father was just twenty-something, he already had a family, and when he was still just twenty-something his first wife started dying slowly, yet so fast. Family and friends told my dad to hope and pray and he did. Sentenced to remain alone among the living, my father lived. He married again.

I grew up in New York, while my father built up a school

for Greek immigrants. In a photograph of my father holding a third baby, a son, his face shines circular and full.

His smile faded after he brought us to the homeland—a grand adventure—where the delight of doing this great patriotic thing waned fast. My father hadn't known what he would find when, with his children still young and his wife happy in America, he moved us all across the ocean to his old home.

He remembered honest people, slow-baked tile roofs, and houses built of stone.

But we found sand and cinderblock, fake wood, and tin. His sisters in New York all said, "Stay here, Andréas," but my father said, "My children have to know who they are." He wanted to build in Plátres, up in the highest mountains, away from all the bustle and the coast and dry plains, where rivers gush and a garden won't dry up in drought. But he had to be practical, so he built a house in the low hills of his own village, close to the city and the sea. We went to school there, learned poetry and history, and finished school.

But the strain of an impossible ideal damaged our united brightness. The moving brought suspicions and tears into the fabric of our family, and a few years into the adventure he started to wear away that square of grass outside.

He would call me out to listen to the poet, point to the ground where I would sit beside his folding chair under a pine, with the thick scent of drying needles all around us. "Few are the moonlit nights I've liked," his radio crackled, and we often lost the station, but my father would adjust the antenna so that we could catch the end.

In Cyprus, you can't keep track of your own heart's mourning because there is your own loneliness, your pain; your family living somewhere else and breaking; and then there is your country, divided, without defense or hope.

>>•<<

Heart muscle tears like any other human thing; after years of perfect self-duplication, our cells can easily make a mistake. When our mother got cancer, though, and our father got heart disease in that same sixth year of life in Cyprus, they did not consider human bodies and the inevitable, inexorable transience of our lives—they blamed the new home, the island destination of my father's choosing; they blamed the strain of a life so far away from where they'd started.

On the night my mother came out of the doctor's office clean, her lymph nodes clear, the cancer gone, my father's voice shivered and his eyes flashed in the light of a street lamp, gleaming and wet—he said, "Thank God—these children have to have a mother."

It was night, there was a moon, we drove home.

Earlier that year, a silent heart attack had scalloped out a flap in my father's heart muscle, scar tissue that's loose and open, like a bay. That little bay inside my father's heart might draw blood in and slow it down. Then it might clot. The little clot would travel up to my father's brain and kill him as it tried to squeeze through capillaries thin as hair. He takes blood thinner and looks at his life waning like a moon.

When he's scratched by a thorn, blood trickles down his arm or leg for hours. To live, my father needs to work, training vines to splintering trellises or planting bulbs for new flowers. He ties saplings to stakes and pulls up weeds and thistles from among the roses, always dodging the poisonous little caterpillars, which bite.

>>•<<

Guardian of the garden now, unable to teach high school history any longer, my father plays teacher at home: "Did you see the moon rise?" Some nights, the moon rises while my mother and brother and I are all done with running and with being outside. We sit watching television, grading papers, rinsing dishes, reading.

For years, my father tried to correct my mother's habit of missing moonrise, of missing everything there was to relish in the homeland. Dad always calls to my mother by name: "Georgia, come and see the moon." We love the inside of the house too much, he says. An air of resignation, almost sneering but too tired for sneering, colors these calls to see the moonrise. My father has grown tired of his family's indifference to the moon, to the movement of stars, to the spectacle in the sky. So he's impatient, resigned to her nonplussed attitude, and yet so eager to indict it and condemn her ingratitude as if the Lord were hosting a party in our yard and this moonshine were His banquet. We won't appreciate the beauty of a young moon in an evening sky when it is tiny as an infant's fingernail, a puncture in the blue-black emptiness. Usually he sits alone to watch it rising. We've already marveled at the milky band that straps around our sky, that band of stars that looks just like a long, narrow cloud. We ignore the planets Venus and Mars with their distinct, tremorless glow. We won't look at the hovering constellations, the cross, the bear.

But on the nights when we do at last answer his command, we sit outside with my father and we all talk together through the rising display. We look up, or across to the horizon where he points. And for a dozen minutes, fifteen maybe, we find something to discuss—politics, the prospect of rain or more heat, our relatives and friends. Each night brings a subtly new shade of glowing crimson. And then the sphere starts to look like hot iron or like raw flesh, open for surgery. I've never found the right words for the wonder of it, and if I think too hard I feel fear; if one of us gasps, then my father looks glad—we have at last grasped the secret of the nighttime, this awful beauty.

>>·<<

In this house of cinderblock and illness, my father splits the nighttime space with me. If Dino is up, he is out, and when he pulls up in a car throbbing hip-hop, he stands behind the hedge of oleander until his cigarette is done. He ducks into his bedroom and sleeps.

My mother sleeps through the night. My father, who grew up without electric light, still dons pajamas as soon as the watering is done. But he can no longer sleep past one, and when I leave my room to get some water, a little air, he is there—shuffling from kitchen to stone patio or back, radio tuned to the truckers' station, kettle boiling for tea made of aniseed and sage. In the nighttime space we share, I have always simply walked around my father. But on nights when there isn't a moon, when we trust our night vision a little too well, we stub our toes, nearly hit the walls. Once or twice, I nearly run into my father.

From the loft, I listen while my father sits there waiting out the dark. I hear the matches struck to light a flame for tea, I hear the kettle and the clink of stainless steel and china. All night, he breaks off little pieces of toast and sharp cheese and munches with bare gums. At three thirty or four he brews the coffee and the smells steal upstairs. On most of my nights I have drifted off to sleep under the siege of morning.

>>·<<

My brother and I fought bitterly as children. Dino threw things at me, wanted to play Monopoly and soccer, begged to play anything, even dolls. I wanted to do my homework alone, play alone, run alone. Hungry for my company, he hit me, kicked me—all for the want of me. At the beach one day, my brother threw a small, sharp stone at the back of my head as I was walking away into the waves. I played the martyr, bled a drop or two, then showed the wound to our parents, who sat watching us from under a flowering acacia on the sand.

I got him punished. We talked about hate, stuck our tongues out and spit.

A year after the silent heart attack that no one noticed, our parents left us in the house all night because my father's white shirt had turned all crimson from the running blood. Our father had lost his last tooth that night, and when he cut his mouth the blood thinner made his blood pour. At the hospital, the doctors tried to give him back enough blood to keep a man alive. We waited. How many rags he reddened that night, and his hands, how the blood stuck to his fingers. How the blood poured down his arms, matted the hair. We opened all the shutters, but there wasn't a moon. My brother went upstairs and clanked back down dragging a half-broken aluminum cot, pushed it into his own room next to his bed, and said, "Sleep here Jo." I slept. After that we didn't fight. Twelve years later, moonless nights make me I think I'm in that room—I hear my brother's breathing—

When do we begin to weep for the living, who must leave us?

When my father went away with my mother to America one summer in order to have a special medical exam, he left

Dino and me in charge of his garden. Neither of us wanted to wake up as early as our father, but you have to water before dawn, so Dino watered after clubbing at four in the morning, or sometimes I rose before the break of day. Dino said, "Can you cook for all my friends, Jo?" and I said, "Sure, just wash my car." Then he swept the floors and I dragged a mop behind him. Dino brought his friends over and filled our father's house with laughing teenage voices, vodka Jell-O shots, and music.

While our father had tubes run through his body, and had test upon excruciating test, we opened up his house, turned on the lights and turned up the music; as our father lay in a bed on the other side of the ocean, we laughed and drank and then we danced.

He came home not cured but tested, tired but all right. Our father inspected the lemon trees leaf by leaf, looked at the poplars, cyclamen, lavender, hyacinth, and jasmine. We lost one geranium, forgotten in the farthest corner of the yard. Oleander still circled the house, along with capers, rosemary, and cyclamen that crept out from between rocks. Our father smiled wide at the blooming orchids, a patch of daisies booming by a pine—"Thank God, thank God"—he smiled—"my children know how to keep things alive."

When do we begin to mourn for those we love; once we begin, how do we end it?

And when we are mourning, do we dance?

We all die in time.

When the moon sets, my father rises. At one in the morning, when his head runs out of sleep, he shuffles out the door in his slippers. Outside, he sips tea and watches the slow spinning of stars, the subtle orbit of planets, and the hurried trajectory of the moon.

I don't really know how to love a man, not even a father. Instead, I open up my intact heart and bow my head and listen for his waning heartbeat. Sometimes we sit together with the scent of watered earth all around us, and then the faded or invisible half of the moon comes out of shadow and we see a full circle, part navy and part bright.

"*Amica silentia lunae*," "Beloved silences of the moon," Seferis writes, translating Horace's Latin lines into a Greek that lingers in our lives today. The moon washes over my father's garden, and all the colors change at night. Gray poplars and the leaves of olive trees reflect light in silver. Our parched grass shines green, and the grayish gravel street looks paved and black. Moonlight washes my father's body, so that in the gleaming he is whole again and strong.

All of us delight a little in the moon, its glow like glass, its craters dark. The blazing rock of light spins into shadow so soon. And as the moon falls through the sky and fades into morning or blackens into more night, I know this truth. My dad, my lonesome father, will look with me tonight at the fading moon with this same thrill, this strange longing, and this, our nighttime knowledge that sun and moon will go on—even as our own small lives run out of light.

Acknowledgments

This book is dedicated to my teachers. My teachers are many; some have served as my formal instructors while others may not know how much they helped me learn. My parents, Georgia and Andréas, were my earliest teachers. My sister Cathy and brother Dino, too, taught me how to be a sister. In high school, Pitsa Georgiadou, Andri Melki, and Christina Kleanthous opened up to me the world of literature.

At Cornell, Gail Holst-Warhaft said *you understand literature, Joanna*, and Lydia Fakundiny made me an essayist in her class The Art of the Essay. At Old Dominion University, Michael Pearson, Janet Peery, Luisa Igloria, Tim Seibles, Sheri Reynolds, Edward Jacobs, Manuela Mourão, David Metzger, Natalie Diaz, Valli Jo Porter, Rebecca Lauren, and Andrea Nolan guided my first steps as a scholar and a writer.

At the University of Missouri, Scott Cairns, Julija Šukys, Alexandra Socarides, Elaine Lawless, Elisa Glick, Maureen Stanton, and E. J. Levy gave me the wisdom and courage I needed to complete my doctoral studies as I came into my own as a lesbian essayist. I am deeply grateful, too, to my other CoMo folks: Beth Peterson, Kavita Pillai, Jen Julian, Martha Kelly, Gabriel Fried, and Erika Patterson. Thank you for reading my words, believing in them, and helping me usher them into the world.

At the Writing Workshops in Greece, I forged life-changing friendships with Carolyn Forché, Natalie Bakopoulos, Allison Wilkins Bakken, and Christopher Bakken. You gave me a community of writers where I finally felt I could belong.

Shreerekha Subramanian, Barbara Hales, Loukia Tsami, and Conor Bracken, colleagues at the University of Houston Clear Lake, read my work and supported me. My new academic home, the English department at Christopher Newport University, has welcomed me and my writing with warmth and enthusiasm, and promises to foster continued creative inquiry (and more books) for years to come. Students too many to name made classroom discussions into thought-adventures that helped me work through so many ideas that ultimately found their way into my book. Teaching them challenged me daily, and they have provided, each semester, a community of writers in which I both received and gave support. Students, too, have been my teachers.

I would finally like to thank the Virginia Center for the Creative Arts for financial support as well as the visionary editors at West Virginia University Press. Along with the generous blind peer reviewers who understood deeply what I sought to do, WVUP believed in this project and made recommendations to make *This Way Back* a better book.

I would also like to express gratitude to journals including *Sinister Wisdom: A Multicultural Lesbian Literary and Art Journal* and *Switchgrass Review* on whose pages I worked out ideas at the heart of this book, and to the publications where the following essays first appeared: "The Rope of Desires," *The Tusculum Review*; "Your Schedule Depends on the Sky" (as "Snow on Sunday"), *St. Katherine's Review*; "She and

I," *Broad River Review*; "Ithacas," *3Elements Review*; "The Other Side," *Crab Orchard Review*; "Wild Honey, Locust Beans," *Arts and Letters*; "Dancing Greek" (short excerpt), *Levure Littéraire*; "Unsent Letter to My Father," *Mary: A Journal of New Writing*; "Out" (part 3), *Vox Magazine*; "Cyprus Pride," *Bellingham Review*; and "Moonlight Elegy" (as "Moonlight"), *Chautauqua*.

Thanks to the children of Costas Montis for permission to reprint lines from their father's poetry in "The Other Side" and to W. W. Norton for permission to reprint lines of poetry by A. R. Ammons.

Notes

This is a selected list of published sources I consulted for these essays. Quotes from unpublished sources and from my own memory are not cited here.

THE ROPE OF DESIRES

7. "Deliver me from a city built . . ." Henry David Thoreau, *Walden and Other Writings of Henry David Thoreau*, ed. Brooks Atkinson (New York: Random House, 1992), 249.
10. "each of us must choose an allegiance—either to the posthuman, the virtual . . ." Robert Pogue Harrison, *The Dominion of the Dead* (Chicago: University of Chicago Press, 2003), 34.
13. "We have worked the earth to death . . ." Harrison, *Dominion of the Dead*, 32.

THE ACTRESS WHO ISN'T ACTING

32. "If you should hear that I have died . . ." "Είκοσι χρόνια χωρίς τη Μελίνα" [Twenty years without Melina], *Iefimerida*, March 2, 2014 (my translation).
33. "enemy of Greek tourism" "Melina Mercouri Is Called 'Enemy of Greek Tourism,' " *New York Times*, June 17, 1967, 17.
35. "the equal value of all." St. Maximus, *The Writings of Maximus the Confessor* (Morrisville: Lulu Books, 2015), Sec. 72.
35. "engrave His beauty on our memory . . ." Maximus, *Writings of Maximus*, Sec. 72.

36. "anything that matters hurts . . ." "Old Loves Go to Paradise," by Maro Vamvounaki, performed by Pyx Lax, on *The Bogeyman Only Sings at Night*, Harvest, 1996 (my translation); "when I see friends . . ." "Dead Good Evenings," by Miltos Paschalides, performed by Dimitris Mitropanos, on *Of Eros and Escape*, Minos, 1998 (my translation).

37. "thirsts to be thirsted for . . ." Maximus, *Writings of Maximus*, Sec. 84.

38. "This is not a funeral . . ." Δημήτρης Χαλιώτης, "Μελίνα Μερχούρη: Να με θυμάσαι και να μ' αγαπάς" [Melina Mercouri: Remember me and love me], *Flash*, April 3, 2011 (my translation).

41. "So-called friends came to warn me . . ." Melina Mercouri, *I Was Born Greek: The Autobiography of Melina Mercouri* (London: Hodder & Stoughton, 1971), 213.

42. "grimly lugubrious drama"; "inevitable climax . . ."; "The situation is slightly Sapphic . . ."; "not a noticeably youthful girl"; "leaps into singing . . ."; "when she kisses . . ." Bosley Crowther, "Screen: Neo-Realism from Athens; 'Stella,' Greek Import, Is at the World Mclodrama Features Melina Mercouri," *New York Times*, June 11, 1957.

46. "The Cause of all things . . ." Quoted in David W. Fagerberg, *On Liturgical Asceticism* (Washington, DC: Catholic University of America Press, 2013), 8.

47. "Mercouri, as a Greek woman . . ." Vassiliki Tsitsopoulou, "Greekness, Gender Stereotypes, and the Hollywood Musical in Jules Dassin's Never on Sunday," *Journal of Modern Greek Studies* 18, no. 1 (2000): 91.

48. "Every act is political . . ." Barbara Gamarekian, "The Wind They Call Mercouri: 'Every act is political—even to eat,' " *New York Times*, October 2, 1987, A14.

ITHACAS

59. "Wise as you've become . . ." C. P. Cavafy, "Ithaca," from *Τα ποιήματα: νέα έκδοση* [The poems: A new edition], ed. G. P. Savvides, vol. 1 *1897–1918* (Athens: Ikaros, 1991), 29–30 (my translation).

69. "Souliot women have not only . . ." "Dance of Zalongo," Greek folk song (my translation).

73. "*to ephebekón oréa kamoméno sóma*" ("the young, beautifully shaped body"), C. P. Cavafy, "27 June 1906, 2 P.M." *Τα ποιήματα: νέα έκδοση* [The poems: A new edition], ed. G. P.

Savvides, vol. 1 *1897–1918*, vol. 2 *1919–1933* (Athens: Ikaros, 1991) (my translation).

THE TEMPLE OF ZEUS

82. "The lack of concern for the erotic root . . ." Audre Lorde, "Uses of the Erotic," in *Sister Outsider* (1984; repr., Berkeley: Crossing Press, 2007), 55.

94. "In any act of thinking, the mind . . ." Anne Carson, *Eros the Bittersweet* (1986, repr. Princeton: Princeton University Press, 2014), 171.

95. "When you consider the radiance . . ." A. R. Ammons, "The City Limits," from *The Complete Poems of A. R. Ammons: Volume 1, 1955–1977* (New York: Norton, 2017), 498.

95. "wife is baking for a funeral" and "until we die . . ." A. R. Ammons, "In View of the Fact," from *Bosh and Flapdoodle: Poems* (New York: Norton, 2005), 29–30.

THE OTHER SIDE

115. "How happy I am . . ." Kaylan Muammar, *The Kemalists: Islamic Revival and the Fate of Secular Turkey* (Amherst, NY: Prometheus, 2005), 442.

122. "rise up and shrug off . . ." Costas Montis, "Moments of the Invasion," *Ἅπαντα Α΄. Ποίηση* [Complete works], vol. 1 (Nicosia: Leventis Foundation, 1987), 229–30 (my translation).

WILD HONEY, LOCUST BEANS

127. "the hungriest country in the world" "Greece: Hungriest Country," *Time*, February 9, 1942.

SHOPPING FOR STORY

147. "innate artistic nature . . ." and "dynamism, sensitivity . . ." *Lefkara Laces or Lefkaritika* (Lefkara Municipality/Ministry of Education and Culture, 2008), https://youtu.be/Nuo1j_-doJQ.

DANCING GREEK

152. "lies in the sea"; "like the backbone of an ass" Archilocus, "Fragment 4," in *The Fragments of Archilochos*, ed. Guy Davenport (Berkeley: University of California Press, 1964), 4.

INHERITANCE LAW

199.   "Yet the question of fidelity . . ." Pascale-Anne Brault and Michael Naas, "Introduction," in *The Work of Mourning*, by Jacques Derrida, ed. Brault and Naas (Chicago: University of Chicago Press, 2003), 23.

WITHOUT GOODBYES

228.   "The only people in the museum were tourists . . ." Orhan Pamuk, "Other Countries, Other Shores," *New York Times*, December 19, 2013.
229.   "I love Cavafy's poetry . . ." Pamuk, "Other Countries."
230.   "And from this exquisite pan-Hellenic mission. . ." C. P. Cavafy, "Days of 200 BC," from *Τα ποιήματα: νέα έκδοση* [The poems: A new edition], ed. G. P. Savvides, vol. 2 *1919–1933* (Athens: Ikaros, 1991), 93–94 (my translation).

EPILOGUE: MOONLIGHT ELEGY

244.   "And now the new moon's come up wrapped . . ." George Seferis, "Days of June '41," from *George Seferis Collected Poems 1924–1955: Bilingual Edition* (Princeton, NJ: Princeton University Press, 1967), 274 (my translation).
245.   "The nightingales won't let you sleep in Plátres . . ." George Seferis, "Helen," from *George Seferis: Collected Poems, 1924–1955: Bilingual Edition* (Princeton, NJ: Princeton University Press, 2016), 354–56 (my translation).